OLD MACKINAW;

OR,

THE FORTRESS OF THE LAKES

AND

ITS SURROUNDINGS.

BY

W. P. STRICKLAND.

PHILADELPHIA:
JAMES CHALLEN & SON,
No. 25 SOUTH SIXTH STREET.
1860.

PHILADELPHIA:
STEREOTYPED BY S. A. GEORGE,
607 SANSOM STREET.

PREFACE.

In the preparation of this volume a large number of works have been consulted, among which the author desires to acknowledge his indebtedness to the following: "The Travels of Baron La Hontan," published in English and French, 1705; "Relations des Jesuits," in three vols., octavo; "Marquette's Journal;" Schoolcraft's works, in three volumes; "Shea's Catholic Missions and Discovery of the Mississippi;" "American Annals;" "Lanman's History of Michigan;" "Parkman's Siege of Pontiac;" "Annals of the West;" "Foster and Whitney's Geological Report;" "Ferris' Great West;" "Disturnell's Trip to the Lakes;" "Lanman's Summer in the Wilderness;" "Pietzell's Lights and Shades of Missionary Life;"

"Life of Rev. John Clark;" "Lectures before the Historical Society of Michigan;" "Mansfield's Mackinaw City;" "Andrews' Report of Lake Trade;" "Heriot's Canada;" "Presbyterian Missions," &c., &c. He desires particularly to mention the works of Schoolcraft, which have thrown more light on Indian history than the productions of any other author. He also desires to acknowledge his indebtedness to Wm. M. Johnson, Esq., of Mackinac Island, for his valuable contributions to the history of that interesting locality. The statistics in relation to that portion of the country embraced in the work are taken from the most recent sources, and are believed to be perfectly reliable."

We are indebted to J. W. Bradley, of Philadelphia, the publisher of "The North American Indians," for the beautiful frontispiece in this work. Mr. Catlin, the author, visited every noted tribe, and, by residing among them, was initiated into many of their secret and hidden mysteries. It is a valuable work.

CONTENTS.

CHAPTER I. PAGE

Mackinaw and its surroundings—Indian legends—Hiawatha—Ottawas and Ojibwas—Pau-pau-ke-wis—San-ge-man—Kau-be-man—An Indian custom—Dedication to the spirits—Au-se-gum-ugs—Exploits of San-ge-man—Point St. Ignatius—Magic lance—Council of peace—Conquests of San-ge-man........ 9

CHAPTER II.

Indian spiritualists—Medicine men—Legends—The spirit-world—Difference between Indian and modern spiritualists—Chusco the spiritualist—Schoolcraft's testimony of—Mode of communicating with spirits—Belief in Satanic agency—Interesting account of clairvoyance........ 19

CHAPTER III.

Marquette's visit to Iroquois Point—Chapel and Fort—Old Mackinaw—The French settlement in the Northwest—Erection of chapel and Fort—The gateway of commerce—The rendezvous of traders, trappers, soldiers, missionaries, and Indians—Description of fort—Courriers des Bois—Expedition of Marquette and Joliet to explore the Mississippi—Green Bay—Fox River—Wisconsin—Mississippi—Peoria Indians—Return trip—Kaskaskia Indians—St. Xavier Missions—Mission to "the Illinois"—Marquette's health declines—Starts out on return trip to Mackinaw—Dies and is buried at mouth of Marquette River—Indians remove his remains to Mackinaw—Funeral cortege—Ceremonies—Burial in the chapel—Changes of time—Schoolcraft on the place of Marquette's burial—Missilimackinac—Name of Jesuit missions........ 39

CHAPTER IV.

La Salle's visit to Mackinaw—English traders—La Hontan's visit—Mackinaw an English fort—Speech of a Chippewa chief—Indian stratagem—Massacre of the English at the fort—Escape of Mr. Alexander Henry—Early white settlement of Mackinaw—Present description—Relations of the Jesuits—Remarkable Phenomena—Parhelia—Subterranean river...... 61

Contents.

CHAPTER V. PAGE

Island of the giant fairies—Possession by the English—Erection of government house—French remain at Old Mackinaw—Finally abandoned—Extent of the island—History—Description—Natural curiosities—Arch Rock—Sugar Loaf Rock—Scull Rock—Dousman's farm—Davenport's farm—Robinson's folly—The Devil's Punch Bowl—Healthful atmosphere—Transparency of the waters—Compared with Saratoga, Cape May, and Mt. Washington as a point for health and recreation—Description of a traveler in 1854—Arrival of steamers and sailing vessels at the port during the year—Mr. Johnson's reminiscences—Indian name of island—Mythology—Three brothers of the great genii—Visit to the subterranean abode of the genii—Vision—Apostrophe of an old Indian chief—Old buildings—Door of Marquette's chapel—John Jacob Astor and the fur trade—Present support of the place—Fort Mackinaw—Fort Holmes—Fine view—Interesting localities—War of 1812—Death of Major Holmes—Soil of the island.... 83

CHAPTER VI.

Lake Superior—Scenery—Transparency of its waters—Climate—Isle Royale—Apostles' Islands—La Point—Thunder Cape—Cariboo Point—A wonderful lake—Romantic scenery—Pictured rocks—Rock Castle—The Grand Portal—The chapel—Fluctuations in the waters of Lake Superior—Curious phenomena—Retrocession of the waters—Mirage—Iron mountains and mines—Description of—Products—Shipments—Copper—Immense boulders—Produce of the mines for 1857—Shipment of copper from the Lake for 1858—Centre of the mining country—Iron mountains—Copper mines of Great Britain—Coal—Mackinaw a great manufacturing point—Key to the Upper Lakes—Commerce of lakes—Growth of cities.............. 105

CHAPTER VII.

Lake Huron—Eastern shore of Michigan—Face of the country—Picturesque view—Rivers—Grand—Saginaw—Cheboy-e-gun—Natural scenery—Fort Gratiot—White Rock—Saginaw Bay—Thunder Bay—Bois Blanc Island—Drummond's Island—British troops—St. Helena Island—Iroquois Woman's Point—Point La Barbe—Point aux Sable—Point St. Vital—Wreck of the Queen City—St. Martin's Island—Fox Point—Moneto pa-maw—Mille au Coquin—Great fishing places—Cross village—Catholic convent... 127

CHAPTER VIII.

Three epochs—The romantic—The military—The agricultural and commercial—An inviting region—Jesuit and Protestant Missions—First Protestant mission—First missionary—Islands of Mackinac and Green Bay—La Pointe—Saut St. Mary—Presbyterians—Baptists—Methodists—Revival at Fort Brady—Ke-wee-naw—Fon du Lac—Shawnees—Pottawatimies—Eagle River—Ontonagon—Camp River—Iroquois Point—Saginaw Indians—Melancholy reflections—Number of Indians in the States and Territories.. 143

CHAPTER IX. PAGE

Indian name of Michigan—Islands—Lanman's Summer in the Wilderness—Plains—Trees—Rivers—A traditionary land—Beautiful description—Official report in relation to the trade of the lakes—Green Bay—Grand Traverse Bay—Beaver Islands—L'Arbre Croche—Boundaries of Lake Michigan—Its connections—Railroad from Fort Wayne to Mackinaw—Recent report of—Amount completed—Land grants 159

CHAPTER X.

Mackinaw, the site for a great central city—The Venice of the lakes—Early importance as a central position—Nicolet—Compared geographically with other points—Immense chain of coast—Future prospects—Temperature—Testimony of the Jesuit fathers—Healthfulness of the climate—Dr. Drake on Mackinaw—Resort for invalids—Water currents of commerce—Surface drained by them—Soil of the northern and southern peninsulas of Michigan—Physical resources—Present proprietors of Mackinaw—Plan of the city—Streets—Avenues—Park—Lots and blocks for churches and public purposes—Institutions of learning and objects of benevolence—Fortifications—Docks and ferries—Materials for building—Harbors—Natural beauty of the site for a city—Mountain ranges—Interior lakes—Fish—Game........ 173

CHAPTER XI.

The entrepot of a vast commerce—Surface drained—Superiority of Mackinaw over Chicago as a commercial point—Exports and imports—Michigan the greatest lumber-growing region in the world—Interminable forests of the choicest pine—Facilities for market—Annual product of the pineries—Lumbering, mining, and fishing interests—Independent of financial crises—Mackinaw the centre of a great railroad system—Lines terminating at this point—North and South National Line—Canada grants—Growth of Northwestern cities—Future growth and prosperity of Mackinaw—Chicago—Legislative provision for opening roads in Michigan—The Forty Acre Homestead Bill—Its provisions...... 205

CHAPTER XII.

The Great Western Valley—Its growth and population—Comparison of Atlantic with interior cities—Relative growth of river and lake cities—Centre of population—Lake tonnage—Progress of the principal centres of population.. 228

CHAPTER XIII.

Michigan Agricultural Reports for 1854—Prof. Thomas' report—Report of J. S. Dixon—Products of States—Climate—Army Meteorological Reports. 255

CHAPTER XIV.

Agricultural interest—Means of transportation—Railways and vessels—Lumber—Vessels cleared—Lake cities and Atlantic ports—Home-market

PAGE

—Breadstuffs—Michigan flour—Monetary panics—Wheat—Importations —Provisions—Fruit—Live stock—Wool—Shipping business—Railroads—Lake Superior trade—Pine lumber trade—Copper interest—Iron interest —Fisheries—Coal mines—Salt—Plaster beds........ 272

CHAPTER XV.

Desirableness of a trip to the Lakes—Routes of travel—Interesting localities —Scenery—Southern coast—Portage Lake—Dr. Houghton—Ontonagon—Apostles' Islands—Return trip—Points of interest—St. Mary's River—Lake St. George—Point de Tour—Lake Michigan—Points of interest—Chicago........ 395

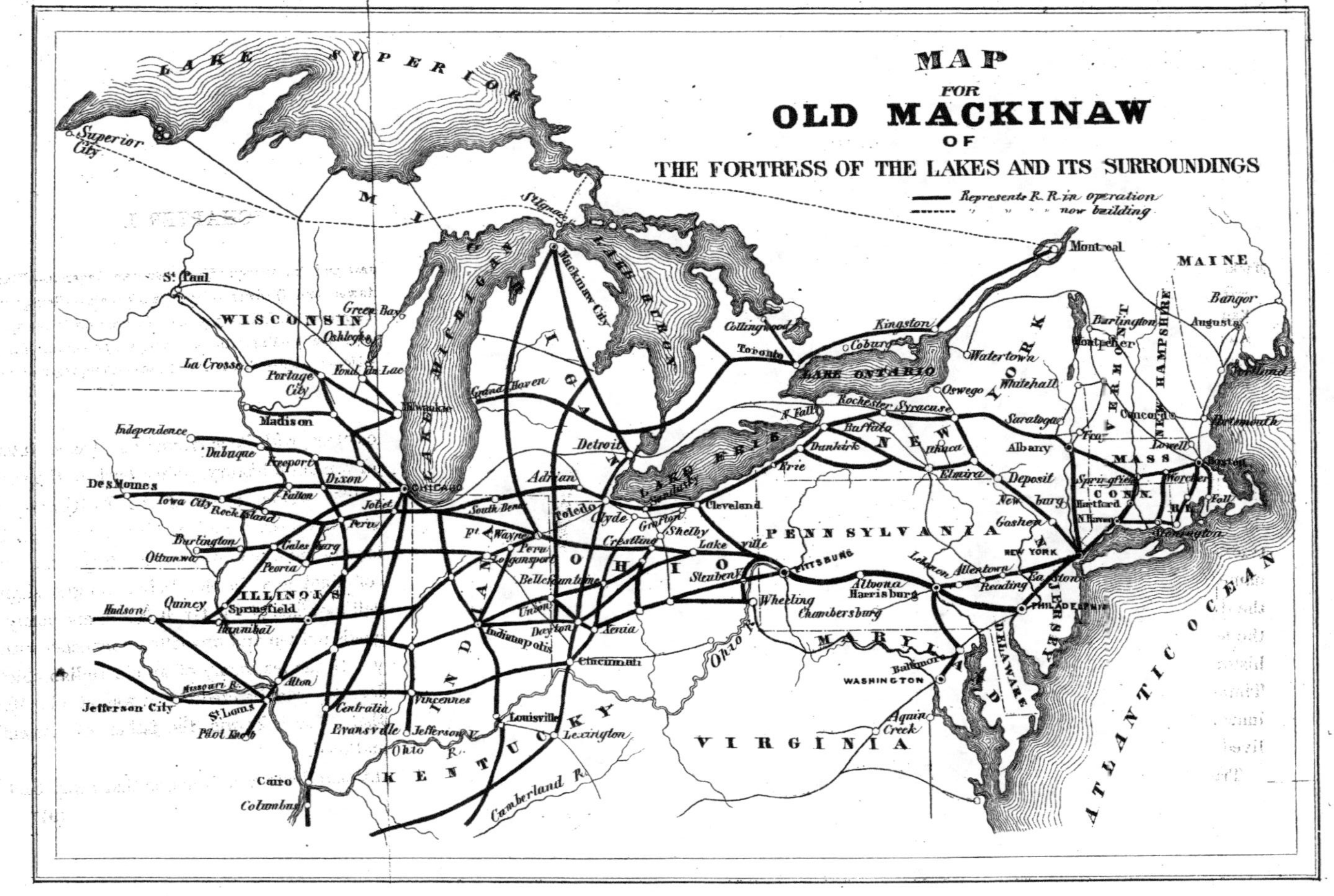
MAP
FOR
OLD MACKINAW
OF
THE FORTRESS OF THE LAKES AND ITS SURROUNDINGS
Represents R. R. in operation
" " now building
LAKE SUPERIOR
LAKE MICHIGAN
LAKE HURON
LAKE ERIE
LAKE ONTARIO
ATLANTIC OCEAN
WISCONSIN
MICHIGAN
ILLINOIS
INDIANA
OHIO
KENTUCKY
PENNSYLVANIA
NEW YORK
VERMONT
NEW HAMPSHIRE
MAINE
MASS
CONN.
NEW JERSEY
DELAWARE
MARYLAND
VIRGINIA
Superior City
St. Paul
Green Bay
La Crosse
Portage City
Madison
Independence
Dubuque
Freeport
Dixon
Des Moines
Iowa City
Rock Island
Fulton
Joliet
Chicago
Burlington
Ottumwa
Peoria
Hudson
Quincy
Springfield
Hannibal
Alton
Jefferson City
Missouri R.
St. Louis
Pilot Knob
Cairo
Columbus
Centralia
Evansville
Vincennes
Ohio R.
Louisville
Lexington
Cumberland R.
Indianapolis
Dayton
Xenia
Cincinnati
Toledo
Detroit
Adrian
Grand Haven
Mackinaw City
Clyde
Cleveland
Shelby
Crestline
Wheeling
Chambersburg
Altoona
Harrisburg
Pittsburg
Washington
Baltimore
Aquia Creek
Philadelphia
Reading
Allentown
New York
Goshen
Deposit
Elmira
Dunkirk
Buffalo
Erie
Rochester
Syracuse
Oswego
Toronto
Collingwood
Kingston
Coburg
Montreal
Watertown
Whitehall
Saratoga
Albany
Troy
Burlington
Montpelier
Concord
Lowell
Bangor
Augusta
Portland
Portsmouth
Boston
Worcester
Springfield
Hartford
Fall River

CHAPTER I.

Mackinaw and its surroundings—Indian legends—Hiawatha —Ottawas and Ojibwas — Paw-pau-ke-wis — San-ge-man— Kau-be-man—An Indian custom—Dedication to the spirits— Au-se-gum-ugs—Exploits of San-ge-man—Point St. Ignatius—Magic lance—Council of Peace—Conquests of San-ge-man.

MACKINAW, with its surroundings, has an interesting and romantic history, going back to the earliest times. The whole region of the Northwest, with its vast wildernesses and mighty lakes, has been traditionally invested with a mystery. The very name of Mackinaw, in the Indian tongue, signifies the dwelling-place of the Great Genii, and many are the legends written and unwritten connected with its history. If the testimony of an old Indian chief at Thunder Bay can be credited, it was at old Mackinaw that Mud-je-ke-wis, the father of Hiawatha, lived and died.

Traditional history informs us that away back in

a remote period of time, the Ottawas and the Ojibwas took up their journey from the Great Salt Lake towards the setting sun. These tribes were never stationary, but were constantly roving about. They were compared by the neighboring tribes to Paw-pau-ke-wis, a name given by the Indians to the light-drifting snow, which blows over the frozen ground in the month of March, now whirling and eddying into gigantic and anon into diminutive drifts. Paw-pau-ke-wis signifies running away. The name was given to a noted Indian chief, fully equal in bravery and daring to Hiawatha, Plu-re-busta, or Man-a-bosho.

The Ottawas and Ojibwas dwelt for a time on the Manitoulin Island in Lake Huron. While the tribes dwelt here, two distinguished Indian youths, by the name of San-ge-man and Kau-be-man, remarkable for their sprightliness, attracted the attention of their particular tribes. Both were the youngest children of their respective families. It was the custom of the Indians to send their boys, when young, to some retired place a short distance from their village, where they were to fast until the manitoes or spirits of the invisible world should appear to them. Temporary lodges were constructed for their accommodation. Those who could not endure the fast enjoined upon them by the Metais or Medicine-men, never rose to any eminence, but were to remain in obscurity. Comparatively few were able to bear the ordeal; but to all who waited the appointed time, and endured the fast, the spiritual guardian appeared and took the direction and control of their subsequent lives. San-ge-man in his first trial fasted seven days, and on the next he tasted food, having been reduced to extreme debility by his long abstinence, during which his mind became exceedingly elevated. In this exaltation his spiritual guide appeared to him. He was the spirit of the serpent who rules in the centre of the earth, and under the dark and mighty waters. This spirit revealed to him his future destiny, and promised him his guardianship through life. San-ge-man grew up and became remarkably strong and powerful. From his brave and reckless daring he was both an object of love and fear to the Ottawas.

About this time, as the legend runs, the former inhabitants of the Manitoulin Island and the adjoining country, who have the name of the Au-se-gum-a-ugs, commenced making inroads upon the settlements of the combined bands, and killed several of their number. Upon this the Ojibwas and Ottawas mustered a war party. San-ge-man, though young, offered himself as a warrior; and, full of heroic daring, went out with the expedition which left the Island in great numbers in their canoes, and crossed over to the main land on the northeast. After traveling a few days they fell upon the war path of their enemies, and soon surprised them. Terrified, they fled before the combined forces; and in the chase, the brave and daring youth outstripped all the rest and succeeded in taking a prisoner in sight of the enemies' village. On their return the Ojibwas and Ottawas were pursued, and being apprised of it by San-ge-man, they made good their escape, while the young brave, being instructed by his guardian spirit, allowed himself to be taken prisoner. His hands were tied, and he was made to walk in the midst of the warriors. At night they encamped, and after partaking of their evening meal, commenced their Indian ceremonies of drumming and shaking the rattle, accompanied with war songs. San-ge-man was asked by the chief of the party, if he could che-qwon-dum, at the same time giving him the rattle. He took it and commenced singing in a low, plaintive tone, which made the warriors exclaim, "He is weak-hearted, a coward, an old woman. Feigning great weakness and cowardice, he stepped up to the

Indian to whom he had surrendered his war club; and taking it, he commenced shaking the rattle, and as he danced round the watch-fire, increasing his speed, and, gradually raising the tone of his voice, he ended the dance by felling a warrior with his club, exclaiming, "a coward, ugh!" Then with terrific yells and the power of a giant, he continued his work of death at every blow. Affrighted, the whole party fled from the watch-fire and left him alone with the slain, all of which he scalped, and returned laden with these terrible trophies of victory to join his companions who returned to the Island.

San-ge-man having by his valor obtained a chieftainship over the Ottawas, started out on the war path and conquered all the country east and north of Lake Huron. The drum and rattle were now heard resounding through all the villages of the combined forces, and they extended their conquests to Saut St. Mary. For the purpose of bettering their condition they removed from the Island to the Detour, or the mouth of the St. Mary's river, where they occupied a deserted village, and there separated, part going up to the Saut, which had also been deserted, and the other portion tarrying in the above village for a year.

At the expiration of this time San-ge-man led a war party towards the west, and reached the present point St. Ignatius, on the north side of the straits where he found a large village. There was also another village a little east of Point St. Ignatius, at a place now called Moran's Bay, and still another at Point Au Chenes on the north shore of Lake Michigan, northeast of the Island of Mackinaw. At these places, old mounds, ditches, and gardens were found, which had existed from an unknown period. From this point a trail led to the Saut through an open country, and these ancient works can be distinctly traced to this day though covered with a heavy growth of timber.

After a hard fight with the inhabitants of these villages, San-ge-man at length succeeded in conquering them, and after expelling them burned all their lodges with the exception of a few at Point St. Ignatius. The inhabitants of this village fled across the straits southward from Point St. Ignatius and located at the point now known as Old Mackinaw, or Mackinaw City.

In the mean time, San-ge-man had returned to the Detour and removed his entire band to Point St. Ignatius. In the following spring while the Ottawas were out in their fields planting corn, a party of

Au-se-gum-ugs crossed over from Old Mackinaw, on the south side of the straits, and killed two of the Ottawa women. San-ge-man at once selected a party of tried warriors, and going down the straits pursued the Au-se-gum-ugs to the River Cheboy-e-gun, whither they had gone on a war expedition against the Mush-co-dan-she-ugs. On a sandy bay a little west of the mouth of the river, they found their enemies' canoes drawn up, they having gone into the interior. Believing that they would soon return, San-ge-man ordered his party to lie in ambush until their return. They were not long in waiting, for on the following day they made their appearance, being heated and weary with their marches, they all stripped and went into the Lake to bathe previous to embarking for Mackinaw. Unsuspicious of danger they played with the sportive waves as they dashed upon the shore, and were swimming and diving in all directions, when the terrific yell of armed warriors broke upon their ears. It was but the work of a moment and one hundred defenseless Indians perished in the waters. When the sad intelligence came to the remainder of the tribe at Mackinaw, they fled towards the Grand River country.

The village now deserted possessing superior attractions to San-ge-man and his warriors, the Ottawas crossed the straits and took possession, and here he remained until after he unfairly succeeded in obtaining the magic lance.

It was while here that a large delegation of Indians of the Mush-co-dan-she-ugs from the Middle village, Bear River, and Grand Traverse came to shake hands and smoke the pipe of peace with him. They had heard of his fame as a mighty warrior. The occasion was one of great rejoicing to the inhabitants of Mackinaw, and all turned out to witness the gathering. San-ge-man and his warriors appeared in council, dressed in richest furs, their heads decorated with eagle feathers, and tufts of hair of many colors. Among all the chiefs there assembled, for proud and noble bearing none excelled the Ottawa. A fur robe covered with scalp-locks hung carelessly over his left shoulder leaving his right arm free while speaking. As the result of these deliberations the bands became united and thus the territory of the Ottawa chief was enlarged.

It was from this point that he sallied forth every summer in war excursions toward the south, conquering the country along the eastern shore of Lake Michigan, extending his conquests to Grand River, and overrunning the country about the present site of Chicago. It was here that he received reinforcements from his old allies the Ojibwas, and extended his conquests down the Illinois River until he reached the "father of waters."

From this place he went forth to the slaughter of the Iroquois at the Detour, and expelled them from the Island of Mackinaw and Point St. Ignatius. From hence he went armed to wage an unnatural war against his relatives the Ojibwas, and was slain by the noble chief Kau-be-man, and it was to this place that the sad news came back of his fate. Thus much for the Indian history of Old Mackinaw.

Equally romantic is the history of the early missionaries and voyagers to this great centre of the Indian tribes. On the far-off shores of the north-western lakes the Jesuit Missionaries planted the cross, erected their chapels, repeated their *pater nosters* and *ave marias*, and sung their *Te Deums*, before the cavaliers landed at Jamestown or the Puritans at Plymouth. Among the Ottawas of Saut St. Marie and the Ojibwas and Hurons of Old Mackinaw, these devoted self-sacrificing followers of Ignatius Loyola commenced their ministrations upwards of two hundred years ago. They were not only the first missionaries among the savages of this north-western wilderness, but they were the first discoverers and explorers of the mighty lakes and rivers of that region. In advance of civilization they penetrated the dense unbroken wilderness, and launched their canoes upon unknown rivers, breaking the silence of their shores with their vesper hymns and matin prayers. The first to visit the ancient seats of heathenism in the old world, they were the first to preach the Gospel among the heathen of the new.

CHAPTER II.

Indian Spiritualists—Medicine men—Legends—The Spirit-world—Difference between Indian and Modern Spiritualists—Chusco the Spiritualist—Schoolcraft's testimony of—Mode of communicating with spirits—Belief in Satanic agency—Interesting account of Clairvoyance.

THE earliest traditions of the various Indian tribes inhabiting this country prove that they have practiced jugglery and all other things pertaining to the secret arts of the old uncivilized nations of the world. Among all the tribes have been found the priests of the occult sciences, and to this day we find Metais, Waubonos, Chees-a-kees and others bearing the common designation of Medicine men. In modern parlance we would call them Professors of Natural Magic, or of Magnetism, or Spiritualism. The difference however between these Indian professors of magic and those of modern date is, that while the latter travel round the country exhibiting their wonderful performances to gaping crowds, at a shilling a head, the former generally shrink from notoriety, and, instead of being anxious to display their marvelous feats, have only been constrained, after urgent entreaty and in particular cases, to exhibit their powers. The Indian magicians have shown more conclusively their power as clairvoyants and spiritualists, than all the rapping, table-tipping mediums of the present day.

Numerous interesting and beautiful Indian legends show their belief in a spiritual world—of a shadowy land beyond the great river. Whether this was obtained by revelations from their spiritual mediums, or derived from a higher source of inspiration, we know not; but most certain it is, that in no belief is the Indian more firmly grounded than that of a spirit-world.

The Indian Chees-a-kees or spiritualists had a different and far more satisfactory mode of communicating with departed spirits than ever modern spiritualists have attained to, or perhaps ever will. Forming, as they did, a connecting link or channel of communication between this world and the world of spirits, they did not affect to speak what the spirit had communicated; or, perhaps, to state it more fully, their organs of speech were not employed by the spirits to communicate revelations from the spirit world; but the spirits themselves spoke, and the responses to inquiries were perfectly audible to them and to all present. In this case all possibility of collusion was out of the question, and the inquirer could tell by the tones of the voice as as well as the manner of the communication, whether the response was genuine or not.

Chusco, a noted old Indian who died on Round Island several years ago, was a spiritualist. He was converted through the labors of Protestant Missionaries, led for many years an exemplary Christian life, and was a communicant in the Presbyterian Church on the Island up to the time of his death. Mr. Schoolcraft in his "Personal Memoirs," in which he gives most interesting reminiscences, running through a period of thirty years among numerous Indian tribes of the northwest, and who has kindly consented to allow us to make what extracts we may desire from his many interesting works, says that "Chusco was the Ottawa spiritualist, and up to his death he believed that he had, while in his heathen state, communication with spirits. Whenever it was deemed proper to obtain this communication, a pyramidal lodge was constructed of poles, eight in number, four inches in diamotor, and from twelve to sixteen feet in height. These poles were set firmly in the ground to the depth of two feet, the earth being beaten around them. The poles being securely imbedded, were then wound tightly with three rows of withes. The lodge was then covered with ap-puck-wois, securely lashed on. The structure was so stoutly and compactly built, that four strong Indians could scarcely move it by their mightiest efforts. The lodge being ready, the spiritualist was taken and covered all over, with the exception of his head, with a canoe sail which was lashed with bois-blanc cords and knotted. This being done, his feet and hands were secured in a like firm manner, causing him to resemble a bundle more than anything else. He would then request the bystanders to place him in the lodge. In a few minutes after entering, the lodge would commence swaying to and fro, with a tremulous motion, accompanied with the sound of a drum and rattle. The spiritualist then commenced chanting in a low, melancholy tone, gradually raising his voice, while the lodge, as if keeping time with his chant, vibrated to and fro with greater violence, and seemed at times as if the force would tear it to pieces.

In the midst of this shaking and singing, the sail and the cords, with which the spiritualist was bound, would be seen to fly out of the top of the lodge with great violence. A silence would then ensue for a short time, the lodge still continuing its tremulous vibrations. Soon a rustling sound would be heard at the top of the lodge indicating the presence of the spirit. The person or persons at whose instance the medium of the spiritualist was invoked, would then propose the question or questions they had to ask of the departed.

An Indian spiritualist, residing at Little Traverse Bay, was once requested to enter a lodge for the purpose of affording a neighboring Indian an opportunity to converse with a departed spirit about his child who was then very sick. The sound of a voice, unfamiliar to the persons assembled, was heard at the top of the lodge, accompanied by singing. The Indian, who recognized the voice, asked if his child would die. The reply was, "It will die the day after to-morrow. You are treated just as you treated a person a few years ago. Do you wish the matter revealed." The inquirer immediately dropped his head and asked no further questions. His child died at the time the spirit stated, and reports, years after, hinted that it had been poisoned, as the father of the deceased child had poisoned a young squaw, and that it was this same person who made the responses.

Old Chusco, after he became a Christian, could not, according to the testimony of Schoolcraft, be made to waver in his belief, that he was visited by spirits in the exhibitions connected with the tight-wound pyramidal, oracular lodge; but he believed they were evil spirits. No cross-questioning could bring out any other testimony. He avowed that, aside from his incantations, he had no part in the shaking of the lodge, never touching the poles at any time, and that the drumming, rattling, singing, and responses were all produced by these spirits.

The following account of Chusco, or Wau-chus-co, from the pen of William M. Johnson, Esq., of Mackinaw Island, will be found to be deeply interesting:

"WAU-CHUS-CO was a noted Indian spiritualist and Clairvoyant, and was born near the head of Lake Michigan—the year not known. He was eight or ten years old, he informed me, when the English garrison was massacred at Old Fort Missilimackinac. He died on Round Island, opposite the village and island of Mackinaw, at an advanced age.

"As he grew up from childhood, he found that he was an orphan, and lived with his uncle, but under the care of his grandmother. Upon attaining the age of fifteen his grandmother and uncle urged him to comply with the ancient custom of their people, which was to fast, and wait for the manifestations of the Gitchey-monedo,—whether he would grant him a guardian spirit or not, to guide and direct him through life. He was told that many young men of his tribe tried to fast, but that hunger overpowered their wishes to obtain a spiritual guardian; he was urged to do his best, and not to yield as others had done.

"Wau-chus-co died in 1839 or '40. He had, for more than ten years previous to his death, led an exemplary Christian life, and was a communicant of the Presbyterian Church on this Island, up to the time of his death. A few days previous to his death, I paid him a visit. 'Come in, come in, nosis!" (grandson) said he. After being seated, and we had lit our pipes; I said to him, 'Ne-me-sho-miss, (my grandfather,) you are now very old and feeble; you cannot expect to live many days; now, tell me the truth, who was it that moved your chees-a-kee lodge when you practiced your spiritual art?' A pause ensued before he answered:—'Nosis, as you are in part of my nation, I will tell you the truth: I know that I will die soon. I fasted ten days when I was a young man, in compliance with the custom of my tribe. While my body was feeble from long fasting, my soul increased in its powers; it appeared to embrace a vast extent of space, and the country within this space, was brought plainly before my vision, with its misty forms and beings—I speak of my spiritual vision. It was, while I was thus lying in a trance, my soul wandering in space, that animals, some of frightful size and form, serpents of monstrous size, and birds of different varieties and plumage, appeared to me and addressed me in human language, proposing to act as my guardian spirits. While my mind embraced these various moving forms, a superior intelligence in the form of man, surrounded by a wild, brilliant light, influenced my soul to select one of the bird-spirits, resembling the kite in look and form, to be the emblem of my guardian spirit, upon whose aid I was to call in time of need, and that he would be always prepared to render me assistance whenever my body and soul should be prepared to receive manifestations. My grandmother roused me to earth again, by inquiring if I needed food: I ate, and with feeble steps, soon returned to our lodge.

"'The first time that I ever chees-a-keed, was on a war expedition toward Chicago, or where it is now located—upon an urgent occasion. We were afraid that our foes would attack us unawares, and as we were also short of provisions, our chief urged me incessantly, until I consented. After preparing my soul and body, by fasting on bitter herbs, &c., I entered the Chees-a-kee lodge, which had been prepared for me:—the presence of my guardian spirit was soon indicated by a violent swaying of the lodge to and fro. "Tell us! tell us! where our enemies are?" cried out the chief and warriors. Soon, the vision of my soul embraced a large extent of country, which I had never before seen—every object was plainly before me—our enemies were in their villages, unsuspicious of danger; their movements and acts I could plainly see; and mentally or spiritually, I could hear their conversation. Game abounded in another direction. Next day we procured provisions, and a few days aftorward a dozen scalps graced our triumphant return to the village of the Cross. I exerted my powers again frequently among my tribe, and, to satisfy them, I permitted them to tie my feet and hands, and lash me round with ropes, as they thought proper. They would then place me in the Chees-a-kee lodge, which would immediately commence shaking and swaying to and for, indicating the presence of my guardian spirit: frequently I saw a bright, luminous light at the top of the lodge, and the words of the spirit would be audible to the spectators outside, who could not understand what was said; while mentally, I understood the words and language spoken.

"'In the year 1815, the American garrison at this post expected a vessel from Detroit, with supplies for the winter—a month had elapsed beyond the time for her arrival, and apprehensions of starvation were entertained; finally, a call was made to me by the commanding officer, through the traders. After due preparation I consented; the Chees-a-kee lodge was surrounded by Indians and whites; I had no sooner commenced shaking my rattle and chanting, than the spirits arrived; the rustling noise they made through the air, was heard, and the sound of their voices was audible to all.

"'The spirits directed my mind toward the southern end of Lake Huron—it lay before me with its bays and islands; the atmosphere looked hazy, resembling our Indian Summer; my vision terminated a little below the mouth of the St. Clair River—there lay the vessel, disabled! the sailors were busy in repairing spars and sails. My soul knew that they would be ready in two days, and that in seven days she would reach this Island, (Mackinaw,) by the south channel, [at that time an unusual route,] and I so revealed it to the inquirers. On the day I mentioned the schooner hove in sight, by the south channel. The captain of the vessel corroborated all I had stated.

"'I am now a praying Indian (Christian). I expect soon to die, Nosis. This is the truth: I possessed a power, or a power possessed me, which I cannot explain or fully describe to you. I never attempted to move the lodge by my own physical powers—I held communion with supernatual beings or souls, who acted upon my soul or mind, revealing to me the knowledge which I have related to you.'

"The foregoing merely gives a few acts of the power exhibited by this remarkable, half-civilized Indian. I could enumerate many instances in which this power has been exhibited among our Indians. These Chees-a-kees had the power of influencing the mind of an Indian at a distance for good or evil, even to the deprivation of life among them: so also in cases of rivalship, as hunters or warriors. This influence has even extended to things material, while in the hands of those influenced. The soul or mind—perhaps nervous system of the individual, being powerfully acted upon by a spiritual battery, greater than the one possessed more or less by all human beings."

In Schoolcraft's "American Indians" an interesting account is given of a woman-spiritualist, who bore the name of the "Prophetess of Che-moi-che-goi-me-gou." Among the Indians she was called "The woman of the blue-robed cloud." The account was given by herself after she had become a member of the Methodist Church and renounced all connection with spirits. The following is her narrative:—

"When I was a girl of about twelve or thirteen years of age, my mother told me to look out for something that would happen to me. Accordingly, one morning early, in the middle of winter, I found an unusual sign, and ran off, as far from the lodge as I could, and remained there until my mother came and found me out. She knew what was the matter, and brought me nearer to the family lodge, and bade me help her in making a small lodge of branches of the spruce tree. She told me to remain there, and keep away from every one, and as a diversion, to keep myself employed in chopping wood, and that she would bring me plenty of prepared bass-wood bark to twist into twine. She told me she would come to see me, in two days, and that in the mean time I must not even taste snow.

"I did as directed; at the end of two days she came to see me. I thought she would surely bring me something to eat, but to my disappointment she brought nothing. I suffered more from *thirst* than hunger, though I felt my stomach gnawing. My mother sat quietly down and said (after ascertaining that I had not tasted anything), 'My child, you are the youngest of your sisters, and none are now left me of all my sons and children, but you *four*' (alluding to her two elder sisters, herself and a little son, still a mere lad). 'Who,' she continued, 'will take care of us poor women? Now, my daughter, listen to me, and try to obey. Blacken your face and fast *really*, that the Master of Life may have pity on you and me, and on us all. Do not, in the least, deviate from my counsels, and in two days more, I will come to you. He will help you, if you are determined to do what is right, and tell me, whether you are favored or not, by the *true* Great Spirit; and if your visions are not good, reject them.' So saying, she departed.

"I took my little hatchet and cut plenty of wood, and twisted the cord that was to be used in sewing *ap-puk-way-oon-un*, or mats for the use of the family. Gradually I began to feel less appetite, but my thirst continued; still I was fearful of touching the snow to allay it, by sucking it, as my mother had told me that if I did so, though secretly, the Great Spirit would see me, and the lesser spirits also, and that my fasting would be of no use. So I continued to fast till the fourth day, when my mother came with a little tin dish, and filling it with snow, she came to my lodge, and was well pleased to find that I had followed her injunctions. She melted the snow, and told me to drink it. I did so, and felt refreshed, but had a desire for more, which she told me would not do, and I contented myself with what she had given me. She again told me to get and follow a good vision—a vision that might not only do us good, but also benefit mankind, if I could. She then left me, and for two days she did not come near me, nor any human being, and I was left to my own reflections. The night of the sixth day, I fancied a voice called to me, and said: 'Poor child! I pity your condition; come, you are invited this way;' and I thought the voice proceeded from a certain distance from my lodge. I obeyed the summons, and going to the spot from which the voice came, found a thin, shining path, like a silver cord, which I followed. It led straight forward, and, it seemed, upward. After going a short distance I stood still and saw on my right hand the new moon, with a flame rising from the top like a candle, which threw around a broad light. On the left appeared the sun, near the point of its setting. I went on, and I beheld on my right the face of Kau-ge-gag-bequa, or the everlasting woman, who told me her name, and said to me, 'I give you my name, and you may give it to another. I also give you that which I have, life everlasting. I give you long life on the earth, and skill in saving life in others. Go, you are called on high.'

"I went on, and saw a man standing with a large, circular body, and rays from his head, like horns. He said, 'Fear not, my name is Monedo Wininees, or the Little man Spirit. I give this name to your first son. It is my life. Go to the place you are called to visit.' I followed the path till I could see that it led up to an opening in the sky, when I heard a voice, and standing still, saw the figure of a man standing near the path, whose head was surrounded with a brilliant halo, and his breast was covered with squares. He said to me: 'Look at me, my name is O-shau-wau-e-geeghick, or the Bright Blue Sky. I am the veil that covers the opening into the sky. Stand and listen to me. Do not be afraid. I am going to endow you with gifts of life, and put you in array that you may withstand and endure. Immediately I saw myself encircled with bright points which rested against me like needles, but gave me no pain, and they fell at my feet. This was repeated several times, and at each time they fell to the ground. He said, 'wait and do not fear, till I have said and done all I am about to do.' I then felt different instruments, first like awls, and then like nails stuck into my flesh, but neither did they give me pain, but, like the needles, fell at my feet as often as they appeared. He then said, 'that is good,' meaning my trial by these points. 'You will see length of days. Advance a little further,' said he. I did so, and stood at the commencement of the opening. 'You have arrived,' said he, 'at the limit you cannot pass. I give you my name, you can give it to another. Now, return! Look around you. There is a conveyance for you. Do not be afraid to get on its back, and when you get to your lodge, you must take that which sustains the human body.' I turned, and saw a kind of fish swimming in the air, and getting upon it as directed, was carried back with celerity, my hair floating behind me in the air. And as soon as I got back, my vision ceased.

"In the morning, being the sixth day of my fast, my mother came with a little bit of dried trout.

But such was my sensitiveness to all sounds, and my increased power of scent, produced by fasting, that before she came in sight I heard her, while a great way off, and when she came in, I could not bear the smell of the fish or herself either. She said, 'I have brought something for you to eat, only a mouthful, to prevent your dying.' She prepared to cook it, but I said, 'Mother, forbear, I do not wish to eat it —the smell is offensive to me.' She accordingly left off preparing to cook the fish, and again encouraged me to persevere, and try to become a comfort to her in her old age, and bereaved state, and left me.

"I attempted to cut wood, as usual, but in the effort I fell back on the snow, from weariness, and lay some time; at last I made an effort and rose, and went to my lodge and lay down. I again saw the vision, and each person who had before spoken to me, and heard the promises of different kinds made to me, and the songs. I went the same path which I had pursued before, and met with the same reception. I also had another vision, or celestial visit, which I shall presently relate. My mother came again on the seventh day, and brough me some pounded corn boiled in *snow-water*, for she said I must not drink water from lake or river. After taking it, I related my vision to her. She said it was good, and spoke to me to continue my fast three days longer. I did so; at the end of which she took me home, and made a feast in honor of my success, and invited a great many guests. I was told to eat sparingly, and to take nothing too hearty or substantial; but this was unnecessary, for my abstinence had made my senses so acute, that all animal food had a gross and disagreeable odor.

"After the seventh day of my fast (she continued), while I was lying in my lodge, I saw a dark, round object descending from the sky like a round stone, and enter my lodge. As it came near, I saw that it had small feet and hands like a human body. It spoke to me and said, 'I give you the gift of seeing into futurity, that you may use it for the benefit of yourself and the Indians—your relations and tribes-people.' It then departed, but as it went away, it assumed wings, and looked to me like the red-headed woodpecker.

"In consequence of being thus favored, I assumed the arts of a medicine-woman and a prophetess; but never those of a Wabeno. The first time I exercised the prophetical art, was at the strong and repeated solicitations of my friends. It was in the winter season, and they were then encamped west of the Wisacoda, or Brule River, of Lake Superior, and between it and the plains west. There were, beside my mother's family and relatives, a considerable number of families. They had been some time at the place, and were near starving, as they could find no game. One evening the chief of the party came into my mother's lodge. I had lain down, and was supposed to be asleep, and he requested of my mother that she would allow me to try my skill to relieve them. My mother spoke to me, and after some conversation, she gave her consent. I told them to build the *Jee-suk-aun,* or prophet's lodge *strong,* and gave particular directions for it. I directed that it should consist of ten posts or saplings, each of a different kind of wood, which I named. When it was finished, and tightly wound with skins, the entire population of the encampment assembled around it, and I went in, taking only a small drum. I immediately knelt down, and holding my head near the ground, in a position as near as may be prostrate, began beating my drum, and reciting my songs or incantations. The lodge commenced shaking violently, by supernatural means. I knew this by the compressed current of air above, and the noise of motion. This being regarded by me, and by all without, as a proof of the presence of the spirits I consulted, I ceased beating and singing, and lay still, waiting for questions in the position I at first assumed.

"The first question put to me was in relation to the game, and *where* it was to be found. The response was given by the orbicular spirit, who had appeared to me. He said, 'How short-sighted you are! If you will go in a *west* direction, you will find game in abundance.' Next day the camp was broken up, and they all moved westward, the hunters, as usual, going far ahead. They had not proceeded far beyond the bounds of their former hunting circle, when they came upon tracks of moose, and that day they killed a female and two young moose, nearly full-grown. They pitched their encampment anew, and had abundance of animal food in this new position.

"My reputation was established by this success, and I was afterward noted in the tribe, in the art of a medicine-woman, and sung the songs which I have given to you."

CHAPTER III

Marquette's visit to Iroquois Point—Chapel and Fort—Old Mackinaw—The French Settlement in the Northwest—Erection of Chapel and Fort—The Gateway of Commerce—The Rendezvous of Traders, Trappers, Soldiers, Missionaries, and Indians—Description of Fort—Courriers des Bois—Expedition of Marquette and Joliet to Explore the Mississippi—Green Bay—Fox River—Wisconsin—Mississippi—Peoria Indians—Return Trip—Kaskaskia Indians—St. Xavier Missions—Mission to "the Illinois"—Marquette's Health declines—Starts out on Return trip to Mackinaw—Dies and is Buried at mouth of Marquette River—Indians remove his Remains to Mackinaw—Funeral Cortege—Ceremonies—Burial in the Chapel—Changes of time—Schoolcraft on the Place of Marquette's Burial—Missilimackinac—Name of Jesuit Missions.

In the year 1670, the devoted and self-sacrificing missionary, Jean Marquette, with a company of Indians of the Huron tribe, subsequently known as the Wyandots from the Georgian Bay, on the northeastern extremity of Lake Huron, entered for the first time the old Indian town on the northern side of the Mackinaw Straits. During the time he was planting his colony, and erecting his chapel at Iroquois Point, which he afterward designated St. Ignace, he resided on the Mackinaw Island. In 1671, he furnished an account of the island and its surroundings, which was published in "The Relations Des Jesuits" He says:

"Missilimackinac is an island famous in these regions, of more than a league in diameter, and elevated in some places by such high cliffs as to be seen more than twelve leagues off. It is situated just in the strait forming the communication between Lakes Huron and Illinois (Michigan). It is the key, and, and as it were, the gate for all the tribes from the south, as the Saut, (St. Marie) is for those of the north, there being in this section of country only those two passages by water, for a great number of nations have to go by one or other of these channels, in order to reach the French settlements.

"This presents a peculiarly favorable opportunity, both for instructing those who pass here, and also for obtaining easy access and conveyance to their places of abode.

"This place is the most noted in these regions for the abundance of its fisheries; for, according to the Indian saying, 'this is the home of the fishes.' Elsewhere, although they exist in large numbers, it is not properly their 'home,' which is in the neighborhood of Missilimackinac.

"In fact, beside the fish common to all the other tribes, as the herring, carp, pike, gold-fish, white-fish and sturgeon, there are found three varieties of the trout—one common; the second of a larger size, three feet long and one foot thick; the third monstrous, for we cannot otherwise describe it—it being so fat that the Indians, who have a peculiar relish for fats, can scarcely eat it. Besides, the supply is such that a single Indian will take forty or fifty of them through the ice, with a single spear, in three hours.

"It is this attraction which has heretofore drawn to a point so advantageous, the greater part of the savages, in this country driven away by fear of the Iroquois. The three tribes at present living on the *Baye des Puans* (Green Bay) as strangers, formerly dwelt on the main land near the middle of this island—some on the borders of Lake Illinois, others on the borders of Lake Huron. A part of them, called *Sauteurs,* had their abode on the main land at the West, and the others look upon this place as their country for passing the winter, when there are no fish at the *Saut.* The Hurons, called *Etonontathronnons,* have lived for some years in the same island, to escape the Iroquois. Four villages of Ottawas had also their abode in this quarter.

"It is worthy of notice that those who bore the name of the island, and called themselves Missilimackinac, were so numerous, that some of the survivors yet living here assure us that they once had thirty villages, all inclosed in a fortification of a league and a half in circuit, when the Iroquois came and defeated them, inflated by a victory they had gained over three thousand men of that nation, who had carried their hostilities as far as the country of the *Agnichronnons.*

"In one word, the quantity of fish, united with the excellence of the soil for Indian corn, has always been a powerful attraction to the tribes in these regions, of which the greater part subsist only on fish, but some on Indian corn. On this account many of these same tribes, perceiving that the peace is likely to be established with the Iroquois, have turned their attention to this point so convenient for a return to their own country, and will follow the examples of those who have made a beginning on the islands of Lake Huron, which by this means will soon be peopled from one end to the other, an event highly desirable to facilitate the instruction of the Indian race, whom it would not be necessary to seek by journeys of two or three hundred leagues on these great lakes, with inconceivable danger and hardships.

"In order to aid the execution of the design, signified to us by many of the savages, of taking up their abode at this point, where some have already passed the winter, hunting in the neighborhood, we ourselves have also wintered here, in order to make arrangements for establishing the mission of *St. Ignace,* from whence it will be easy to have access to all the Indians of Lake Huron, when the several tribes shall have settled each on its own lands.

"With these advantages, the place has also its inconveniences, particularly for the French, who are not yet familiar, as are the savages, with the different kinds of fishery, in which the latter are trained from their birth; the winds and the tides occasion no small embarrassment to the fishermen.

"The winds: For this is the central point between the three great lakes which surround it, and which seem incessantly tossing ball at each other. For no sooner has the wind ceased blowing from Lake Michigan than Lake Huron hurls back the gale it has received, and Lake Superior in its turn, sends forth its blasts from another quarter, and thus the game is played from one to the other—and as these lakes are of vast extent, the winds cannot be otherwise than boisterous, especially during the autumn."

"Old Mackinaw," the Indian name of which is Pe-quod-e-non-ge, an Indian town on the south side of the Straits, became the place of the first French settlement northwest of Fort Frontenac, or Cadaraeque on Lake Ontario. The settlement was made by father Marquette, in 1671. Pe-quod-e-non-ge, as we have seen in a previous Chapter, with its coasts and islands before it, has been the theatre of some of the most exciting and interesting events in Indian history, previous to the arrival of the "white man." It was the Metropolis of a portion of the Ojibwa and Ottawa nations. It was there that their Congresses met, to adopt a policy which terminated in the conquest of the country south of it —it was there that the tramping feet of thousands of plumed and painted warriors shook Pe-quod-e-non-ge, while dancing their war dances—it was from there that the startling sound of the war yell of these thousands was wafted to the adjacent coast and islands, making the peaceful welkin ring with their unearthly shouts of victory or death. In process of time a Chapel and Fort were erected, and it became a strong-hold and trading post of the greatest importance to the entire region of the northwest, being the gateway of commerce between the St. Lawrence and the Mississippi, and also the grand avenue to the Upper Lakes of the north, and the rendezvous of the traders, merchants, trappers, soldiers, missionaries and Indians of the whole northwest. Villages of Hurons and Ottawas were located in the vicinity of the Fort and Chapel. The Fort inclosed an area of about several acres, and was surrounded with cedar pickets. The remains of the fort and buildings can still be seen. On an eminence not far from the fort, the Ottawas erected a fortification. Within the inclosure of the Fort and adjoining the Chapel, the Jesuits erected a College, the first institution of the kind in the Western country. It was also the great depot for the *Courriers des Bois,* or rangers of the woods, who, from their distant excursions, would congregate here. The goods which they had brought from Canada, for the purpose of exchanging for furs with the Indians of Green Bay and Illinois, and along the shores of Lake Superior, and the region lying between that and the banks of the Mississippi, had to be deposited here, and they were usually on hand a long time before they could be disposed of and transferred to the distant marts of trade.

In the year 1672, while Marquette was engaged in his duties as priest at the Chapel, the site of which now bears the name of St. Ignatius, and also employed in instructing the Indian youth of the villages, he was visited by Joliet, a member of the same order who bore a commission from Frontenac, then Governor of Canada, empowering him to select Marquette as a companion and enter upon a voyage of discovery. The winter was spent by these men in making preparations to carry out the commands of their superiors. The specific object of their mission was to explore the Mississippi, which was supposed to empty into the Gulf of California. That all possible information might be gained in regard to this unknown river, Marquette held conversations with all the noted Indian explorers and trappers, as well as the rangers of the woods within his reach. From the information thus gained he made out a map of the river, including its source and direction, and all the streams known to empty into it.

Spring at length came, and on a bright, beautiful morning in the month of May, having bid adieu to his charge at his mission, and commended his flock to God, Marquette and his companion, with five others selected for the purpose, entered their bark canoes with paddles in hand, and St. Ignatius was soon lost to the sight of the devoted missionary forever. After sailing along the Straits they entered Lake Michigan, and continued their voyage until they arrived at Green Bay, passed the mouth of the Menominee River, finally reaching that of the Fox River. On the 7th of June, having sailed upwards of two hundred miles, the voyagers reached the mission of St. Francis Xavier. They had now reached the limit of all former French or English discoveries. The new and unknown West spread out before them, and the thousand dangers and hardships by river and land, heightened by tales of horror related to them by the Indians, were presented to their imagination. Resolutely determined to prosecute the enterprise committed to their charge, they knelt upon the shore of Fox River to renew their devotions and obtain the divine guidance and protection. Encouraged by past success, and urged on by a strong faith, they launched their canoes upon the bosom of the Fox River, and breaking the silence of its shores by the dip of their paddles, they sailed up its current. When they reached the rapids of that river, it was with difficulty they were enabled to proceed. There was not power enough in the paddles of the two canoes to stem the current, and they were obliged to wade up the rapids on the jagged rocks, and thus tow them along. Having made the voyage of the Fox they arrived at the portage, and taking their canoes containing their provision and clothes upon their shoulders, they reached the Wisconsin and launched them upon that stream. They had no longer to breast a rapid current, as the waters of the Wisconsin flowed west. With renewed courage they prosecuted their voyage, and after ten days their hearts were made glad at the sight of the broad and beautiful river which they were entering, and which they supposed would bear them to the far-off western sea. They had reached the "father of waters." No sight could be more charming than that which presented itself to their vision as they beheld on either side, alternately stretching away to a vast distance, immense forests of mountain and plain.

At length, on the 25th of June, as they were sailing along near the eastern shore, they discovered foot-prints in the sand. At sight of these they landed and fastening their canoes, that they might again look upon the face of human beings, they followed an Indian path which led up the bank. They were not long in finding two Indian villages, which proved to be those of the "Pewarias" and "Moing-wenas." In answer to a question proposed by Marquette, who addressed them in Indian, and inquired who they were; they answered, "We are Illinois." After an exchange of friendly greetings with these peaceable Indians, the voyagers re-embarked and passed on down the river. They continued on their downward passage until they reached the mouth of the Missouri, which poured its turbid flood into the Mississippi; and still further until they passed the mouth of the Ohio, and then on down until they passed the Arkansas, and arrived within thirty miles of the mouth of the Mississippi. It was not necessary to proceed any further to satisfy the explorers that the river entered into the Gulf of Mexico, instead of that of California.

Having accomplished the end of the expedition, the company started out upon their return trip on the 17th of July. When they reached the mouth of the Illinois river, they determined on returning by that route to Mackinaw. Arriving at the portage of that river they fell in with a tribe of Indians who called themselves the Kaskaskias, who kindly volunteered to conduct them to Lake Michigan, where in due time they arrived. After sailing along the western shore of the lake they again found themselves at Green Bay, and were heartily welcomed by the brethren at the mission of St. Francis Xavier. Worn down with fatigue, Marquette determined to remain here to recruit his health before returning to his missionary labors. He spent his time at this mission post in copying his journal of the voyage down the Mississippi and back, which he accompanied by a map of the river and country, and sent by the Ottawa flotilla to his superiors at Montreal. The return of this flotilla brought him orders for the establishment of a mission among the Illinois, with whom he had so friendly an interview on his exploring voyage. Having passed the winter and succeeding summer at the St. Xavier mission, he started out in the fall for Kaskaskia. The difficulties of the journey were such, it having to be accomplished by land and water, that his health, which had been greatly enfeebled by his former voyage, was not sufficient to enable him to endure the cold winds of winter which had set in before the completion of the journey. On reaching the Chicago River it was found closed, and he did not consider it prudent to undertake an over-land journey. He therefore resolved to winter at that point, and giving his Indian companions who accompanied him the proper instructions and pious counsel, he sent them back to Green Bay. Two Frenchmen made an arrangement to remain with him during the winter. The nearest persons to their lodge were fifty miles distant. They were French trappers and traders, one of whom bore the title of a doctor. This latter person being informed of Marquette's ill-health paid him a visit, and did what he could for his relief. He also received friendly offices from the Indians in the neighborhood, a party of whom proposed to carry him and all his baggage to the contemplated mission at Kaskaskia. His health, however, was such that it did not allow him to accept their kind offer, and he was obliged to remain in his camp during the winter.

Spring at length returned after a long and dreary winter, and Marquette, with some Indian companions, started out for the upper waters of the Illinois River. In about two weeks he reached Kaskaskia, and at once entered upon the duties of his mission. After having instructed the Indians, so as to enable them to understand the objects of his mission to them, he called them all together in the open prairie, where he had erected a rude altar surmounted by the cross, and adorned with pictures of the Virgin Mary. The chiefs and warriors, and the whole tribe, were addressed by him in their native tongue. He made a number of presents to them, the more effectually to gain their affections and confidence, and then related to them the simple story of the cross, after which he celebrated mass. The scene was truly impressive, and the effect upon the sons of the forest was all that the missionary could desire. Bright and cheering were the prospects of converting the Kaskaskias to Christianity, but the devoted missionary was doomed to disappointment. His former malady returned, and assumed a type of so alarming a nature, that he was satisfied his labors on earth would soon come to an end.

Thoughts of his beloved mission at Mackinaw, where he had spent so many days in preaching to Ottawas and Hurons, and in teaching their youth Christian science, filled his mind; and the Christian, not to say natural, desire of his heart, was again to bow in the Chapel of St. Ignatius, and again behold the parents and children of his former charge. Having received the last rites of the church he set out to the lake, accompanied by the Kaskaskias who sorrowed much at his departure, but who were comforted by the dying missionary, who assured them that another would soon be sent to take his place. When they reached the shore of Lake Michigan the Indians returned, and with his two French companions Marquette embarked in a canoe upon its waters. As they coasted along the eastern shore of the lake the health of Marquette continued to fail, and he at last became so weak that when they landed to encamp for the night they had to lift him out of the canoe. Much further they could not proceed, as the journey of life with the missionary was rapidly drawing to a close.

Conscious of his approaching dissolution, as they were gently gliding along the shore, he directed his companions to paddle into the mouth of a small river which they were nearing, and pointing to an eminence not far from the bank, he languidly said, "Bury me there." That river, to this day, bears the name of the lamented Marquette. On landing they erected a bark cabin, and stretched the dying missionary as comfortably as they could beneath its humble roof. Having blessed some water with the usual ceremonies of the Catholic Church, he gave his companions directions how to proceed in his last moments. He instructed them also in regard to the manner in which they were to arrange his body when dead, and the ceremonies to be performed when it was committed to the earth. He then, for the last time, heard the confessions of his companions, encouraging them to rely on the mercy and protection of God, and then sent them away to take the repose they so much needed. After a few hours he felt that he was about taking his last sleep, and calling them, he took his crucifix and placing it in their hands, pronounced in a clear voice his profession of faith, thanking the Almighty for the favor of permitting him to die a Jesuit Missionary. Then calmly folding his arms upon his breast with the name of Jesus on his lips, and his eyes raised to heaven, while over his face beamed the radiance of immortality, he passed away to the land of the blest.

In conformity with the directions of the deceased, in due time his companions prepared the body for burial, and to the sound of his Chapel bell bore it slowly and solemnly to the place designated, where they committed it to the dust, and erected a rude cross to point out to the passing traveler the place of his grave.

James Marquette was of a most ancient and honorable family of the city of Laon, France. Born at the ancient seat of his family, in the year 1637, he was, through his pious mother, Rose de la Salle, allied to the venerable John Baptist de la Salle, the founder of the institute known as the Brothers of the Christian Schools. At the age of seventeen he entered the Society of Jesus, and after two years of study and self-examination had passed away, he was, as is usual with the young Jesuits, employed in teaching, which position he held for twelve years. No sooner had he been invested with the priesthood, than his desire to become in all things an imitator of his chosen patron, St. Francis Xavier, induced him to seek a mission in some land that knew not God, that he might labor there to his latest breath, and die unaided and alone. His desire was gratified. For nine years he labored among the Indians, and was able to preach to them in ten different languages; but he rests from his labors, and his works follow him. He died, May 18, 1675.

The Indians of Mackinaw and vicinity, and also those of Kaskaskia, were in great sorrow when the tidings of Marquette's death reached them. Not long after this melancholy event, a large company of Ojibwas, Ottawas, and Hurons, who had been out on a hunting expedition, landed their canoes at the mouth of the Marquette river, with the intention of removing his remains to Mackinaw. They had heard of his desire to have his body interred in the consecrated ground of St. Ignatius, and they had resolved that the dying wish of the missionary should be fulfilled. As they stood around in silence and gazed upon the cross that marked the place of his burial, the hearts of the stern warriors were moved. The bones of the missionary were dug up and placed in a neat box of bark made for the occasion, and the numerous canoes which formed a large fleet started from the mouth of the river with nothing but the sighs of the Indians, and the dip of the paddles to break the silence of the scene. As they advanced towards Mackinaw, the funeral cortege was met by a large number of canoes bearing Ottawas, Hurons, and Iroquois, and still others shot out ever and anon to join the fleet.

When they arrived in sight of the Point, and beheld the cross of St. Ignatius as if painted against the northern sky, the missionaries in charge came out to the beach clad in vestments adapted to the occasion. How was the scene heightened when the priests commenced, as the canoe bearing the remains of Marquette neared the shore, to chant the requiem for the dead. The whole population was out, entirely covering the beach, and as the procession marched up to the Chapel with cross and prayer, and tapers burning, and laid the bark box beneath a pall made in the form of a coffin, the sons and daughters of the forest wept. After the funeral service was ended, the coffin was placed in a vault in the middle of the church, where the Catholic historian says, "Marquette reposes as the guardian angel of the Ottawa missions."

"He was the first and last white man who ever had such an assembly of the wild sons of the forest to attend him to his grave.

"So many stirring events succeeded each other after this period—first, the war between the English Colonists, and the French; then the Colonists with the Indians, the Revolutionary War, the Indian Wars, and finally the War of 1812, with the death of all those who witnessed his burial, including the Fathers who officiated at the time, whose papers were lost, together with the total destruction and evacuation of this mission station for many years, naturally obliterated all recollections of the transaction, which accounts for the total ignorance of the present inhabitants of Point St. Ignatius respecting it. The locality of his grave is lost; but only until the Archangel's trump, at the last, shall summon him from his narrow grave, with those plumed and painted warriors who now lie around him."

The Missionaries who succeeded Marquette, at

Mackinaw, continued their labors until 1706, when, finding it useless to continue the mission, or struggle any longer with superstition and vice, they burned down their College and Chapel, and returned to Quebec. The governor, alarmed at this step, at last promised to enforce the laws against the dissolute French, and prevailed on Father Marest to return. Soon after the Ottawas, discontented at Detroit, a French post, which was served by the Recollects, and where the blood of a Recollect had been shed in a riot, began to move back to Mackinaw, and the mission was renewed. In 1721, Charlevoix visited this mission, and this is the last we hear of it.

Nearly two hundred years have passed away since that event. The Chapel of St. Ignatius has passed away, and with it the Chapel, and Fort, and College at Old Mackinaw. Nothing is left but the stone walls and stumps of the pickets which surrounded them, and which may be seen to this day. To the Catholic, this consecrated spot, the site of one of their first Chapels, and their first College in the great northwest, must possess unusual interest. As there is a difference of opinion in relation to the burial place of Marquette, whether it was on the north or south side of the Straits, we give the following from "Schoolcraft's Discovery of the Sources of the Mississippi." He says: "They carried his body to the Mission of Old Mackinaw, of which he was the founder, where it was interred. It is known that the Mission of Mackinaw fell on the downfall of the Jesuits. When the post of Mackinaw was removed from the peninsula to the island, which was about 1780, the bones of the Missionary were transferred to the old Catholic burial ground, in the village on the island. There they remained till a land or property question arose to agitate the Church, and when the crisis happened the whole grave-yard was disturbed, and his bones, with others, were transferred to the Indian village of La Crosse, which is in the vicinity of L'Arbre Croche, Michigan."

There is a difference of opinion also as to the point from whence Marquette and his companions started for the discovery of the Mississippi. Schoolcraft says: "Wherever Missilimackinac is mentioned in the Missionary letters, or in the history of this period, it is the ancient Fort on the apex of the Michigan peninsula that is alluded to." In his Introduction to the above work, he says, that "Father Marquette, after laying the foundation of Missilimackinac, proceeded in company with Sieur Joliet, up the Fox River of Green Bay, and crossing the portage into the Wisconsin, entered the Mississippi in 1673."

It is an established fact, that Marquette organized the Mission at Old Mackinaw, in the year 1671, subsequently to that at the opposite point, and that he remained there until the year 1673, when he embarked with Joliet on his exploring tour of the Mississippi. Charelvoix places the Mission of St. Ignace, on the south side of the Straits, adjoining the Fort, and has made no such designation on the north side, showing at least that this mission was more modern than the other. Nearly all the Jesuit Missions bore the name of St. Ignatius, in honor of their founder, as those of the Franciscans bore the name of St. Francis. Ignatius Loyola and Francis Xavier were the founders of these sects.

CHAPTER IV.

La Salle's visit to Mackinaw—English traders—La Hontan's visit—Mackinaw an English fort—Speech of a Chippewa Chief—Indian stratagem—Massacre of the English at the fort—Escape of Mr. Alexander Henry—Early white settlement of Mackinaw—Present description—Relations of the Jesuits — Remarkable phenomena — Parhelia — Subterranean river.

IN the summer of 1679 the Griffin, built by La Salle and his company on the shore of Lake Erie, at the present site of the town of Erie, passed up the St. Clair, sailed over the Huron, and entering the Straits, found a safe harbor at Old Mackinaw. La Salle's expedition passed eight or nine years at this place, and from hence they penetrated the country in all directions. At the same time it continued to be the summer resort of numerous Indian tribes who came here to trade and engage in the wild sports and recreations peculiar to the savage race. As a city of peace, it was regarded in the same light that the ancient Hebrews regarded their cities of Refuge, and among those who congregated here all animosities were forgotten. The smoke of the calumet of peace always ascended, and the war cry never as yet has been heard in its streets.

In Heriot's Travels, published in 1807, we find the following interesting item:

'In 1671 Father Marquette came hither with a party of Hurons, whom he prevailed on to form a settlement. A fort was constructed, and it afterward became an important spot. It was the place of general assemblage for all the French who went to traffic with the distant nations. It was the asylum of all savages who came to exchange their furs for merchandise. When individuals belonging to tribes at war with each other came thither, and met on commercial adventure, their animosities were suspended."

Notwithstanding San-ge-man and his warriors had braved the dangers of the Straits and had slain a hundred of their enemies whose residence was here, yet it was not in the town that they were slain. No blood was ever shed by Indian hands within its precincts up to this period, and had it remained in possession of the French the terrible scenes subsequently enacted within its streets would in all probability never have occurred, and Old Mackinaw would have been a city of Refuge to this day.

The English, excited by the emoluments derived from the fur trade, desired to secure a share in this lucrative traffic of the northwestern Lakes. They, accordingly, in the year 1686, fitted out an expedition, and through the interposition of the Fox Indians, whose friendship they secured by valuable presents; the expedition reached Old Mackinaw, the "Queen of the Lakes," and found the El Dorado they had so long desired.

The following interesting description, from Parkman's "History of the Conspiracy of Pontiac," of a voyage by an English merchant to Old Mackinaw about this time, will be in place here: "Passing the fort and settlement of Detroit, he soon enters Lake St. Clair, which seems like a broad basin filled to overflowing, while along its far distant verge a faint line of forests separates the water from the sky, He crosses the lake, and his voyagers next urge his canoe against the current of the great river above. At length Lake Huron opens before him, stretching its liquid expanse like an ocean to the furthest horizon. His canoe skirts the eastern shore of Michigan, where the forest rises like a wall from the water's edge, and as he advances onward, an endless line of stiff and shaggy fir trees hung with long mosses, fringe the shore with an aspect of desolation. Passing on his right the extensive Island of Bois Blanc, he sees nearly in front the beautiful Island of Mackinaw rising with its white cliffs and green foliage from the broad breast of waters. He does not steer toward it, for at that day the Indians were its only tenants, but keeps along the main shore to the left, while his voyagers raise their song and chorus. Doubling a point he sees before him the red flag of England swelling lazily in the wind, and the palisades and wooden bastions of Fort Mackinaw standing close upon the margin of the lake. On the beach canoes are drawn up, and Canadians and Indians are idly lounging. A little beyond the fort is a cluster of white Canadian houses roofed with bark and protected by fences of strong round pickets. The trader enters the gate and sees before him an extensive square area, surrounded by high palisades. Numerous houses, barracks, and other buildings form a smaller square within, and in the vacant place which they enclose appear the red uniforms of British soldiers, the grey coats of the Canadians, and the gaudy Indian blankets mingled in picturesque confusion, while a multitude of squaws with children of every hue stroll restlessly about the place. Such was old fort Mackinaw in 1763."

La Hontan, who visited Mackinaw in 1688, says: "It is a place of great importance. It is not above half a league distant from the Illinese (Michigan) Lake. Here the Hurons and Ottawas have each of them a village, the one being severed from the other by a single palisado, but the Ottawas are beginning to build a fort upon a hill that stands but one thousand or twelve hundred paces off. In this place the Jesuits have a little house or college adjoining to a church, and inclosed with pales that separate it from the village of the Hurons. The Courriers de Bois have but a very small settlement here, at the same time it is not inconsiderable, as being the staple of all the goods that they truck with the south and west savages; for they cannot avoid passing this way when they go to the seats of the Illinese and the Oumamis on to the Bay des Puanto, and to the River Mississippi. Missilimackinac is situated very advantageously, for the Iroquese dare not venture with their sorry canoes to cross the stright of the Illinese Lake, which is two leagues over; besides that the Lake of the Hurons is too rough for such slender boats, and as they cannot come to it by water, so they cannot approach it by land by reason of the marshes, fens, and little rivers which it would be very difficult to cross, not to mention that the stright of the Illinese Lake lies still in their way."

As rivals of the French, the English were never regarded with favor by the various Indian tribes. Constant encroachments by the English from year to year, though they were lavish of their gifts did not tend to soften the hostility of the tribes. Thus matters continued until Mackinaw passed into the hands of the English, which event took place after the fall of Quebec in the year 1759. This transfer of jurisdiction from a people that the Indians loved to one that they experienced a growing hate for during three-quarters of a century, filled them with a spirit of revenge. Such was the dislike of the Indians of Mackinaw to the English, that when Alexander Henry visited that place in 1761, he was obliged to conceal the fact that he was an Englishman and disguise himself as a Canadian voyager. On the way he was frequently warned by the Indans to turn back, as he would not be received at Mackinaw, and as there were no British soldiers there as yet, he was assured that his visit would be attend with great hazard. He still persisted, however, and finally, with his canoes laden with goods he reached the fort, which, we have before remarked, was surrounded with palisades, and occupied the high ground immediately back from the beach. When he entered the village he met with a cold reception, and the inhabitants did all in their power to alarm and discourage him.

Soon after his arrival he received the very unpleasant intelligence, that a large number of Chippewas were coming from the neighboring villages in their canoes to call upon him. Under ordinary circumstances this information would not have excited any alarm, but as the French of Mackinaw as well as the Indians were alike hostile to the English trader, it was no difficult matter to apprehend danger. At length the Indians, about sixty in number, arrived, each with a tomahawk in one hand and a scalping knife in the other. The garrison at this time contained about ninety soldiers, a commander and two officers. Beside the small arms, on the bastions were mounted two small pieces of brass cannon. Beside Henry, there were four English merchants at the fort. After the Indians were introduced to Henry and his English brethren, their chief presented him with a few strings of wampum and addressed them as follows:

"Englishmen, it is to you that I speak, and I demand your attention. You know that the French

King is our father. He promised to be such, and we in turn promised to be his children. This promise we have kept. It is you that have made war with this our father. You are his enemy, and how then could you have the boldness to venture among us, his children. You know that his enemies are ours. We are informed that our father, the King of France, is old and infirm, and that being fatigued with making war upon your nation, he has fallen asleep. During this sleep you have taken advantage of him and possessed yourselves of Canada. But his nap is almost at an end. I think I hear him already stirring and inquiring for his children, and when he does awake what must become of you? He will utterly destroy you. Although you have conquered the French you have not conquered us. We are not your slaves. These lakes, these woods and mountains are left to us by our ancestors, they are our inheritance and we will part with them to none. Your nation supposes that we, like the white people, cannot live without bread, and pork, and beef, but you ought to know that He, the Great Spirit and Master of Life, has provided food for us in these spacious lakes and on these woody mountains.

Our father, the King of France, employed our young men to make war upon your nation. In this warfare many of them have been killed, and it is our custom to retaliate until such time as the spirits of the slain are satisfied. But the spirits of the slain are to be satisfied in one of two ways; the first is by the spilling the blood of the nation by which they fell, the other by covering the bodies of the dead, and thus allaying the resentment of their relations. This is done by making presents. Your king has never sent us any presents, nor entered into any treaty with us, wherefore he and we are still at war, and until he does these things we must consider that we have no other father or friend among the white men than the King of France. But for you, we have taken into consideration that you have ventured among us in the expectation that we would not molest you. You do not come around with the intention to make war. You come in peace to trade with us, and supply us with necessaries, of which we are in much need. We shall regard you, therefore, as a brother, and you may sleep tranquilly without fear of the Chippewas. As a token of friendship we present you with this pipe to smoke."

Henry was afterwards visited by a party of two hundred Ottawa warriors from *L'Arbre Croche*, about seventy miles southwest of Mackinaw. One of the Chiefs addressed him thus:—

"Englishmen: We, the Ottawas, were some time since informed of your arrival in this country, and of your having brought with you the goods we so much need. At this news we were greatly pleased, believing that, through your assistance, our wives and children would be able to pass another winter; but, what was our surprise, when a few days ago we were informed the goods which we had expected were intended for us were on the eve of departure for distant countries, some of which are inhabited by our enemies. These accounts being spread, our wives and children came to us crying, and desiring that we should go to the Fort to learn with our ears the truth or falsehood. We accordingly embarked, almost naked as you see, and on our arrival here we have inquired into the accounts, and found them true. We see your canoes ready to depart, and find your men engaged for the Mississippi and other distant regions. Under these circumstances we have considered the affair, and you are now sent for that you may hear our determination, which is, that you shall give each of our men, young and old, merchandise and ammunition to the amount of fifty beaver skins on credit, and for which

I have no doubt of their paying you in the summer, on their return from their wintering."

The demands of the Indians upon the English, and their dissatisfaction arising therefrom, had the effect to rouse the different tribes, and they were noticed assembling from the surrounding country in great numbers, and gathering in the vicinity of Mackinaw. One night four hundred Indians lay around the Fort, evidently plotting mischief. A Chippewa chief apprised Henry of the impending danger; but when the suspicions were communicated to the Commandant of the Fort, Major Etherington, he took no notice of it, supposing that the Indians only resorted to this for the purpose of intimidation. The next day being the King's birthday, the Indians proposed to celebrate it by a game of *baggatiway*. It was played with bat and ball, and the contestants were the Chippewas and Sacs. Major Etherington was present at the game, and bet largely on the side of the Chippewas. In the midst of the game, when all were in a high state of excitement, a warrior struck the ball and sent it whizzing over the palisade into the Fort. Instantly the Indian war yell was heard, and the savages rushed within the gate, not however for the ball, but to tomahawk and scalp every Englishman within the

Fort. The French stood by as silent spectators of the bloody scene, and were not attacked.

Henry witnessed the dreadful slaughter from his window, and being unarmed he hastened out, and springing over a low fence which divided his house from that of M. Langlade, the French Interpreter, entered the latter, and requested some one to direct him to a place of safety. Langlade hearing the request, replied that he could do nothing for him. At that moment a slave belonging to Langlade, of the Pawnee tribe of Indians, took him to a door which she opened, and informed him that it led to the garret where he might conceal himself. She then locked the door and took away the key. Through a hole in the wall Henry could have a complete view of the Fort. He beheld the heaps of the slain, and heard the savage yells, until the last victim was dispatched. Having finished the work of death in the Fort, the Indians went out to search the houses. Some Indians entered Langlade's house and asked if there were any Englishmen concealed in it. He replied that he did not know, they might search for themselves. At length they opened the garret door and ascended the stairs, but Henry had concealed himself among a heap of birch-bark vessels, which had been used in making maple sugar, and thus escaped. Fatigued and exhausted, he lay down on a mat and went to sleep, and while in this condition he was surprised by the wife of Langlade, who remarked that the Indians had killed all the English, but she hoped he might escape. Fearing, however, that she would fall a prey to their vengeance if it was found that an Englishman was concealed in her house, she at length revealed the place of Henry's concealment, giving as a reason therefor, that if he should be found her children would be destroyed. Unlocking the door, she was followed by several Indians, who were led by Wenniway, a noted chief. At sight of him the chief seized him with one hand, and brandishing a large carving knife, was about to plunge it into his heart, when he dropped his arm, saying, "I won't kill you. My brother, Musinigon, was slain by the English, and you shall take his place and be called after him." He was carried to L'Arbre Croche as a prisoner, where he was rescued by a band of three hundred Ottawas, by whom he was returned to Mackinaw, and finally ransomed by his Indian friend Wawatam. At the capture of the place only one trader, M. Tracy, lost his life. Captain Etherington was carried away by some Indians from the scene of slaughter. Seventy of the English troops were slain. An Englishman, by the name of Solomon, saved himself by hiding under a heap of corn, and his boy was saved by creeping up a chimney, where he remained two days. A number of canoes, filled with English traders, arriving soon after the massacre, they were seized, and the traders, dragged through the water, were beaten and marched by the Indians to the prison lodge. After they had completed the work of destruction, the Indians, about four hundred in number, entertaining apprehensions that they would be attacked by the English, and the Indians who had joined them, took refuge on the Island of Mackinac, Wawatam fearing that Henry would be butchered by the savages in their drunken revels, took him out to a cave, where he lay concealed for one night on a heap of human bones. As the Fort was not destroyed, it was subsequently reoccupied by British soldiers, and the removal to the Island did not take place until about the year 1780.

Old Mackinaw, the theatre of so many thrilling scenes and tragic incidents, has a history as a white settlement, reaching back to 1620, the year of the landing of the Pilgrims at Plymouth. W. M. Johnson, Esq., of Mackinac Island, in describing its history, says: "Mackinaw City," for such has become the name of this wonderful point, "with its coasts and the islands before it, has been the theatre of some of the most exciting and interesting events in Indian history, previous to the arrival of the 'white man.' It was the metropolis of a portion of the Ojibwa and Ottawa nations. It was there that their Congresses met, to adopt a policy which terminated in the conquest of the country south of it; it was there that the tramping feet of thousands of plumed and painted warriors shook Pe-quod-e-nonge—the Indian name—while dancing their war dances, it was from thence that the startling sound of the war yell of these thousands was wafted to the adjacent coast and islands, making the peaceful welkin ring with their unearthly shouts of victory or death.

"How remarkable, in reflecting upon the early and sound judgment of the Indians in seizing upon the points commanding all the natural avenues and passes of the Lakes, when it is considered that there selections must necessarily have been the result of an intimate knowledge with the geographical features of the country! This has been yearly proved by the re-occupation of posts and places long neglected, but the importance of which has become evident in proportion as we have set a just value upon the Indian's judgment, with the natural advantages of the country. Perhaps in no instance, is this more strikingly exemplified than in Mackinaw City, the commanding position of which, although always known to the Indians, Traders, and Missionaries, and lately confirmed by Military Scientific Europeans; *but as yet not perceived by our Government.* It is the only point which can control the passage of the Straits of Mackinaw, and also the Indians living in numerous villages south of the Straits. The Island of Mackinac was merely occupied by the English to escape a second massacre as in 1763; and which occupancy our Government has blindly followed, believing it, as an evidence of English military skill and judgment in the selection of commanding posts, while they at that period did not make this selection with any reference to a future hostile maritime power who might wish to pass, or force a passage through the Straits.

"The land rises gradually from the water at Mackinaw City, until it reaches an elevation of seventy-five feet, from which beautiful and picturesque views are obtained of the waters of the Straits, with the numerous Islands sleeping on its bosom. The prospect from the City is beautiful, beyond description—the Battery at New York can only be compared to it, which is like it in its location. The

SUGAR-LOAF—MACKINAC.

MACKINAC ISLAND

1. Lover's Leap. 2. Harbor. 3. Village. 4. Fort. 5. Signal. 6. Sugar Loaf. 7. Mission. 8. Robinson's Folly.

visitor will enjoy the view presented of the Islands, Points, and adjacent shores; especially on a calm day, for the lake, and the green woods upon isle and promontory, lie with a sleepy stillness before him, enhancing the beauty of the prospect; and when the mind contemplates the events of two hundred and fifty years ago, when thousands of the red sons of the forest passed and repassed the site upon which he now stands, he will appreciate more fully the rapid strides of civilization.

"Two hundred and fifty years ago, bark canoes only dotted the surface of the Lake; this spell of quiet was then broken a few years afterward by the boisterous Canadian *Voyageur* with his songs, as he rowed or paddled his *bateaux* and large northwest canoe. Now, the roaring noise of the wheels of steamers, the shrill whistle of the propeller, and the whitening sails of hundreds of vessels have succeeded to the past age of darkness and quiet. Civilization and commerce have broken the charm which beautified Indian scenery in years forever gone by."

A work, published under the auspices of the Canadian Government, in three large octavo volumes, French, entitled "Relations of the Jesuits," containing the most remarkable events that transpired in the missions of the Jesuits in New France, furnishes valuable information of the missions in the Mackinaw region. Among the remarkable phenomena which came under the observation of the Jesuit Fathers in Mackinaw, was the appearance of a parhelion on the 21st of January, 1671. This remarkable phenomenon occurred about two hours before sunset. It presented the form of a great crescent with its points turned toward the sun. At the same time two other suns appeared, equidistant from it, partly covered by a cloud having all the colors of the rainbow, very luminous and dazzling to the eye. The Indians said it was a premonition of great cold, which followed soon after. On the 16th March the same parhelion appeared, and was seen from three different places more than fifty leagues apart. The observer at the Mackinaw mission saw three suns distant some half league from each other. They were seen twice the same day, one hour before sunrise and one hour before sunset. In the morning they were on the south side of the true sun, and in the evening on the west side. That on the south side was so accurate that it was difficult to distinguish it from the true sun, excepting that it was partly surrounded by a scarlet band on the side toward the sun. That on the other side had more the appearance of an oval iris than a sun, nevertheless it was an image like those which painters adorn with golden rays, giving it a very magnificent appearance.

The same parhelion was seen on the island of Manitou in Lake Huron, and accompanied by a very remarkable appearance. Three suns appeared in the west, parallel with the earth. They were equal in size, but not in beauty. The true sun was west-by-southwest, and the false sun on each side. At the same time were seen parts of two circles parallel to the horizon, having the colors of the rainbow, beside a fourth part of the circle perpendicular to the horizon, having nearly the same color, touched the false sun, which was in the southwest, and cutting the half circle parallel to the horizon, was mingled and lost in its rays. The false suns disappeared from time to time, and even the true sun. Finally, a fourth sun was seen placed in a right line. When the false suns disappeared they left after them two rainbows, as beautiful as their own light. The Indians, who attributed all these signs to the Genii, and who believe that they are married, wanted to know of the missionary if these were not the wives of the sun. At this question it occurred to him that a favorable opportunity was presented for explaining to them the mysteries of the Trinity. On the next day the Indian women, who before would not come to hear prayers, came and presented their children to be baptized.

At the Saut St. Mary, seven false suns appeared around the true sun. The true sun was in the centre of a circle formed by the colors of the rainbow. On either side were two false suns, and also one above and one below. These four were placed on the circumference of the circle, and at equal distances directly opposite from each other. Beside this, another circle of the same color as the first, but much larger, rested the upper part of its circumference in the centre of the true sun, while below and on either side were the false suns. All these eight luminaries made a grand spectacle.

Auroras, even in midsummer, are of frequent occurrence, and exhibit a brilliancy and extent rarely observed in lower latitudes. The phenomena which most frequently occur are the following: A dark cloud tinged on the upper edge with a pale luminous haze, skirts the northern horizon. From this streaks of orange and blue colored light flash up, and often reach a point south of the zenith. They rapidly increase and decrease, giving to the whole hemisphere the appearance of luminous waves and occasionally forming perfect corona. They commence shortly after sunset and continue during the night. The voyagers regard them as the precursors of storms and gales, and our own observations have confirmed the result. Occasionally broad belts of light are seen spanning the whole arc of the heavens, of sufficient brilliancy to enable one to read. In the winter these phenomena are much more frequent, and the ground appears tinged with a crimson hue.

We find in these relations of the Jesuits other matters of equal interest. The fathers of the missions in and around the Straits of Mackinaw gave it as their opinion, that the waters of Lake Superior entered into the Straits by a subterranean passage, and in support of it, mention the wonderful fact that the current floats against the wind, and notwithstanding it drives furiously in one direction, vessels are enabled to sail in a contrary direction as rapidly as though the wind were not blowing. In addition to this, they refer to the constant boiling up of the waters. Without admitting this theory, they affirmed that it was impossible to explain two things. The first is, that without such subterranean passage it is impossible to tell what becomes of the waters of Lake Superior. This vast lake has but one visible outlet, namely, the river of the Saut, while it receives into its bosom the waters of a large number of rivers, some twelve of which are of greater dimensions than the Saut. What then, they ask, becomes of all these waters if they do not find an issue through a subterranean river. The second reason for their belief in this theory is the impossibility to explain from whence come the waters of Lake Huron and Lake Michigan? But very few rivers flow into these lakes, and their size is such as to justify the belief that they must be supplied through the subterranean river entering into the Straits.

CHAPTER V.

Island of the Giant Fairies—Possession by the English—Erection of Government house—French remain at Old Mackinaw—Finally abandoned—Extent of the Island—History—Description — Natural curiosities — Arch Rock — Sugar Loaf Rock—Scull Rock—Dousman's Farm—Davenport's Farm—Robinson's Folly—The Devil's Punch Bowl—Healthful atmosphere—Transparency of the waters—Compared with Saratoga, Cape May, and Mt. Washington as a point for health and recreation—Description of a traveler in 1854—Arrival of steamers and sailing vessels at the port during the year Mr. Johnson's reminiscences—Indian name of Island—Mythology—Three brothers of the great Genii—Visit to the subterranean abode of the Genii—Vision—Apostrophe of an old Indian Chief—Old buildings—Door of Marquette's Chapel—John Jacob Astor and the fur trade—Present support of the place—Fort Mackinaw—Fort Holmes—Fine view—Interesting localities—War of 1812—Death of Major Holmes—Soil of the Island.

THE old fort having been deserted by the English, as we have noticed in a previous chapter, and they having fled to the Island of Mackinaw, which, in the

Indian name, signifies Island of the giant fairies, preparations were made for a settlement. Sir Wm. Johnston called a grand council with those Indians who had been engaged in the massacre at Old Mackinaw. By this council, which was held in 1764, the spring following the siege, a way was opened for St. Clair to negotiate for the island, and also for the grants previously made by the Indians to the French for military purposes. The first thing done after the island had been obtained was the erection of a government house. The French and others who still remained at Old Mackinaw, amounting only to about three hundred, continued a few years, when they finally left, and everything was suffered to go into decay. A desolation reigned over it for many years, and, on account of the bloody siege, that point, which was the most attractive as well as the most important to Indians, French, and English in all the Lake region was, as if by common consent, abandoned.

The "New Mackinaw," as it is called, distant seven miles from the Old, is on an island about nine miles in circumference, and covers an area of six thousand acres. Its extreme elevation above the lake is about three hundred and twelve feet. The village and fortress are situated on the southeastern extremity of

ARCH ROCK.

ROCK CASTLE—PICTURED ROCKS.

the island, where there is a good harbor protected by a water battery. The island remained in possession of the British until 1793, when it was surrendered to the United States. It was retaken in 1812, but restored again by the treaty of Ghent, in 1814. It is situated in North lat. 45° 54′, West lon. 84° 30′ from Greenwich, being 7° 30′ west from Washington. It is three hundred and fifty miles north of Chicago and about three hundred miles north from Detroit, and about two hundred and fifty miles west of Collingswood, Canada. The fort stands on an elevated ground about two hundred feet above the water. The town contains at present three hotels, six boarding houses, eight dry-goods stores, and seven groceries. Its public buildings are a Court House, Jail, Custom House, Post Office, and Express Office. There are two Churches, the Roman Catholic and Presbyterian.

The first thing we shall notice as a natural attraction on the island, is what is called "The Arch Rock." This is a natural arch projecting from the precipice on the northeastern side of the island, about a mile from the fort, and elevated about one hundred and forty feet above the level of the water. Its abutments are formed of calcareous rock, and have been produced by the falling down of great masses of rock, leaving a chasm of eighty or ninety feet in height, and covered by the arch which spans it of fifty or sixty feet sweep. The scene presented by cliff and chasm is one of wild grandeur. Like the Natural Bridge of Virginia, it possesses an attraction to all fond of natural curiosities, sufficient of itself to justify a visit to the northern lakes. The view from the beach is particularly grand. Before you is a magnificent arch suspended in mid air. Indian tradition says that this wonderful arch was formed by the giant spirits who inhabited this island. Geological tradition, however, indicates that it was formed by the action of the waters, which were at a remote period much higher than at the present time.

The next object which strikes the attention of the visitors is the "Sugar Loaf Rock," a high, isolated, conical rock which, resting upon the elevated plateau that forms the next highest point of the island from that of Fort Holmes, exhibits a rise of some sixty to eighty feet. This is but little less than the elevation of the ridge which forms the crowning plan of the island, and upon which the dismantled post of Fort Holmes is seen, being separated therefrom by a distance not exceeding one hundred and fifty yards. By what violent throe of nature it has become severed from the adjacent ridge, of which it no doubt, formed a part, is matter of curious inquiry. Has nature done this by gradual recession, or by the slow upheaval of the land? On inspection, this rock is found cavernous, slightly crystalline, with its strata distorted in every conceivable direction. In its crevices grow a few cedars and vines. As the visitor approaches it by the road side its effect is grand and imposing; still more so, perhaps, when beheld from the top of the ridge, where its isolated position with its bold form, breaking the outline of the island, strikes the beholder with wonder and admiration.

Robinson's Folly is a high bluff, northeast from the village of Mackinaw, half a mile from the mission house. Soon after the settlement of the modern Mackinaw, Capt. Robinson, of the English army, then commanding this port, had a summer house built on the brow of this bluff, now called Robinson's Folly, for the purpose of enjoying the prospect from that cool and elevated spot. Often he and his brother officers resorted there during the summer days, to while away lonely and tedious hours. Pipes, cigars, and wine, were brought into requisition. No Englishman at that period was without them; in fact, no hospitality or entertainment was complete without them.

They were indeed isolated; the nearest white settlements being then Detroit, Green Bay. Saut St. Mary, and Chicago. Communications with these places were not frequent.

A few years after, from the action of the elements, the brow of the bluff, where Robinson's Folly stood, was precipitated to the base of the rock, where the fragments can now be seen, which disastrous event gave rise to its name.

The "Scull Rock," half a mile or three quarters northwest from the rear of Fort Mackinaw, is chiefly noted for a cavern, which appears to have been a receptacle for human bones, many of which were still to be observed about its mouth a few years ago. The entrance is low and narrow, and seems to promise little to reward the labors of exploration. It is here probably that Alexander Henry was secreted by the chief Wawatam after the horrid massacre of the British garrison at Old Mackinaw.

Chimney Rock well repays the trouble of a visit, with the other points of interest on the island.

Dousman's Farm, two miles west from the Village of Mackinaw, consists of a section of land; the road to the English or British landing passes through it, also to Scott's or Flinn's Cave, which is on the northwestern portion of the farm. There are three springs of cold delicious water on this farm, two of them are shaded by beech and maple trees. This farm yields yearly from eighty to one hundred tons of hay, besides a large quantity of potatoes and other farm produce.

Davenport's Farm, about one and a half miles from the village, is situated on the southwestern portion of the Island. At the base of the bluff, on the south part of this farm, is the Devil's Caves, and near them is a beautiful spring of clear cold water, shaded by evergreens and other trees. Half way up the bluff, which is nearly, if not fully, three hundred feet high at this point; stands out, detached from the limestone, an isolated rock, in appearance similar to the Sugar Loaf Rock, which some persons have called the Lover's Leap; it is worth the trouble of a visit, which a few minutes walk from the village accomplishes. There are several points called Lover's Leap, so called by romantic visitors, within the last few years. A gentleman from Chicago, has purchased this farm, and report says that several summer-houses are to be built upon it, which will enhance the beauty of this locality.

Wm. M. Johnston Esq., furnishes the following tradition of Lover's Leap:

"The huge rock called the 'Lover's Leap' is situated

about one mile west of the village of Mackinaw. It is a high perpendicular bluff, one hundred and fifty to two hundred feet in height, rising boldly from the shore of the lake. A solitary pine tree formerly stood upon its brow, which some Vandal has cut down.

"Long before the pale faces profaned this island home of the Genii, a young Ojibwa girl, just maturing into womanhood, often wandered there, and gazed from its dizzy heights and witnessed the receding canoes of the large war parties of the combined bands of the Ojibwas and Ottawas speeding south, seeking for fame and scalps.

"It was there she often sat, mused and hummed the songs Ge-niw-e-gwon loved; this spot was endeared to her, for it was there that she and Ge-niw-e-gwon first met and exchanged words of love, and found an affinity of souls existing between them. It was there she often sat and sang the Ojibwa love song—

> 'Mong-e-do-gwain, in-de-nain-dum,
> Mong-e-do-gwain, in-de-nain-dum,
> Wain-shung-ish-ween, neen-e-mo-shane,
> Wain-shung-ish-ween, neen-e-mo-shane,
> A-nee-wau-wau-sau-bo-a-zode,
> A-nee-wau-wau-sau-bo-a-zode.'

I give but one verse, which may be translated as follows:

A loon, I thought was looming,
A loon, I thought was looming:
Why! it is he, my lover,
Why! it is he, my lover;
His paddle, in the waters gleaming,
His paddle in the waters gleaming.

"From this bluff she often watched and listened for the return of the war parties, for amongst them she knew was Ge-niw-e-gwon; his head decorated with war-eagle plumes, which none but a brave could sport. The west wind often wafted far in advance the shouts of victory and death, as they shouted and sang upon leaving Pe-quod-e-nong (Old Mackinaw), to make the traverse to the Spirit, or Fairiy Island.

"One season, when the war party returned, she could not distinguish his familiar and loving war shout. Her spirit, told her that he had gone to the Spirit-Land of the west. It was so: an enemy's arrow had pierced his breast, and after his body was placed leaning against a tree, his face fronting his enemies, he died; but ere he died he wished the mourning warriors to remember him to the sweet maid of his heart. Thus he died far away from home and the friends he loved.

" Me-she-ne-mock-e-nung-o-qua's heart hushed its

beatings, and all the warm emotions of that heart, were chilled and dead. The moving, living spirit of her beloved Ge-niw-e-gwon, she witnessed continually beckoning her to follow him to the happy hunting grounds of spirits in the west—he appeared to her in human shape, but was invisible to others of his tribe.

"One morning her body was found mangled at the foot of the bluff. The soul had thrown aside its covering of earth, and had gone to join the spirit of her beloved Ge-niw-e-gwon, to travel together to the land of spirits."

Another point of interest and curiosity is the Devil's Punch Bowl, situated south from the gateway, as you enter the farm of the late J. Dousman, Esq.

This Island which rises like a gem on the brow of the lakes, is favored by the clearest and most healthful atmosphere, and washed by the purest and most transparent water in the world, imparting the most pleasurable sensations imaginable. When this enchanting region shall become fully known, Saratoga, Cape May, and Mount Washington will be forgotten by those who fly from the heat and dust of our inland cities, to breathe a pure air and drink health-giving waters.

A traveler in 1854, thus describes this interesting locality, "Everything on the island is a curiosity, the roads or streets that wind around the harbor or among the grove-like forests of the island, are naturally pebbled and macadamized, the buildings are of every style, from an Indian lodge to an English house, the island is covered with charming natural scenery, from the beautiful to the grand, and one may spend weeks constantly finding new objects of interest, and new scenes of beauty. The steamers all call here on their way to and from Chicago, and hundreds of small sail vessels in the fishing trade have here their head quarters. Drawn upon the pebbled beach, or gliding about the bay, are bark canoes, and the far-famed Mackinaw boats, without number. These last are the perfection of light sail boats, and I have often been astonished at seeing them far out in the lake, beating up against winds that were next to gales."

We are indebted to Mr. Johnston for the following official list, giving the number of sail vessels and steamers that have passed through the Straits of Mackinaw during the *day time*, as reported to the Revenue department, for six months, ending September 30th, 1859.

	Barques.	Brigs.	Schr's.	Steamers.
April, ...	14	9	101	47
May..........	9	11	177	82
June,.........	15	13	221	194
Next 3 mon's	98	61	764	353
	136	94	1263	586

Total, 2079.

It would be a pretty correct estimate to add at least one-third more of the total number for those that passed during the night,—which would be a very low estimate of the shipping passing through our straits.

But few of the vessels passing through the straits leave the main channel, and go to the island some miles out of the way.

The lake traffic has of late years become perfectly enormous, the increase of the western navigation being unprecedented. For example, three thousand and sixty-five steamers passed up from Lake Erie to Lakes Huron and Superior, by Detroit, in 1859, and three thousand one hundred and twenty-one passed down. The greatest number up in a single day was eighty-five—down seventy-three. Detroit statistics show that five steamers, five propellers, four barques, seven brigs, and eighty-five schooners have been more or less engaged in the Lake Superior trade during the past season. Forty vessels left during the season for European and seaboard ports, some of which have returned, and one has taken her second departure. Navigation at Detroit opened March 14th, and closed December 15th.

William Johnston, Esq., who has long resided on the island, says: 'The Indians, from the earliest times, have always regarded the Island of Mackinaw with veneration. The Indian name is 'Moc-che-ne-mock-e-nug-gonge,' which, as before stated, signifies Island of Great or Giant Fairies.

"Indian mythology relates that three brothers of great or giant Fairies, occupied different Islands in this section of the country. The eldest occupied the Island Missillimackinac, the second lived on the Island Tim-au Rin-ange-onge, in Lake Michigan, now called Pottawattime Island, the youngest inhabited an Island called Pe-quoge-me-nis, in Lake Huron. The heathen Indians, to this day, look upon them with awe and veneration, and in passing to and fro, by their shores, still offer to the Great Spirits tobacco and other offerings, to propitiate their good-will. The stories they relate of these Great Fairies, are very interesting and worthy of record.

"The present southern gate of Fort Mackinac overlooks the spot, where in olden times a door existed, to the entrance of the subterraneous abode of these Giant Fairies. An Indian Chees-a-kee, or spiritualist, who once encamped within the limits of the present garrison, related, that some time during the night, after he had fallen asleep, a fairy touched him and beckoned him to follow. He obeyed and his spirit went with the fairy; they entered the subterraneous abode, through an opening beneath the present gate near the base of the hill. He there witnessed the giant spirits in solemn conclave in what appeared to be a large beautiful wigwam. After being there some time, lost in wonder and admiration, the chief spirit directed one of the lesser ones, to show the Indian spirit out and conduct him back to his body. This Indian could never be induced to divulge the particulars of what he witnessed in his mysterious visit.

An old Indian chief upon leaving this island, to visit his friends in Lake Superior, thus soliloquized, as he sat on the deck of McKnight's splendid steamer, the Illinois, while the darkness began dimly to shadow forth the deep blue outlines of the island:

"'Moc-che-ne-mock-e-nug-gonge, thou Isle of the clear, deep-water Lake, how, soothing it is from amidst the curling smoke of my opawgun (pipe), to trace thy deep blue outlines in the distance; to call from memory's tablets the traditions and stories connected with thy sacred and mystic character, how sacred the regard, with which thou hast been once clothed by our Indian seers of gone-by days; how, pleasant in imagination for the mind to picture and view, as if now present, the time when the Great Spirit allowed a peaceful stillness to dwell around thee, when only light and balmy winds were permitted to pass over thee, hardly ruffling the mirror surface of the waters that surrounded thee. Nothing then disturbed thy quiet and deep solitude, but the chippering of birds, and the rustling of the leaves of the silver-barked birch; or to hear, by evening twilight the sound of the giant Fairies as they with rapid step, and giddy whirl, dance their mystic dance on thy lime-stone battlements.'

"Several old buildings are now standing, the frames of which were brought from old Mackinaw in the year 1764, which gives an odd and venerable appearance to the village. Mr. Schoolcraft had the door of Marquette's Chapel pointed out to him, which had been brought over from Mackinaw, and hung to one of the edifices of the town.

"The village formely received its greatest support from the fur trade, when in the hands of the late John Jacob Astor, Esq., being, at that time, the outfitting and furnishing place for the Indian trade. His

9

outfits extended then to the head waters of the Mississippi, on the northwest, south to Chicago, southwest by the way of Green Bay, to the Mississippi, and Missouri Rivers, in fact his business was carried on throughout all the then northwest Indian country. This trade became extinct in 1834, when Mr. Astor, sold out to Ramsey Crooks, Esq., of New York, and others, but it lacked the energy and controlling influence which had been characteristic of Mr. Astor's business, and after languishing a few years, the new company became involved and their outposts were discontinued.

"The place since then has been mostly supported from the fisheries, which are excellent and extensive. It is estimated that twenty thousand barrels of white fish and trout are exported from this country alone annually, estimated worth, at this point, about one hundred and fifty thousand dollars. A material support is also derived from the immense amount of trade.

"The population is fluctuating, owing to the influx of strangers seeking health, traders, and Indians; but the permanent inhabitants of the village are about one thousand and fourteen, as per census of 1854.

"Fort Mackinac stands on a rocky eminence immediately above the town, and is at present garrisoned by a company of United States troops: a chaplain (Episcopalian) is attached to the garrison, and services are held there every Sabbath. Fort Holmes occupies the highest bluff of the island, and is not at present occupied: this fortress was erected by the English, while they held possession of the island, during the last war, and by them named Fort George. But after the surrender of the island in 1814, the name was altered in compliment to the memory of Major Holmes of the United States Army, who fell in the unfortunate attack upon the island by Col. Croghan. The gallant Holmes was killed a little below the rise of ground, as you descend toward the Dousman farm-house, on your way to the British landing. On Fort Holmes is a triangular station for the government engineers, who have been at work some years in the straits.

"Visitors mounting the station on a still clear day, have a view of this island, the straits with its curves, islands and points, and the adjacent shores, which well repays them, especially on a calm day, for the lake and green woods lie in stillness before them, taking the mind for hundreds of years back, to the time when thousands of warriors occupied the prominent points brought within view.

"Off to the northwest, some four or five miles, lies

the mixed Canadian and Indian settlement of Point St. Ignace and Moran Bay, with a few farms, which give a more agreeable view to the otherwise sameness of wood and water. There the Indians, called the Au-se-gum-ugs, lived until driven away by the Ojibwas and Ottawas, as they extended their conquests south and west. There also the Iroquois were permitted to locate and live before the French reached and settled on the St. Lawrence, there some of the Iroquois were massacred and driven off by the Ojibwas and Ottawas. North of this can be seen the outlines of the bluff called "Rabbit Sitting," northeasterly the St. Martin Islands, the entrance of the Chenoux, and the dividing ridge between this and the Saut St. Mary. On the northeast can be seen the Detour, and to the south, Bois Blanc Light-House, and the Cheboy-e-gun; and on the west the Straits of Lake Michigan, with Waugoohance Point and Light-House.

"To the northwest of the ridge, where the woods slope by a gradual descent to the shores of the Island, is the place at which the English in the last war (1812), from six to eight hundred strong, composed of a few English, Canadians, the majority being Indians, landed at night, and having secured Michael Dousman's cattle, at his farm adjoining the landing, and succeeded during the night in reaching the hollow, which may be seen on the way from Fort Mackinac to Fort Holmes, a little northwest of the present parade-ground, or nearly opposite the northwest rear gate of the present fort, with their cannon, which by daylight, was placed in battery on the knoll south of the hollow before alluded to, which by its position completely commanded the western gate and the garrison itself, took their station.

"At dawn the citizens of the village were roused, and told to flee to a place called the Distillery, west of the present village, as the English troops were about to attack the American fort, and that the English commanding officer had pledged his word for the safety of the lives of those citizens who would flee to the place designated. This was the first intimation the citizens had of war being declared between the United States and Great Britain. Soon a cannon shot was fired over the fort, its booming being also the first intimation the American garrison had of the country being in a state of war. An English officer appeared with a flag to summon the garrison to surrender, stating the overwhelming force they had in command. The American garrison, being short of one full company of men, was surrendered, and the few troops taken and sent to

Detroit on parole. After this the English built and occupied Fort George, (now called Fort Holmes) between the years 1812 and 1814. The English government paid ten thousand pounds as prize-money to the volunteers and soldiers, and merchandise and arms to the Indians. In the year 1836 I examined the list or pay-roll for this prize-money; the names of all those who participated in the taking of Fort Mackinac were there enrolled, the money was divided according to rank, and each person receipted for his individual share.

"It is worth knowing, that by the treaty of Paris, of 1783, acknowledging the independence of the United States, and fixing its boundaries, Fort Mackinac fell under the jurisdiction of the United States, and was surrendered, according to McKenzie, in 1794. In 1812 it was taken, as before stated, by the English and their Indian allies. It resisted an attack from a strong detachment of the American army and navy in 1814, under Col. Croghan, and was finally restored to the United States by the treaty of Ghent.

"In 1814 Col. Croghan landed at the English Landing, under cover of the guns of the American vessels. The troops moved from the landing, and had reached Mr. M. Dousman's farm-house. The skirm ishing with the English and Indians had already commenced. East from the house is a ridge over which the road lay. On this ridge and back of it, also on each side of the road, the English were posted in force. The gallant Major Holmes, on reaching the clearing near the house, formed his men for a charge upon the enemy posted on the ridge. To encourage his troops he led the charge. The English and Indians, seeing the strong force, had commenced retreating, when an English sergeant thought he might as well discharge the cannon before retreating with his comrades, so accordingly applied the match. At this instant, Major Holmes was either killed by a grape shot, or by an accidental musket ball. His death threw the Americans into a panic, and they immediately commenced a retreat, which ended in confusion.

"When the fleet first appeared before the island, there was only one company of troops in the fort—had Col. Croghan then summoned it to surrender, it would have been given up; but he sailed away, went and burnt the trading-houses at Old St. Joseph's Island, and from thence sent an expedition to the Saut St. Mary, under Major Holmes, who burned the North West Fur Company Houses on the Canada side, and carried away all the personal property of individuals on the American side. Thus ten or twenty days were lost. In the mean time, the Indians had come to the defense of Fort Mackinac, and, on the second appearance of Col. Croghan, they were prepared, and our troops shamefully defeated.

"This island, although the bluffs present the appearance of sterility, is covered with a strong soil, which is continually renovated by the spontaneous decomposition of calcareous rock. The common growth of trees on the island are the sugar-maple, beech, birch, white and yellow pine, white and red spruce, balsam fir, white cedar, iron wood, and the poplar; the trees now seen are the second and third growth. On the northwestern part of Mr. Dousman's farm, a few of the old patriarchs of the forest are still standing."

CHAPTER VI.

Lake Superior—Scenery—Transparency of its waters—Climate—Isle Royale — Apostles' Islands—La Point—Thunder Cape—Cariboo Point—A wonderful lake—Romantic scenery—Pictured Rocks—Rock Castle—The Grand Portal—The Chapel—Fluctuations in the waters of Lake Superior—Curious phenomena — Retrocession of the waters — Mirage—Iron mountains and mines—Description of—Products—Shipments—Copper — Immense boulders — Produce of the mines for 1857—Shipment of copper from the Lake for 1858—Centre of the mining country—Iron Mountains—Copper mines of Great Britain—Coal—Mackinaw, a great manufacturing point — Key to the Upper Lakes — Commerce of Lakes — Growth of cities.

LAKE SUPERIOR, though it possesses not all the vastness of the ocean, is yet equal in sublimity. In gazing upon its surface, whether spread out like a vast mirror reflecting the varying tints of the sky, or ruffled by gently curling waves, or lashed into fury by the tempest, one is impressed with the idea of the Infinite. It is known to be the largest body of fresh water on the globe, being nearly four hundred miles long from east to west, and one hundred and thirty wide. It is the grand reservoir from whence proceed the waters of Michigan, Huron, and Erie. It gives birth to Niagara, the wonder of the world, fills the basin of Ontario, and rolls a mighty flood down the St. Lawrence to the Atlantic.

This lake lies in the bosom of a mountainous region, where the Indian yet reigns and roams in his wonted freedom. Except an occasional picketed fort or trading house, it is yet a perfect wilderness. The entire country is rocky and covered with a stunted growth of vegetation such as is usual in high latitudes. The waters of this lake are marvelously clear, and, even at midsummer, are exceedingly cold. Mr. Charles Lanman, who has written a most admirable book, entitled "Summer in the Wilderness," says, "In passing along its rocky shores, in my frail canoe, I have often been alarmed at the sight of a sunken boulder, which I fancied must be near the top, and on further investigation have found myself to be upward of twenty feet from the danger of a concussion. I have frequently lowered a white rag to the depth of one hundred feet and been able to discern its every fold or stain. The color of the water near the shore is a deep green; but off soundings it has all the dark blue of the ocean."

Speaking of the climate, he says: "In midsummer it is beyond compare, the air is soft and bracing at the same time. A healthier region does not exist on the earth, an assertion corroborated by the fact, that the inhabitants usually live to an advanced age, notwithstanding the many hardships. The common diseases of mankind are here comparatively unknown, and I have never seen an individual whose breast did not swell with a new emotion of delight as he inhaled the air of this northern wilderness."

The largest island in Lake Superior is Isle Royale. It is forty miles in length and from six to ten miles in width. Its hills reach an altitude of four hundred feet. During the winter season it is entirely uninhabited, but in the summer it is frequently visited, particularly by copper speculators. Near the western extremity of the lake are the Apostles' Islands, which are detachments of a peninsula running out in the same direction with Keweenaw, which is known as La Point. The group consist of three islands, which rise like gems from the water. There is a dreamy summer about them which make them enticing as the Hesperides of the ancients.

The two most prominent peninsulas are Thunder Cape and Cariboo Point. Thunder Cape is about fourteen hundred feet high. It looms up against the sky in grandeur, and is a most romantic spot. Cariboo Point is less lofty and grand in its appearance, but is celebrated for its unknown hieroglyphics painted upon its summits by a race which has long since passed away. In the vicinity of the bluff are found the most beautiful agates in the world.

In the northeastern part of the lake is an island situated about twenty miles from the Canadian shore, which has a wonderful lake in its centre, about one mile in length. It is as beautiful as it is wonderful. It is imbosomed in the fastnesses of perpendicular cliffs, which rise to a height of seven hundred feet. It has but one outlet and is impassable even to a canoe. At the opening of this narrow chasm stands a column of solid rock which has a base of about one hundred feet in diameter. The column rises, gradually tapering until it reaches a height of eight hundred feet. A solitary pine surmounts the summit of this wonderful column. There it stands like the sentinel of this calm, deep lake, whose silence and solitude are rarely ever broken, and whose tranquil bosom has never been ruffled by the slightest breeze.

The scenery on the shores of Lake Superior is in some places of the most romantic character. About one hundred miles west of Saut St. Mary, a range

ROCK CHAPEL.

THE CASTLES.

of cliffs are to be seen, what has been called the "Pictured Rocks." They are a series of sandstone bluffs extending along the shore of the lake for about five miles, and rising, in most places vertically from the water, from fifty to two hundred feet in height. These towering cliffs have been worn away by the action of the lake, which for centuries has dashed an ocean-like surf against their base. The surface of these rocks has been, in large portions, strangely colored by bands of brilliant hues, which present to the eye of the voyager a singularly pleasing appearance. One of these cliffs resembles so much the turreted entrance and arched portal of some old feudal castle that it has been called "Rock Castle." Beyond this is another architectural curiosity, denominated "The Grand Portal," which consists of an arched opening in the rocks. The cliff is composed of a vast mass, of a rectilinear shape, projecting out into the lake six hundred feet, and presenting a front of three hundred feet, and rising to a height of two hundred feet. An entrance has been excavated from one side to the other, opening out into large vaulted passages which communicate with the great dome, some three hundred feet from the front of the cliff. The Grand Portal, which opens out on the lake, is of magnificent dimensions, being one hundred feet high, and one hundred and sixty-eight feet wide at the water level. The distance from the verge of the cliff, over the arch to the water, is one hundred and thirty-three feet, leaving three feet for the thickness of the rock above the arch itself. The extreme height of the cliff is about fifty feet more, making in all one hundred and eighty-three feet. It is impossible, adequately, to describe this wonderful scene. The vast dimensions of the cavern, the vaulted passages, the rare combination of colors, the varied effects of the light as it streams through the great arch and falls on the different objects; the deep, emerald green of the water, the unvarying swell of the lake, keeping up a succession of musical echoes; the reverberation of one's voice coming back with startling effect, must all be seen and heard to be fully appreciated.

Not far from this point is "The chapel" of the voyagers which nature has cut out of the cliff thirty or forty feet above the lake. The interior consists of a spacious vaulted apartment. An arched roof from ten to twenty feet in thickness rests on four gigantic columns of rock. These columns consist of finely stratified rock, and have been worn into curious shapes. At the base of one of these pillars an arched cavity or niche has been cut, access to which is had by a flight of steps formed by the projecting strata. The arrangement of the whole resembles very much the pulpit of a church, while the arched canopy in front, opening out to the voluted interior, with a flat tabular mass rising to a convenient height for a desk, and an isolated block resembling an altar, all fashioned as appropriately as if formed by the hand of man, constantly impresses one that he is within the walls of a church.

In the Geological Report, made by Foster and Whitney, to Congress, we find the following remark: "It is a matter of surprise, that so far as we know, none of our artists, have visited this region, and given to the world representations of scenery, so striking and so different from any which can be found elsewhere. We can hardly conceive of any thing more worthy of the artist's pencil, and if the tide of pleasure-travel should once be turned in this direction, it seems not unreasonable to suppose, that a fashionable hotel may yet be built under the shade of the pine groves near the chapel, and a trip thither become as common as one to Niagara now is."

Beyond the grand portal, the rock, being less exposed to the force of the waves, bears fewer marks of their destructive action. The entrance to Chapel river is at the most easterly extremity of a sandy beach, which extends for a quarter of a mile, and affords a convenient landing place, while the drift terrace elevated about thirty feet above the level of the lake, being an open pine plain, affords excellent camping ground, and is the most central and convenient spot for the traveler to pitch his tent, while he examines the most interesting localities in the series which occur in the vicinity, particularly the Castle and the Chapel.

One who had resided upon the shores of Lake Superior for several summers says, "Our attention has been directed to the fluctuations in the level of its waters, and while we have failed to detect any ebb and flow corresponding with the tidal action, we have on the other hand noticed certain extraordinary swells, which appear to be independent of the action of the sun and moon." The Jesuit Fathers in 1670–1, had their attention called to these extraordinary swells. In their "Relations," they say, "We found at one time the motion of the waters to be regular and at others extremely fluctuating. We have noticed however, that at full moon and new moon, the tides change once a day for eight or ten days, while during the remainder of the time there is hardly any change perceptible. The currents set almost invariably in one direction, namely toward Lake Michigan, and they almost invariably set against the wind, sometimes with great force."

Mackenzie who wrote in 1789, relates a very curious phenomenon, which occurred at Grand Portage, on Lake Superior, and for which no obvious cause could be assigned. He says, "the water withdrew, leaving the ground dry, which had never before been visible, the fall being equal to four perpendicular feet, and rushing back with great velocity above the common mark. It continued thus rising and falling for several hours, gradually increasing until it stopped at its usual height."

Professor Mather, who observed the barometer at Copper Harbor during the prevalence of one of these fluctuations, remarks, "As a general thing, fluctuations in the barometer accompanied the fluctuations in the level of the water, but sometimes the water level varied rapidly in the harbor, while no such variations occurred in the barometer at the place of observation. The variations in the level of the water may be caused by varied barometric pressure of the air on the water, either at the place of observation or at some distant points. A local increased pressure of the atmosphere at the place of observation would lower the water level, where there is a wide expanse of water; or a diminished pressure, under the same circumstances, would cause the water to rise above its usual level."

In the summer of 1834, according to the report of Foster and Whitney, made to Congress, in 1850, an extraordinary retrocession of the waters took place at Saut St. Mary. The river here is nearly a mile in width, and the depth of the water over the sandstone rapids is about two and a half feet. The phenomenon occurred at noon. The day was calm but cloudy; the water retired suddenly, leaving the bed of the river bare, except for the distance of about twenty rods where the channel is deepest, and remained so for the space of an hour. Persons went out and caught fish in the pools formed in the rocky cavities. The return of the waters was sudden and presented a sublime spectacle. They came down like an immense surge, roaring and foaming, and those who had incautiously wandered into the river bed, had barely time to escape being overwhelmed. A similar event occurred in 1842, when the current set back from the rapids, and the water rose upward of two feet above the usual mark.

In 1845, Foster and Whitney, while coasting in an open boat between Copper Harbor and Eagle River, observed the water rise up, at a distance of a fourth of a mile to the northwest, to the height of twenty feet. It curled over like an immense surge, crested with foam and swept toward the shore. It was succeeded by two or three swells of less magnitude, when the lake resumed its former tranquillity. At the same time the mirage was beautifully displayed, and imaginary islands were seen along the horizon. In 1849, they witnessed at Rock Harbor, Isle Royale, the ebbing and flowing of the water, recurring at intervals of fifteen or twenty minutes, during the entire afternoon.

The difference between the temperature of the air and the lake, gives rise to a variety of optical illusions known as *mirage*. Mountains are seen with inverted cones, headlands project from the shore where none exist. Islands clothed with verdure or girt with cliffs rise up from the bosom of the lake. On approaching Keweenaw Point, Mount Houghton, is the first object to greet the eye of the mariner. In peculiar stages of the atmosphere, its summit is seen inverted in the sky long before the mountain itself is visible. On the north shore the Paps, two elevated mountains near the entrance of Neepigon Bay, at one time appear like hour glasses, and at another like craters, emitting long columns of smoke, which gradually settles around their cones.

The mines and minerals of the northwest constitute the most striking feature of the country, and at the present time one of the great sources of its wealth.

The centre of the mining country is called the Superior country, or the northern peninsula of Michigan, but there is no reason to believe it is confined to this region. Coal and iron, the most valuable of all minerals are found in various places in the northwest. The principal and most valuable minerals found west of Mackinaw, are iron, copper, and lead. A general view of the mineral region may be found in Owen's Geological Survey of Iowa, Wisconsin, Minnesota, and Superior. Great beds of iron are found in ridges or cliffs, some of which rise up to an immense height. Some of these ore-beds of Lake Superior are fifteen feet in thickness, and one of them contains iron enough to supply the world for ages. Above them are immense forests, suitable for charcoal.

The discovery of the iron mountains and mines of Lake Superior was made in 1846, but they were not fully developed until the year 1855, when the ship canal at Saut St. Mary was completed. The mines are from three to sixteen miles from Marquette, a thriving village of upward of one thousand inhabitants, overlooking the lake, about one hundred and forty miles above the Saut. The mine nearest the lake is about two and a half miles distant from Marquette, and bears the name of Eureka. The ore is said to be of surpassing richness, and yields an iron of the best quality, adapted to cutlery. The Jackson iron mountain, and the Cleveland iron mountain, are fourteen and sixteen miles distant. They send to Marquette an aggregate of one thousand tons per week. These mountains rise gradually to the height of six or seven hundred feet, and are a solid mass of iron ore, yielding from 50 to 60 per cent. of the best iron. The New England iron mountain is two and a half miles beyond the Cleveland mountain, and abounds with ore of equal richness. A mile or two further is the Burt mountain, and the same may be said of this, both as it regards quantity and quality, as of the others. A railroad has been constructed from Marquette to the iron regions, and immense quantities of ore and iron are transported over it daily.

All the hills and mountains surrounding Lake Superior, abound in valuable minerals of which copper is the most abundant. It exists in every variety of form. According to the opinion of the lamented Houghton, this region contains the most extensive copper mines in the known world. The native copper boulder discovered by the traveler Henry in the bed of the Ontonagon river, and now in Washington, originally weighed thirty-eight hundred pounds. A copper mass of the same material, found near Copper Harbor, weighed twelve hundred pounds. At Copper Falls, there is a vein of solid ore which measures nine feet in depth, and seven and a half inches in thickness. At Eagle river a boulder was found weighing seventeen hundred pounds. The number of mining companies in operation on the American shore is upward of a hundred.

The Minnesota mine, fifteen miles from Ontonagon, during the year ending January 1, 1857, produced 3,718,403 pounds of copper. The Cliff mine during the year, produced 3,291,229 pounds of copper. The Portage Lake District, including Isle Royale, Portage, Huron, Quincy and Pewabic shipped 539 tons of copper in 1857.

The Lake Superior miners estimate the total shipment of copper mineral from the lake during the year 1858, at 6,008 tons, of an average purity of 67 per cent—making the product of ingot copper about 4,000 tons, worth in the market at present $1,840,000. Estimating the population of the copper region at 6,500 persons, this gives an annual product of about $280 for each man, woman and child. The shipments were as follows: From Keweenaw Point 2,180 tons; from Portage Lake 1,152 tons; from Ontonagon District 2,676 tons; total 6,008 tons.

The extent and importance of the copper mines of Superior, in relation to the general trade in that metal, may be estimated by the following account of the amount of pure copper produced in other parts of the world. The United Kingdom of Great Britian 14,465 tons, Norway 7,200 tons, Russia 4,000, Mexico 500, Hesse Cassel 500, Hartz Mountains 212, Sweden 2,000, Hungary 2,000, East Germany 443; making a total, out of America, of 30,820 tons. The single District of Ontonagon can produce as much copper as the entire Kingdom of Great Britain. The copper mines of the United States, are doing their part as effectually in adding to the solid wealth of the country, as the gold mines of California, or the silver mines of the Arizonia. The copper mining countries are another illustration of the principle upon which success is based, namely, that concentrated talent, effort and capital are necessary to a development of the resources of a country.

When we look into the manufacture of this article, we shall find a new element in the future growth of towns to arise in this region. At present, a large portion of this copper is shipped abroad to be smelted.

But is there not every reason, as well of economy as of material, for carrying on smelting, and all other manufacturing processes, at the point of production? The cost of transporting the raw material is greater than that of carrying the manufactured product. But when all the elements of successful manufacturing exist where the raw material is found, then the economy of the process is doubled. Of metals, of navigation, of food, we have shown there is an inexhaustible supply. But there is also coal near enough to supply the last and only material which might be supposed wanting. Coal is found in the Southern Peninsula of Michigan, in abundance and of good quality. This coal is found at Jackson and at Lansing. This was a matter of so much importance that Prof. Douglas, of the State University, proceeded immediately to analyze it.

The following are the principal results of his analysis. It was made chiefly in reference to the manufacture of gas:—

"The coal was of the bituminous variety, having a jet black color and slaty structure. It was readily ignited, burning with a dull flame and smoke, the fragments comminuting more or less by the heat. It had a specific gravity of about 1.25.

100 parts gave violatile matter 50.780, sulphur

4.028, iron 4.400, ash 8.400, carbon (not volatilized) 41.600.

The value of coal for the manufacture of gas is usually estimated by the amount of volatile matter it yields at a full red-heat."

Of ten samples of English coal, this had more volatile matter than six. Of American coals, it had more of the burning principle than any, except one. The quality of this coal is unquestionably good, and its distance from Mackinaw is no objection, since access can be obtained both by water and railroad. Both the coal and iron used in the manufactures of Cincinnati are brought from places distant from one hundred to five hundred miles; and yet scarcely any place in America has prospered more by manufactures than the Queen of the West. Mackinaw has more than the advantages of Cincinnati for manufactures. It not only has iron and coal, but copper and lead, near enough for all the purposes of successful manufacture. Favorable indications of coal exist within fifty miles south of the Straits, and indications also exist of lead. When we consider these facts, and the vast extent of country, of inland oceans, and of streams around it, why should not Mackinaw be a point of concentration for manufactures, as well as of distribution for commerce?

Mackinaw is centrally situated in the mineral region, and with coal and hard wood for charcoal in perpetual abundance, and the cheapest possible mode of transportation, will become a great manufacturing point, and be able to manufacture innumerable articles, which are now made in Europe, and which our people have been compelled to import for use, simply because the material hitherto employed has been of a quality unsuitable for such purposes. Besides the healthful and bracing temperature of this locality, when compared with Ohio and Pennsylvania, whose summers are found to be exceedingly enervating, especially to those employed in the manufacture of iron, affords advantages, and offers inducements which cannot be overlooked, since in the physical strength and comfort of the workmen, is involved the all-important question of economy. If it should be asked, is the site such that a great city can be built upon it, without imperial wealth, like to that of St. Petersburg, or with the artificial foundations like to those of Chicago, or bankrupting successive companies like Cairo on the Ohio,—the answer is at hand and decisive. At Mackinaw there are no marshes to fill up or drain, no tide sands, no flood-washed banks, no narrow and isolated rocks or ridges, to intercept the progress of commercial growth and activity. On the contrary, the lake rises under the heaviest rains but little, and breaks its waves on a dry shore rising gradually far above its level. There is no better natural site for the foundation of a city in the world, nor one possessing more inviting or beautiful surroundings, and when we consider its available resources, it is evident that nothing can prevent its rise and progress. The straits are so completely the key of the Upper Lakes, Mackinaw must, as in the days of the fur trade, unlock the vast treasures of the entire northwest. The shore of Lake Superior, being but about fifty miles north of Mackinaw and dependent on a canal navigation, annually navigable sixty days less than the straits, on account of ice, to say nothing of breakage, it is perfectly obvious that there can be no competing city further north.

The following from the Toledo Blade shows the immense importance of this point as a key position:

"The immense commerce of the lakes, the growth of which has been unparalleled by anything in the the history of the world, and the vast mineral, timber and agricultural resources of their shores, which are even now, only beginning to attract attention, may well awaken a desire on the part of enterprise to get possession of the key position which is to command

and unlock the future treasures of this vast empire. Already, six important commercial cities, with an aggregate population of about 350,000 inhabitants, have sprung up on these island waters, and are the most flourishing of any away from the Atlantic coast. Others are struggling into notoriety on the borders of Lake Superior, and must, at no very distant time, become important and active places of business. But the place of all others, where we would expect a city to spring up and grow rapidly into importance, is still undeveloped.

"The Straits of Mackinaw, four and a half miles wide, make the only natural ferry communication between the great peninsula, enclosed by the lakes and the rich mineral region lying on the southern border of Lake Superior; and must, hence, be the terminus of all the great railroad lines that traverse Michigan longitudinally and compete for the trade north of the straits, now rapidly growing up into importance. It must therefore be the point of radiation, eastward, through Canada; westward through the mineral region; and southward, through Michigan. Canada has already made grants of land for several important roads which must ultimately reach the straits; and lines are also provided for by government grants, from the straits through the Northern Peninsula, and from the straits southward to Fort

Wayne by the way of Grand Rapids, and to Toledo, through Lansing. The culminating point being thus settled for several roads, all others will naturally centre at the same crossing, even if the coast line had not made such a thing inevitable.

"The point which projects northward into the lake, from the Michigan Peninsula, to form this strait, is admirably located for a great city. It is the site of old Fort Mackinaw, and in health and commercial position, can have no rival in those southern waters. This point has been selected by a company of capitalists, on which to plant the commercial city of the north; the Venice of the Lakes, foreshadowed in the extract which we have placed at the head of the article. This new city is to bear the name of the ancient fort and strait, and to be called Mackinaw. It will hold the key of all the northern lakes; and should its growth be marked by energy and enterprise, will command the trade of the greatest mining region in the world; be the chief depot of the northern fisheries; the outlet of an immense lumber trade; and the focus of a great network of railways, communicating with tropics on the south, and stretching out its iron arms, at no distant day, to the Atlantic on the east, and Pacific on the west.

The proposed city will have the advantage of the

most salubrious climate to be found in the temperate zone, and will be the resort of those seeking health, as well as those seeking wealth. It has a northern position, being on the same parallel as Montreal; but the winters are equable, and the summers though short, are mild and pleasant, being modified by the great body of water which stretches out on every side, except at the south. As a manufacturing point it may well command universal attention. The Lake Superior iron is known to be the best in the world, and coal and wood are at hand in the greatest abundance; while communication by water is so wide as to leave nothing to desire on that head. It should be as famous for smelting as Swansea, in England, for it must have unbounded supplies of iron and copper ore.

"But we have no space to speak of its commercial position. It must be seen at a glance that, as all the produce which flows through Chicago, Milwaukee, and the great West must sweep by on its way to the East, and all the goods and merchandise of the East, must be borne by its wharves on their way to the West, that it cannot fail to be a point which must spring at once into importance. The government, too, must have a fort, a light-house, and custom-house there, which with the fisheries, must supply a large profitable business to its earlier population."

CHAPTER VII.

Lake Huron—Eastern shore of Michigan—Face of the country—Picturesque view—Rivers — Grand—Saginaw—Cheboy-e-gun—Natural scenery—Fort Gratiot—White Rock—Saginaw Bay—Thunder Bay—Bois Blanc Island—Drummond's Island — British Troops — St. Helena Island — Iroquois Woman's Point—Point La Barbe—Point aux Sable—Point St. Vital—Wreck of the Queen City—St. Martin's Island—Fox Point—Moneto pa-maw—Mille au Coquin—Great fishing places—Cross Village—Catholic Convent.

LAKE HURON, which, with Lake Erie and St. Clair, washes the eastern boundary of the southern peninsula of Michigan, is two hundred and fifty miles long and its average width is about one hundred miles. Its depth is about eight hundred feet. The southeastern shore of Michigan presents a level surface covered with a dense forest, at points meeting the edge of the bank. The trees of this heavily-timbered land, with their massive shafts standing close together, "cast a gloomy grandeur over the scene, and when stripped of their foliage appear like the black colonnade of a sylvan temple." In advancing into the interior, a picturesque and rolling country opens to view, covered with oak-openings or groves of white oak thinly scattered over the ground, having the appearance of stately parks. The appearance of the surface of the country is as if it was covered with mounds, arranged without order, sometimes rising from thirty to two hundred feet in height, producing a delightful alternation of hill and dale, which is sometimes varied by a rich prairie or burr-oak grove.

The principal rivers of the State are the Grand, St. Joseph's, Kalamazoo, the Raisin, the Clinton, the Huron, and the Rouge. The Grand is two hundred and seventy miles in length, and has a free navigation for steamboats which ply regularly between Lake Michigan and Grand Rapids, a distance of forty miles. The Saginaw empties into Lake Huron and is navigable for sixty miles. These, with the others we have named, interlock their branches running through different parts of southern Michigan, and while they beautify the landscape they afford water-power and fertilize the soil.

The river Cheboy-e-gun is the largest stream in the northern portion of the lower peninsula and empties into the Straits of Mackinaw opposite Bois

Blanc Island. At its mouth is a village containing two steam saw mills and one water saw mill. A light-house stands a mile or two east from this point. Brook-trout, bass, pike, pickerel, and perch, are caught at the entrance of the river. In the fall and spring numerous water-fowl resort to the upper forks of the river and to the small lakes forming its sources. These lakes also abound with a great variety of fish, which can be taken by spearing.

The natural scenery of Michigan is imposing. The extensive tracts of dense forests, clothed with the richest verdure, fresh as when it first came from the hands of the Creator; the prairies and lakes which abound, the wide parks, whose soil is entirely covered for miles with large and rich flowers, present a striking and agreeable contrast. The beech and black walnut, the elm, the maple, the hickory, and the oaks of different species and large size, the lind and the bass-wood, and various other kinds of forest trees, plainly indicate the fertility of the soil from whence they spring. Grape vines often hang from the branches a foot in circumference, clustering around their trunks, or thickening the undergrowth along the banks of rivers; and, while the glades open to the sun like cultivated grounds, the more thickly-timbered forests, shut out from the sky by the mass of vegetation, present in summer a gloomy twilight.

In traveling along the main roads of Michigan, splendid tracts of park-like lawns sweep along the path for miles covered with flowers, broken by prairies, thick forests, and lakes.

Fort Gratiot stands at the foot of Lake Huron and commands the entrance to the upper lakes. Advancing along the western shore of this lake the voyager sees a long, alluvial bank covered with a forest of pine, poplar, beech, and hemlock.

On advancing further the banks become more elevated until they rise to forty feet in height. About fifty miles from Fort Gratiot, a large rock rises to the surface of the lake, a mile or so from the shore, which is called the "White Rock." From the earliest period this rock has been regarded as an altar or a landmark. It was to the early voyagers a beacon to guide them in their course; but to the Indians it was a place of oblation, where they offered sacrifices to the spirits of the lakes.

Saginaw Bay is a large indentation of the shoreline like to that of Green Bay in Lake Michigan, but not so large. Near its centre are a number of small islands. Twenty miles from its mouth stands the thriving town of Saginaw. From the north-westerly cape of Saginaw Bay to Flat Rock Point, the shore of Lake Huron presents a bank of alluvial soil, with a margin of sand along its border intersected with frequent masses of limestone rock, in some places ground to fragments by the surging of the waves.

Thunder Bay is also another indentation made by the Lake. It was thus called from the impression that at this point the air was more than ordinarily charged with electricity.

Bois Blanc Island, at the head of Lake Huron, stretches in the form of a crescent between the Island of Mackinac and the lower peninsula of Michigan. It is from ten to twelve miles in length by three or four in breadth. The lower part of this island is sandy, but the larger portion of it is covered with a fertile soil bearing a forest of elm, maple, oak, ash, white-wood and beech. It has been surveyed and a government light-house stands on its eastern point.

In the northern part of Lake Michigan are located Beaver Islands. There are five or six of this group bearing different names. Big Beaver is the most considerable, and contains perhaps forty square miles. These islands all lie in the vicinity of each other, and within a few miles northwest of Grand

and Little Traverse Bays in Lake Michigan. The Big Beaver was, up to July, 1856, in possession of the Mormons, who claimed it as a gift from the Lord.

Another interesting locality is Drummond's Island, between the Detour and the False Detour. It was taken possession of by the British troops when they surrendered Fort Mackinaw in 1814. On this island they built a fort and formed quite a settlement. Upon an examination of the boundary line between the United States and Great Britain, it was ascertained that this island was within the jurisdiction of the former, and it was accordingly evacuated by the British in 1828. The British subjects living on the island followed the troops, and the place was soon deserted and became a desolation.

St. Helena Island is a small island near the Straits of Mackinaw, not far from the shore of the northern peninsula, containing a few acres over a section of land. It is a great fishing station, and enjoys a good harbor protected from westerly winds. Its owner, who has exiled himself *a la Napoleon,* spends his time in fishing, and other pursuits adapted to his mind.

In addition to the numerous islands constituting the surroundings of Mackinaw there are a number of interesting localities denominated "Points, that we must not omit to mention. The first, because the most important, and one which is connected with many historic associations which we shall direct attention to, is the "Iroquois Woman's Point," the Indian name for Point St. Ignatius on the opposite side of the straits from Mackinaw, distant between three and four miles, about the same as from the Battery at New York to Staten Island. The original inhabitants with their descendants have long since passed away. Its present occupants are principally Canadians. It has a Catholic chapel.

Point La Barbe, opposite to Green Island Shoals and Mackinaw, is a projection of the upper peninsula into the straits. It is four miles distant from Gross Cape, and derives its name from a custom which prevailed among the Indian traders in olden time on their annual return to Mackinaw of stopping here and putting on their best apparel before making their appearance among the people of that place.

About half way between Mackinaw and Cheboy-e-gun, a projection from the lower peninsula into the straits, is Point aux Sable. Point St. Vital is a cape projecting into Lake Huron from the south-eastern extremity of the upper peninsula. There is a reef of rocks off this point where the steamer Queen City was wrecked. On a clear day this point may be seen from Fort Holmes, and it presents an enchanting view. The St. Martin's Islands are also in full view from this point.

In the southwestern part of the straits, about twenty miles distant from Mackinaw, is Fox Point. A light-house has been erected on a shoal extending out two miles into the lake. Moneto-pa-maw is a high bluff still further west, on the shore of Michigan, where there are fine fisheries, and is a place of considerable resort. Further west, near the mouth of the Mille au Coquin river which empties into Michigan, there are also excellent fisheries, and to those who are fond of this kind of sport apart from the profit connected with it, there is no place in the world possessing half the attractions as Mackinaw and its surroundings, while the "Mackinaw trout," with the "Mackinaw boat" and the "Mackinaw blanket," are famous over the world.

Between Little Traverse and Mackinaw is the village of Cross, or La Crosse. The following interesting account of a visit to that place is taken from the Mackinaw Herald in 1859:

"The name of this village—'Cross,' recalls to one's mind, some reminiscences connected with the early history of the Indian Missions. Suffice it to observe, that it derives its name from the circumstance of a large cross having stood for many years on the brow of the hill, on which the present Indian village stands, planted there by some of the followers of James Marquette, during their explorations and missions in this part of the country. The old cross was of oak, and was still standing about forty-five years ago. Recently it has been replaced by another. An old Indian, called *The Short-Arm*, over whose head some eighty winters had passed, was still living in 1836, and who, when a little boy, recollected to have seen the last Missionary of this place. 'I am old, my children,' said the aged Missionary, 'and I wish to die among my own people—I must leave you.' He left; and in the course of time the Arbre-Croche Indians relapsed into Paganism. They continued in this state until a young Christian Ottawa, named *Aw-taw-weesh*, who had just returned from among the Catholic Algonquins in Canada, appeared among them and taught religion. He became also, in some respects, what Cadmus was of old, or Guess among the Cherokees—the first teacher of letters, among his people. As writing paper was then scarce, at least among the Indians, he taught them to write on birch bark, with sharpened sticks, instead of pens.

This man is still living. He is now old, poor, almost entirely blind; and although having been a real benefactor to his people, he may go down to his grave, unpitied, and unknown.

"But awakened by his teachings, the Indians afterward called loudly on Missionaries to come among them, and they have had them during the past thirty or forty years.

"At this day two Catholic Clergymen and a Convent of four Brothers and twelve Sisters—being a religious community, of the Third Order of St. Francis—are stationed at this place. But, to return: As rough voyaging generally gives keen appetite, so the party did ample justice to the eatables, which had been prepared by the Indians. Perhaps some reader at a distance might suppose this supper to have been taken in a *wigwam;* with the fire-place in the centre, a hole above for the escape of smoke; and the party squatting down upon the ground, with legs crossed in tailor fashion, around a single dish: no, no; but it was prepared in a good, substantial house; on a table with a table-cloth, with crockery, dishes, tea-cups and saucers, and knives and forks, such as are used by common white folks. Then there stood the waiters, ready to assist the double-handed manipulations going on at the table. At a convenient hour, the party separated for the night;

the agent was put in possession of the clergyman's house, then temporarily absent on a mission, by the Rev. Mr. Weikamp, the Superior of the Convent.

"The next day, after the forenoon services of the church at the village, the agent and party, according to previous invitation, went to the Convent for dinner. Arrived there, they were introduced first into a log cabin, situated at some distance in the rear of the convent, occupied by the four Brothers, belonging to the order, and the Rev. Superior. He occupies a single room, in real new-settler style. This is his sitting-room, library, study and bed-room. He has traveled in Europe, and some parts of Asia; he has various objects of curiosity; and among these is a silver coin of about the size and value of a Mexican quarter of a dollar, which he brought with him from Jerusalem. This piece of money is said to be one of the kind of which Judas received thirty pieces, from the chief priests and magistrates, the price for which he sold his Divine Master. Another thing, is a Turkish pipe, with its long, pliable stem, with which the lover of the 'weed' could regale himself without being annoyed by the smoke, as usual; for the pipe, which is made somewhat in the shape and of the size of a small decanter and half-filled with water is so arranged that while the wet tobacco is burning in the cup on the top, the smoke, during suction at the stem, descends through a tube into the water, and none of it escapes visibly, into the open air. The Rev. Mr. Weikamp, the Superior, is a German, and speaks English fluently. He is in the prime of life, and is full of energy and perseverance. He is not one of those who, from the fact of belonging to a religious order, may be supposed to be gloomy, with head bowed down, not hardly daring to cast his eyes up into the beautiful light of the heavens; but he converses with freedom, ease and assurance; and he relishes a joke as well as any man, when it comes *a propos.* A fanciful peculiarity, though nothing strange in it, attends his steps wherever he goes, in the shape of a small black dog called "Finnie," with a string of small horse-bells round his neck. "Finnie" has two black, watery and glistening spots in his head for eyes, which seem ready to shoot out from their sockets, especially when spoken to. When told in German, to speak, 'Finnie' begins to tremble—he shakes his head—jingles his bells; and utters a kind of guttural snuffling, and half-suppressed growl or bark. But, as we are not acquainted with the German language, we cannot say, that "Finnie" pronounces it well!

"Dinner being announced at the convent, the party

went over with the Superior to partake of it. Everything about the table was scrupulously neat—an abundance of the substantials of good living had been prepared by the Sisters. Some time after dinner the vesper bell rang at the convent; and by special permission, the party were shown into the choir usually occupied by the Brothers alone during the services of the church. This was on one side of the altar; and on the other, was a similar choir for the sisters. In the body of the church, the Indians or others are admitted. For a few moments after entering, all was silence;—but the priest having intoned the vespers, the sweet tones of a large melodeon suddenly swelled through the sanctuary, mingling with the voices of the sisters. This for a time had a singular effect. To hear music in these wild woods, far away from civilized society where instrumental music forms part of the ordinary pleasures and amenities of life, served to recall to one's memory other days and other climes. After vespers, the Superior of the convent conducted the party through the building to view it. The dimensions are: 160 feet long, 80 wide, and 28 feet high. There are two court yards, each 40 by 40 feet, and the church also 40 by 40, placed between them. When finished, this building will contain 108 bedrooms, a large schoolroom, carpenter and blacksmith shops, dining-rooms, kitchen, store-rooms, halls, corridors, &c. It will be separated into two parts; one to be occupied exclusively by the Sisters, and the other by the Brothers. At the time of this visit, there were some cultivated flowers yet in bloom in the court-yard. So much for the material building: and now a hasty sketch of this religious order may not be unacceptable to some of our readers.

"This religious community, is the Third Order of St. Francis, of Assisi, instituted in Europe by this saint in 1221. It was established for persons married or single living in the world, united by certain pious exercises, compatible with a secular state. It soon spread over all Europe, and even kings and queens on their thrones vied with the poorest peasants in eagerly entering this order, to share the labors of the mission within its sphere, and to participate in its spiritual benefits. Among the persons of this order, who were expelled from their cloister homes during the revolution which agitated Europe in 1848, was Sister Teresa Hackelmayer. This nun, at the proposal of a missionary father in America, and by permission of her Superior, came to New York in the winter of 1851, to establish a community of her order in that State. But meeting with disappointment there, she finally established a convent at Oldenburg, in the State of Indiana. In 1851, a second convent of this order was founded at Nojoshing, four miles from Milwaukee, on Lake Michigan. In 1853, the Rev. J. B. Weikamp founded, in West Chicago, the third convent of this order, and also formed a community of Brothers;—and in October 1855, with the understanding of Bishop Baraga, then Vicar Apostolic of Upper Michigan, he transferred those two communities to 'Cross Village'—his present location.

The company having ranged through the building, as observed, took a walk outside. From the south side of the convent, a broad walk is laid out reaching to an inclosure of some forty feet square, at the distance of about fifteen rods. Another and narrower walk through the centre of this inclosure leads to a small square building, on the opposite side, having a four-sided roof meeting in a point, and surmounted by a cross. On entering this building, a lounge or settee, stands in front, and on the wall above it, hangs a piece of board or canvass, painted black, on which are human skulls of different sizes, each with two cross bones painted in white. A trap-door is raised from the floor, and a deep, spacious vault is opened to view: this is the place of burial for the Superior of the convent. On the outside, the spaces on either side of the little walk are intended to be the last resting-places of the brothers and sisters. It is a solemn thought to see men thus prepare deliberately for *Death!* But as the party retraced their steps in such cheerful, good humor, loitering toward the convent, one might have supposed that the beautiful weather, the bright sunshine, and the bracing air had, for the time, scattered away all thoughts of death. Among the questions proposed to the Superior was, 'Whether at any time the brothers and sisters were allowed to have social, familiar intercourse with each other?' The Superior answered, in substance, that they were not; nor even allowed to speak to each other, without permission of the Superior. 'Then according to your principle,' some one rejoined, 'the world would soon come to an end!' The remark raised a general laugh, in which the Superior himself joined heartily."

CHAPTER VIII.

Three epochs—The romantic—The military—The agricultural and commercial—An inviting region—Jesuit and Protestant missions — First Protestant mission — First missionary — Islands of Mackinac and Green Bay—La Pointe—Saut St. Mary—Presbyterians — Baptists — Methodists — Revival at Fort Brady — Ke-wee-naw—Fon du Lac—Shawnees—Pottawatimies—Eagle River—Ontonagon—Camp River—Iroquois Point—Saginaw Indians—Melancholy reflections—Number of Indians in the States and Territories.

THE history of this region, in the language of one, exhibits three distinct and strongly marked epochs. The first may be properly denominated the romantic, which extends to the year 1760, when its dominion passed from the hands of the French to the English. This was the period when the first beams of civilization had scarcely penetrated its forests, and the paddles of the French fur trader swept the lakes, and the boat songs of the *voyageurs* awakened the tribes on their wild and romantic shores.

The second epoch is the military, which commenced with the Pontaic war, running down through the successive struggles of the British, the Indians, and the Americans, to obtain dominion of the country, and ending with the victory of Commodore Perry, the defeat of Proctor, the victory of General Harrison and the death of Tecumseh, the leader of the Anglo-savage conspiracy on the banks of the Thames.

The third may be denominated the enterprising, the hardy, the mechanical, and working period, commencing with the opening of the country to emigrant settlers, the age of agriculture, commerce, and manufactures, of harbors, cities, canals, and railroads, when the landscapes of the forest were meted out by the compass and chain of the surveyor, when its lakes and rivers were sounded, and their capacity, to turn the wheel of a mill or to float a ship, were demonstrated, thus opening up avenues of commerce and industry. Its wild and savage character has passed away, and given place to civilization, religion, and commerce, inviting the denizens of over-crowded cities to its broad lakes and beautiful rivers, its rich mines and fertile prairies, and promising a rapid and abundant remuneration for toil.

We have alluded to the labors and sacrifices of the Jesuit missionaries in the early period of the history of the northwest, and it is right and proper that the labors of the Protestant missionaries, though of a much later period, should not be forgotten. The Jesuit fathers were not alone in sacrifice and toil in introducing the Gospel among the tribes of the northwest. The first Protestant missions established in this region, as far as we have been able to learn, were those of the Presbyterian Church on the Island of Mackinac and at Green Bay.

The first missionary who visited Mackinaw was the Rev. David Bacon, father of the Rev. Leonard Bacon, D. D., of New Haven. He was sent out by the Connecticut Missionary Society in 1800, and commenced his mission in Detroit, where, after remaining a year or two, he relinquished his field to a Moravian missionary, Rev. Mr. Denky, and visited the Indians on the Maumee. From this he returned to Detroit, and from thence went to Mackinac, where he remained until the missionary society was compelled, from want of funds, to recall their missionary.

The following interesting account was given by C. J. Walker, Esq., before the Historical Society of Detroit:

"The Connecticut Missionary Society is, I believe, the oldest Missionary Association in America. It was organized in June, 1795, the General Association of Connecticut, at its annual meeting that year, having organized itself into a society of that name. Its object was 'to Christianize the heathen in North America, and to support and promote Christian knowledge in the new settlements within the United States.' For some years its efforts were principally directed to sending missionaries 'to the new settlements in Vermont, New York, and Pennsylvania,' and subsequently 'New Connecticut,' or the Western Reserve of Ohio, became an important field of its operations. The trustees, in June, 1800, determined 'that a discreet man, animated by the love of God and souls, of a good common education, be sought for, to travel among the Indian tribes south and west of Lake Erie, to explore their situation and learn their feelings with respect to Christianity, and so far as he has opportunity to teach them its doctrines and duties.' A very sensible letter of 'Instructions' was adopted and a long message 'to the Indian tribes bordering on Lake Erie' prepared, showing very little knowledge of Indian mind and character. Mr. David Bacon presented himself as a candidate for this somewhat unpromising field of labor. His son says he was one of those men who are called visionary and enthusiasts by men of more prosaic and plodding temperament. He had not a liberal education, but was a man of eminent intellectual powers and of intensely thoughtful habits, and beside a deep religious experience, he had endeavored dilligently to fit himself for a missionary life, the self-denying labors of which he ardently coveted. On examination Mr. Bacon was accepted.

"On the 8th of August, 1800, Mr. Bacon left Hartford on foot with his pack upon his back, and on the 4th of September he was at Buffalo, having walked most of the distance. On the 8th, he left on a vessel for this city, which he reached after a quick and pleasant voyage on the 11th. He was made welcome at the house of the commandant, Major Hunt, where, I believe, his first religious services were held. Gen. Uriah Tracy, of Litchfield, Conn., General Agent of the United States for the Western Indians, was then here, and, together with the local Indian agent, Jonathan Schieffelin, took an active interest in the mission of Mr. Bacon. John Askin, Esq., the same liberal-minded merchant, who so essentially befriended the Moravians twenty years before, and Benjamin Huntington, a merchant here, formerly of Norwich, Conn., rendered him valuable information and assistance. Learning from those sources that the Delawares at Sandusky, were about to remove, that the Wyandottes were mostly Catholics, and that there were no other Indians 'south and west of Lake Erie,' among whom there was an inviting field of labor, his attention was turned to the north, and, with the advice of these judicious friends, on the 13th of September, he took passage with General Tracy in a government vessel bound for Mackinac, and went to Harson's Island, at the head of Lake St. Clair, near which there was quite an Indian settlement. Although only forty miles distant, he did not reach there until the 17th, being four days upon the voyage. Jacob Harson or Harsing, as it was originally spelled, the proprietor of this island, was an Albany Dutchman, who, in 1766, on appointment of Sir Wm. Johnson, came to Niagara as Indian blacksmith and gunsmith, and his original commission or letter of appointment, written by Sir William, is now before me. On the breaking out of the Revolution, finding Mr. Harson friendly to the Americans, the British stripped him of his property and sent him, sorely against his will, to this frontier. He established himself upon the island as early as 1786, where his descendants now reside, acquired great influence with the Indians, and lived in a very comfortable manner. He received Mr. Bacon in this beautiful retreat, with great kindness and hospitality, and he thanks the Lord that he is provided a comfortable house, a convenient study, and as good a bed and as good board as I should have had if I had remained in Connecticut. I know of no place in the State of New York so healthy as this, I believe the water and the air as pure here as in any part of New England, and I have never been before where venison and wild geese and ducks were so plenty, or where there was such a rich variety of fresh-water fish. There were many Indians in the vicinity. Mr. Harson encouraged the establishment of a mission, and Mr. Bacon deemed it a most favorable opening. Bernardus Harson, a son of Jacob, was engaged as interpreter. He returned to Detroit on the same vessel with General Tracy, Sept. 30th, to attend an Indian Council which was held here on the 7th of October, when he was formally introduced to the Indians by General Tracy, and was most favorably received. He returned to the island and remained until the Indians departed for their winter hunting grounds, when he left for Connecticut, where he arrived about the middle of December. He was soon ordained to the ministry, and I believe married, for he returned with a young wife of whom nothing is heard previously.

"Late in January 1801, Mr. Bacon commenced his

return journey with his wife and her brother, Beaumont Parks, Esq., now of Springfield, Illinois, a young man who came with him to learn the Chippewa language and to become a teacher. The sleighing leaving them they remained at Bloomfield, Ontario county, New York, until spring, and did not reach here until May 9th. Mr. Bacon's plan was to remain at Detroit, until he became so familar with the Indian language that he could successfully prosecute his mission. He remained here until the spring of 1802, holding regular religious services in the Council House. For a time he preached twice upon the Sabbath, but the afternoon attendance being thin, he accepted a call from the settlement on the river Rouge to preach to them half a day. To aid in defraying expenses he commenced keeping a school in the house where he lived on St. James street, just in the rear of the Masonic Hall, and in this he was assisted by his wife. One at least of our present fellow citizens was a pupil of Mr. Bacon, and has pleasant memories of that little school. Amid many discouragements the study of the Chippewa was pursued by this missionary family, and although they made 'but slow progress' and it was 'hard work to commit their words to memory' and 'extremely difficult to construct a sentence according to the idioms of their language,' they 'hope and expect we shall be able to surmount every difficulty.'

"While thus toilfully but hopefully preparing for his anticipated work, getting acquainted with Indians, their life and character, and as yet uncertain at what precise point to commence his mission, Mr. Denhey, a Moravian missionary, desired to occupy the field upon the St. Clair River, which Mr. Bacon in some measure occupied the year before, and to this Mr. Bacon assented. His attention had been called to Mackinac and L'Arbre Croche, but he resolved to visit the Indians upon the Maumee, and ascertain by personal interviews and examination what encouragement there was for a mission in that vicinity. For this purpose, with his brother-in-law and a hired man, on 29th of April, 1802, he left in a canoe for the 'Miami,' as the Maumee was then called. He found most of the Indian chiefs engaged in a drunken debauch, and it was not until the 14th of May, and after repeated efforts, that he succeeded in gathering a full council, and addressing them upon the subject of establishing a mission among them. He felt it his duty to have translated the message sent to the Indians by the Missionary Society. The poor savages listened courteously to this long piece of abstruse theological narrative and argument, but they must have been terribly, bored, notwithstanding Mr. Bacon's efforts to 'express the ideas in language better adapted to the capacity and more agreeable to their ways of speaking.' No wonder that Little Otter was 'too unwell to attend in the afternoon.' After this translation. Mr. Bacon made a well conceived speech of considerable length, setting forth the advantages which the Indians would derive from a mission. There was no little point in the polished reproof of Little Otter, in the commencement of his speech, who said: 'Now brother, if you will listen to us we will give you an answer. But it is our way to be very short. Our white brothers, when they make speeches, are very lengthy. They read and write so much that they get in a great many little things. But it is not so with your red brothers. When we go on any great business and have any great things to say, we say them in a few words.' With no little ingenuity, but with apparent courtesy, these sons of the forest declined a mission in their midst. The gist of the reply is contained in the following sentence: 'Brother, your religion is very good; but it is only good for white people. It will not do for Indians, they are quite a different sort of people.'

"On the following day Mr. Bacon started for Detroit, and remained here until June 2d, when, with his family, he removed to Missilimackinac, then the great centre of Indian population in our Territory. Here he remained until August 1804, perfecting himself in the language, teaching, preaching and pursuing the other labors incident to his mission. He very clearly saw that a successful Indian mission involved no inconsiderable expenditure in establishing schools and in educating the Indians in agriculture and the ruder arts of civilization. These expenditures were too large for the means of the Missionary Society, and in January, 1804, they directed the mission to abandoned, and that Mr. Bacon should remove to the Western Reserve. The intelligence of this reached Mr. Bacon in July, and in August he removed and became the first founder of the town of Tallmadge, Ohio. Thus ended this first Protestant effort to convert the Indians of Michigan to the faith of the cross. It was while Mr. Bacon was residing here that Rev. Dr. Bacon was born. We may therefore, with pride, claim him as a native of our beautiful city."

Sometime after a mission was established at La Pointe near the southern extremity of Lake Superior. The Mission at Mackinac was subsequently revived and continued until 1837, when the population had so entirely changed, and the Indians had discontinued their visits for purposes of trade, that it was deemed best to abandon it, which was done, and the property sold. The Rev. Mr. Pitezel, in his "Lights and Shade of Missionary Life," who visited the island in 1843, thus speaks of this mission: "We visited the mission establishment once under the care of the Presbyterian Church, but now abandoned. It is a spacious building, and was once thronged with native and half-bred children and youth, there educated at vast expense. Little of the fruit of this self-sacrificing labor is thought now to be apparent, but the revelations of eternity may show that here was a necessary and a very important link in the chain of events, connected with the Christianization of benighted pagans." During the time of Mr. Pitezel's visit, a large number of Indians of different tribes had assembled at the island, for the purpose of receiving their annuity, among which were several Christian Indians, from Saut St. Mary, Grand Traverse, and elsewhere. The Rev. Mr. Daugherty, a Presbyterian minister, from the latter place, accompanied his Indians, and had his tent among them for the purpose of keeping his sheep from the hands of the woolfish white man, who would first rob him of his religion, and then of his money.

In 1828, the Baptists established a mission at Saut St. Mary. This mission was opened under the most favorable auspices by the Rev. A. Bingham, and continued in a state of prosperity for many years. In 1843 it was still under the superintendence of the Rev. Mr. Bingham, who for twenty years had been laboring to bring the Indians under Christian influence. Indian children were boarded in the mission establishment, and a school was kept up, which, in the language of one, would have been a credit to any land. The Rev. Mr. Porter, a Congregationalist missionary, also labored here. The labors of these missionaries were greatly blessed, and numbers of officers and soldiers at the fort and garrison, as well as Indians, were converted.

The Baptist missionaries extended their labors to various points on the northern peninsula and on the shores of Lake Superior.

The Methodists commenced a mission at Saut St. Mary, under the labors of "John Sunday," a converted Indian, soon after that established by the Baptists. In 1831 a portion of the Oneida Indians removed to Green Bay, and the Rev. John Clark was sent out as a missionary among them the following year. In a report made by the missionary to the Board, he thus describes his field of labor: "The white settlement is located on the left bank of the Fox River, extending up the river about five miles from the head of the bay. The population is about one thousand, but greatly amalgamated with the Menominee Indians, over whom it is said they have great influence. The Indian settlement is about twenty-five miles from this place, on the left bank of the Fox river." Mr. Clark preached at this settlement and at Green Bay on alternate Sabbaths. Messrs. Marsh and Stevens, of the Presbyterian church, were located here, laboring among the Stockbridge Indians and kindly welcomed Mr. Clark among them. These Indians emigrated from Stockbridge, Mass., and were at one time under the pastoral care of Jonathan Edwards. While this distinguished divine was missionary among these Indians, at Stockbridge, he wrote his famous "Treatise on the Will." Mr. Clark was cordially received by the Indian agent, Mr. Schoolcraft.

In 1833, he visited Saut St. Mary, and found a revival in progress. Nearly all the officers, and thirty or forty soldiers, in Fort Brady had been converted. The command was soon after removed to Chicago, and was succeeded by another. A gracious revival followed his labors at the fort, and officers and soldiers were seen bowing at the same altar, happy in the enjoyment of a common salvation. Still holding his connection with Green Bay, he visited that place and preached in Fort Howard and also among his Indians who had removed to Duck Creek.

At Ke-wee-naw, John Sunday commenced a mission among the Chippewas, and in 1834 Mr. Clark visited that interesting field. He continued to superintend the missions in this region, until he volunteered as a missionary for Texas, and the superintendence of the Indian mission was given to the Rev. W. H. Brockway. The Rev. Mr. Pitezel labored at Ke-wee-naw with great success for several years, preaching at the different mines on the shores of Lake Superior. The Methodists also established a mission at Fon du Lac near the east shore of the Winnebago Lake. In the year 1830, a branch mission was organized among the Wyandottes and Shawnees on the Huron river, and also one among the Pottawatimees at Fort Clark on the Fox river, at which place, in 1837, upward of one hundred were converted.

In 1847 a mission was established at the Cliff Mine, on Eagle River, a stream which empties into Lake Superior, about twenty miles west of Copper

Harbor. The Methodists have missions also at Ontonagon and Carp River, all of which are more or less prosperous.

At present this church has maintained missions and schools among small bands of Indians collected on reserves in Isabella and Oceana counties in the lower peninsula of Michigan. The Indians at the old mission in the vicinity of Saut St. Mary, are assembling at Iroquois Point at the lower end of Lake Superior, and are supplied with a missionary. A mission was also established in the Bay Shore Reservation, among the Saginaw Indians, which still exists.

It is a matter of melancholy reflection, that the immense tribes, each of which could muster thousands of warriors in this vast region, have dwindled down to small and feeble bands. The same remark will apply to all the tribes in North America. The race is rapidly passing away, and the nation, like that of Edom, will at no distant day become entirely extinct. The last report of the Secretary of the Interior, states, that the whole number of Indians within the limits of the States and Territories of the Union, does not now exceed three hundred and twenty-five thousand.

CHAPTER IX.

Indian name of Michigan—Islands—Lanman's Summer in the wilderness — Plains—Trees—Rivers—A traditionary land—Beautiful description—Official report in relation to the trade of the lakes — Green Bay — Grand Traverse Bay—Beaver Islands—L'Arbre Croche—Boundaries of Lake Michigan—Its connections—Railroad from Fort Wayne to Mackinaw—Recent report of—Amount completed—Land grants.

THE Indian name of the State of Michigan, is Michi-sawg-ye-gan, the meaning of which in the Algonquin tongue is the Lake country. Surrounded as it is almost entirely by water, it possesses all the advantages of an island. It has numerous streams which are clear and beautiful, abounding in fish. The surface of the western half (we allude now to the lower or southern peninsula) is destitute of rocks, and undulating. In the language of Lanman in his "Summer in the Wilderness," "It is here that the loveliest of lakes and streams and prairies are to be found. No one who has never witnessed them can form any idea of the exquisite beauty of the thousand lakes which gem the western part of Michigan. They are the brightest and purest mirrors the virgin sky has ever used to adorn herself. On the banks of these lakes, grow in rich profusion, the rose, the violet, the lily and the sweet brier.

"A great proportion of Michigan is covered with white-oak openings. Standing on a gentle hill, the eye wanders away for miles over an undulating surface, obstructed only by the trunks of lofty trees,—above you a green canopy, and beneath, a carpet of velvet grass, sprinkled with flowers of every hue and form.

"The prairies are another interesting feature of Michigan scenery. They meet the traveler at every point, and of many sizes, seeming often like so many lakes, being often studded with wooded islands, and surrounded by shores of forests. This soil is a deep black sand. Grass is their natural production, although corn, oats and potatoes flourish upon them. Never can I forget the first time I entered White Pigeon Prairie. Sleeping beneath the shadows of sunset, as it was, the effect upon me was like that which is felt on first beholding the ocean,—overpowering awe. All that the poet has said about these gardens of the desert is true.

"Burr Oak Plains. The only difference between these and the oak openings, is the character of the trees and the evenness of their surface. The soil is a mixture of sand and black loam. They have the appearance of cultivated orchards, or English parks; and on places where the foot of the white man has never trod, a carriage and four could easily pass through. They produce both wheat and corn.

"The wet prairies have the appearance of submerged land. In them the grass is often six or seven feet high. They are the resort of water-fowl, musk-rats, and otters.

"But the best and most fertile soil in Michigan is that designated by the title of timbered land. It costs more to prepare it for the plough, but when once the soil is sown it yields a thousand-fold. And with regard to their beauty and magnificence, the innumerable forests of this State are not surpassed by any in the world, whether we consider the variety or grandeur of their production. This timber is needed for prairie States, Lake cities, and exports.

"A friend of mine, now residing in western Michigan, and who once spent several years in Europe, thus writes respecting this region:

"'Oh, such trees as we have here! Magnificent,

tall, large-leafed, umbrageous. Vallombrosa, the far-famed Vallombrosa of Tuscany, is nothing to the thousand Vallombrosas here! A fig for your Italian scenery! This is the country where nature reigns in her virgin beauty; where trees grow, where corn grows; where men grow better than they do anywhere else in the world. This is the land to study nature in all her luxuriant charms, under glorious green branches, among singing birds and laughing streams; this is the land to hear the cooing of the turtle-dove, in far, deep, cool, sylvan bowers; to feel your soul expand under the mighty influences of nature in her primitive beauty and strength.'

"The principal inland rivers of Michigan, are the Grand River, the Kalamazoo, the St. Joseph, the Saginaw, and the Raisin. The first three empty into Lake Michigan, and are about seventy miles apart. Their average length is about two hundred and fifty miles, and they are about thirty or forty rods in width. At present, they are navigable about half their length for small steamboats and bateaux. Their bed is of limestone, covered with pebbles. I was a passenger on board the Matilda Barney, on her first trip,—the first steamer that ever ascended the St. Joseph, which I consider the most perfectly beautiful stream that I ever have seen. I remember well the many flocks of wild turkeys and herds of deer that the 'iron horse' frightened in his winding career. The Indian canoe is now giving way to the more costly but less beautiful row-boat, and those rivers are becoming deeper and deeper every day. Instead of the howl of the wolf, the songs of husbandmen now echo through their vales, where may be found many comfortable dwellings.

"The Saginaw runs toward the north and empties into Lake Huron,—that same Huron which has been celebrated in song by the young poet, Louis L. Noble. This river is navigable for sixty miles. The river Raisin is a winding stream, emptying into Lake Erie, called so from the quantity of grapes that cluster on its banks. Its Indian name is Nummasepee, signifying River of Sturgeons. Sweet river! whose murmurs have so often been my lullaby, mayst thou continue in thy beauty forever. Are there not streams like thee flowing through the paradise of God?

"Notwithstanding the comparative newness of Michigan, its general aspect is ancient. The ruin of many an old fort may be discovered on its borders, reminding the beholder of wrong and outrage, blood and strife. This was once the home of noble but oppressed nations. Here lived and loved the Algonquin and Shawnese Indians; the names of whose warrior chiefs—Pontiac the proud, and Tecumseh the brave—will long be treasured in history. I have stood upon their graves, which are marked only by a blighted tree and an unhewn stone, and have sighed deeply as I remembered their deeds. But they have gone—gone like the lightning of a summer day!

"It is traditionary land. For we are told that the Indian hunters of old saw fairies and genii floating over its lakes and streams, and dancing through its lonely forests. In these did they believe, and to please them was their religion.

"The historian, James H. Lanning, Esq., of this State, thus writes, in alluding to the olden times: 'The streams rolled their liquid silver to the lake, broken only by the fish that flashed in their current, or the swan that floated upon their surface. Vegetation flourished alone. Roses bloomed and died, only to be trampled by the deer or savage; and strawberries studded the ground like rubies, where the green and sunny hillsides reposed amid the silence, like sleeping infants in the lap of the forest. The rattlesnake glided undisturbed through its prairies; and the fog which hung in clouds over its stagnant marshes spread no pestilence. The panther, the fox, the deer, the wolf, and bear, roamed fearless through the more remote parts of the domain, for there were none to dispute with them their inheritance. But clouds thickened. In the darkness of midnight, and silence of the wilderness, the tomahawk and scalping knife were forged for their work of death. Speeches were made by the savages under the voiceless stars, which were heard by none save God and their allies; and the war-song echoed from the banks of lakes where had never been heard the footsteps of civilized man.'

"Then followed the horrors of war; then and there were enacted the triumphs of revenge. But those sounds have died away; traced only on the page of history, those deeds. The voice of rural labor, the clink of the hammer, and the sound of Sabbath-bells now echo in those forests and vales. The plough is making deep furrows in its soil, and the sound of the anvil is in every part. A well-endowed University, and seminaries of learning are there. Railroads and canals, like veins of health, are gliding to its noble heart. The red man, in his original grandeur and state of nature, has passed away from its more fertile borders; and his bitterest enemy, the pale face is master of his possessions."

From a report made, by order of Congress, by

Israel D. Andrews, in 1853, in relation to the trade of the great lakes and rivers, we extract the following:—"Michigan is the second of the great lakes in size, being inferior only to Lake Superior, and in regard to situation and the quality of the surrounding soil and the climate is, in many respects, preferable to them all. Its southern extremity, rising south in fertile regions, nearly two degrees to the south of Albany, and the whole of its great southern peninsula being imbosomed in fresh waters, its climate is mild and equable, as its soil is rich and productive. The lake is three hundred miles long by sixty in breadth, and contains sixteen thousand nine hundred and eighty-one square miles, having a mean depth of nine hundred feet. On the western shore it has the great indentation of Green Bay; itself equal to the largest lakes in England, being one hundred miles long and thirty broad. It is well sheltered at its mouth by the Traverse Islands, and has for its affluent the outlet of Winnebago and the Fox River.

"Grand Traverse Bay is a considerable inlet of Lake Michigan, which sets up into the lower peninsula, one hundred miles south from the Island of Mackinac. It is a good farming and lumbering country. There are two mission stations and six or seven steam and water mills located at this point. It is now an organized county called Grand Traverse. The county seat is at Grand Traverse City, West Bay, where they have a court-house and jail.

"L'Arbre Croche Village is an old Indian town, situated about twenty-five miles southwest from Mackinaw, on the lower peninsula. It is composed mostly of Indians. It has a Catholic Church and a Home Mission Station, with a teacher and other assistants to instruct the Indians in the English language. It has extensive clearings for miles, along the banks of the lake shore, and extending from one to six miles back into the interior, indicating that once a large population must have inhabited this section of the country.

"The principal tributaries of Lake Michigan are the Manistee, Great Kalamazoo, and St. Joseph's rivers, from the southern peninsula of Michigan, the Des-Plaines, the O Plaines and Chee rivers, from Indiana, Illinois, and from the northern peninsula, the Menominee, Escambia, Noquet, White Fish and Manistee rivers. The lake is bounded to the eastward by the rich and fertile land of the southern peninsula, sending out vast quantities of all the cereal grains, equal if not superior in quality to any raised in the United States. It is bounded on the south and southwest by Indiana and Illinois, which supply corn and beef of the finest quality, in superabundance, for exportation. On the west it is bounded by the productive grain and grazing lands and lumber district of Wisconsin, and on the northwest and north by the invaluable and not yet half-explored mineral district of northern Michigan.

"The natural outlet of its commerce, as of its waters, is by the Straits of Mackinaw into Lake Huron, thence by the St. Clair River down to the lower marts. Of internal communications it already possesses many, both by canal and railroad, equal to those almost of any of the older States, in length and availability, and inferior to none in importance. First, it has the Green Bay, Lake Winnebago, and Fox River improvement connecting it with the Wisconsin River, by which it has access to the Mississippi River, and thereby enjoys the commerce of its upper valleys, and its rich lower lands and prosperous States;—and second, the Illinois and Michigan canal, rendering the great commercial valley of the Illinois tributary to its commerce. By railways, perfected and projected, it has, or will soon have, connection with the Mississippi in its upper tributaries and lead regions by way of the Milwaukee and Mississippi, and Chicago and Galena lines. To the eastward, by the Michigan Central and Southern

Railroad, it communicates with the lake shore road, and thence with all the eastern lines from Buffalo to Boston. To the southward it will speedily be united by the great system of projected railroads.

"A road is now in progress extending from Fort Wayne, Indiana, to Mackinaw. From a recent report made of this road, which will prove of vast importance in developing the immense resources of Michigan, we extract the following:—

"The distance from point to point, as measured by the engineers, are as follow:

"From Fort Wayne to the 'Air-line Railroad, Indiana, 28 miles; the Air-line railroad, to Wolcottville, 6; Wolcottville to Lagrange, 10; Lagrange to Lima, 5; Lima to Sturgis, Mich., 5½; Sturgis to Mendon, 14; Mendon to Brady, 8; Brady to Kalamazoo, 12; Kalamazoo to Grand Rapids, 47; Grand Rapids to Laphamville, 13; Laphamville to Little Traverse Bay, 169; Little Traverse to the Straits of Mackinaw, 27. Total; 344.

"The work of construction now performed, is mostly between Wolcottville and Kalamazoo. Between Lagrange and Sturgis the earth-work and bridges are nearly done—$1,500 will complete it for the ties. About one-fourth of the earth-work, bridges and ties, of the remainder of the line from Wolcott-

15

ville to Kalamazoo, is done. Between Kalamazoo and Grand Rapids, work to the amount of $8,000 has been done.

"The construction of the road bed, bridging, ties, ballasting, &c., from Kalamazoo to the north bank of the Muskegon River, one hundred and three miles, is let to Daniel Beckel, Esq., of Dayton, Ohio. Near two hundred hands are engaged on the work—on the twenty miles north of Grand Rapids. It is the intention of the company, as we are informed, to complete this twenty miles early the coming summer.

"We are informed by the annual report, that on July 21st, $216,316 18 had been collected and expended.

"The land grant made by Congress is of great value. The portion of the road to which it attaches, extends from Grand Rapids to Little Traverse Bay; the precise length of which is, as adopted by the proper departments at Washington, one hundred and eighty-two miles and three thousand and sixty-seven feet. Under the rules of adjustment adopted by the department, the quantity of lands granted will be somewhere from 600,000 to 674,164 acres.

"These lands are generally timbered farm lands—of the best quality, in timber, soil and water. Some are pine lands, some pine and hard wood mixed; and a small portion are cedar swamp lands. But there is none too much of either description for the value of the lands and the prosperity of the country. Nature has distributed and interspersed them in such proportions as will best contribute to the support of a populous and well improved agricultural country. The great bulk of these lands are what are generally denominated 'beech and sugar-tree lands.' The soil is generally rich sandy loam. The estimated value of the lands, when the road is completed, has been put, by different parties, from $4 to $10 per acre.

"The lands granted are the odd numbered sections within six miles of the line; and if any such sections are sold or pre-empted, then the company has the right to select other sections outside of the six miles and within fifteen miles of the road, to make up such deficit.

"The odd numbered sections, outside of the six-mile limits, and within the fifteen-mile limits, are set apart to this company, out of which to select lands to make up any deficit that may occur in the six miles.

"By those best acquainted with the value of these lands—and who are familiar with that portion of the

State—they are estimated at $10 per acre, on the completion of the road. This will give the company the sum of $6,600,000. And if the road when fully equipped costs $30,000 per mile, then the gross cost will be $10,500,000; which by the proceeds of the land grant will be reduced to the sum of $3,900,000, and will reduce the actual cost of the road to $11, 142,85 per mile. Anything like fair success in the construction of the road will enable the company to do it, after applying the proceeds of the land grant, for about *eleven thousand dollars per mile.* Such a result will not only give to the country all the advantages of this much-needed work; but when done the capital stock must prove to be a good paying investment."

CHAPTER X.

Mackinaw, the site for a great central city—The Venice of the lakes—Early importance as a central position—Nicolet —Compared geographically with other points — Immense chain of coast — Future prospects — Temperature — Testimony of the Jesuit fathers—Healthfulness of the climate —Dr. Drake on Mackinaw — Resort for invalids — Water currents of commerce—Surface drained by them—Soil of the northern and southern peninsulas of Michigan—Physical resources—Present proprietors of Mackinaw—Plan of the city—Streets—Avenues—Park—Lots and blocks for churches and public purposes—Institutions of learning and objects of benevolence—Fortifications—Docks and ferries—Materials for building—Harbors—Natural beauty of the site for a city—Mountain ranges—Interior lakes—Fish—Game.

FERRIS, in his "States and Territories of the Great West," says: "If one were to point out, on the map of North America, a site for a great central city in the lake region, it would be in the immediate vicinity of the Straits of Mackinaw. A city so located would have the command of the mineral trade, the fisheries, the furs, and the lumber, of the entire

North. It might become the metropolis of a great commercial empire. It would be the Venice of the Lakes." Mackinaw, both straits and peninsula, was so naturally the key point of the great system of northern lakes and their connection with the Mississippi, that while the New England colonies were yet but infant and feeble settlements, the Indians of the northwest, the Jesuit missionaries, the French voyagers, all made Mackinaw the point from whence they diverged—in all directions. When Philadelphia and Baltimore had not begun, and when the sites of Pittsburg, Cincinnati, and St. Louis were unknown places in the wilderness, Nicolet took his departure from Quebec in search of the mysterious river of the west. In passing to meet the Indians at Green Bay, he was the first to notice the Straits of Mackinaw. About thirty years after, James Marquette established, on the northern shore of the straits, the Mission of St. Ignace. Here, amidst the wilds and solitudes of the North American forests, and on the shores of its great inland seas, Marquette and Joliet planned their expedition as we have already described, and it was Mackinaw and not New Orleans or New York that the lines radiated from to the earliest settlements of the west.

Mackinaw presents one of the most remarkable

geographical positions on the earth. Constantinople on the Bosphorus, the Straits of Gibraltar, Singapore on the Strait of Malacca, and the Isthmus of Panama, are the only ones which seem to present a parallel. The two former have been for ages renowned as the most important in the commercial world. Singapore has rapidly become the key and centre of Asiatic navigation, at which may be found the shipping and people of all commercial nations, and Panama is now the subject of negotiation among the most powerful nations with a view to the exceeding importance of its commercial position. Geographically, Mackinaw is not inferior to either. From the northwest to the southeast, midland of the North American continent, there stretches a vast chain of lakes and river dividing the continent nearly midway. This chain of Lakes and rivers is in the whole nearly three thousand miles long. At the Straits of Mackinaw the whole system of land and water centres. The three greatest lakes of this system, Superior, Huron, and Michigan, are spread around, pointing to the straits, while between them three vast peninsulas of land press down upon the waters until they are compressed into a river of four miles in width. On the north is the peninsula of Canada, on the south that of Michigan, and on the west that of the copper region, all of which are divided only by the narrow Straits of Mackinaw. Here are three inland seas of near eighty thousand square miles and about five thousand miles of coast. From coast to coast and isle to isle of this immense expanse of waters, navigation must be kept up, increasing with the ever-increasing population on their shores till tens of millions are congregated around. Of all this vast navigation and increasing commerce, Mackinaw is the natural centre around which it exists, and toward which it must tend by an inevitable law of necessity. Superior, Huron, and Michigan have no water outlet to each other but that which flows through the Straits of Mackinaw, and its geographical position is unrivaled in America. Whoever lives twenty years from this time will find Mackinaw a populous and wealthy city, the Queen of the Lakes.

If any serious objection be made to the site of a city at this place, it can only be that the climate is *supposed* to be cold. But, what is climate? Climate is relative and composed of many elements. The first is temperature, as determined by *latitude*. The Straits of Mackinaw are in the latitude of 45° 46′. North of this lies a part of Canada, containing at least a million of inhabitants. North of this latitude lies the city of Quebec in America; London, Paris, Amsterdam, Berlin, Vienna, Warsaw, Copenhagen, Moscow, and St. Petersburg, in Europe; Odessa and Astracan, in Asia. North of it, are in Prussia, Poland, and Russia, dense populations, and a great agricultural production. The latitude of Mackinaw, therefore, is in the midst of that temperate zone, where commerce, population, cities, and the arts have most flourished. The climate, however, is actually milder than the latitude represents. The isothermal line, which passes through Mackinaw, also passes in Wisconsin, nearly as low as 43°, and in the east also deflects south. This is the true line of vegetation; and thus it appears that the actual climate of Mackinaw is about that of 43° 30′. The same isothermal linc, passes through Prussia and Poland, the finest grain countries of Europe. The climate of the straits is, therefore, as favorable as that of most civilized States, either for the production of food or the pursuits of commerce.

The Marquette Journal gives some items relative to the winter of that locality. The mercury was not below zero until the evening of January 8th, and then only 2° below. The highest point reached in January, was 20° above, and lowest 16° below zero. In February, the highest point was 55° above, the lowest 20° below zero. The average temperature for the three winter months had been about 15° above zero. In the "Relations of the Jesuits," 3d. volume, 1671, it is stated that that the "winter in Mackinaw is short, not commencing until after Christmas and closing the middle of March, at which time spring begins."

The Lake Superior Journal for February 23, 1859, says:—

"We are now within five days of the first spring month, and have scarcely had a brush of winter yet. But very few days has the thermometer been below zero, and but a single day as low as ten degrees below. Most of the time it has been mild. For two weeks past, there has been a blandness and mellowness in the atmosphere, which was enough to cause the moodiest heart to sing for joy. There was a flare-up, however, for a single day (the 20th), when the storm descended, the wind blew, and there was great commotion in the elements, but the next day all was calm and delightful as before. We have quite a depth of snow on the ground, have had fine sleighing since the 10th of November. But our bay has not been closed more than a week at a time this winter, and but a few days in all. It is open now, and 'the stern monarch of the year,' seems to be melting away into spring.

"In regard to the healthfulness of Mackinaw, it may be remarked that the northern regions of the earth are everywhere the most healthy. Yet there are differences in situation and exposure which make differences in health. Mackinaw has now been known and settled for two hundred years, a period long enough to have both tested its healthiness, and created a permanent reputation. The Jesuit Missionaries, the frontier traders, and the French voyageurs, have lived and died there; yet we have never heard of any prevalent disease, or local miasm. It seems to have been the favorite resort of all the frontiers men, who inhabited or hunted in the region of the Northern Lakes. In recent years, it has been visited by men of science, and accomplished physicians, and their report has been uniformly in favor of its superior healthiness. Dr. Drake, who visited Mackinaw in 1842, for the express purpose of examining the climate and topography, says, "From this description, it appears, that the conditions which are held to be necessary to the generation of autumnal fever, are at their *minimum* in this place; and when we consider this fact, with its latitude nearly 46°, and its altitude above the sea, from six to eight hundred feet, we are prepared to find it almost exempt from that disease; and such from the testimony of its inhabitants is the fact, especially in reference to the intermittent fevers, which, I was assured by many respectable persons, never originated among the people, and would cease spontaneously in those who returned, or came with it from other places.'

"Speaking of this region as a place of resort for invalids, the same writer says:

"'The three great reservoirs of clear and cold water, Lakes Huron, Michigan, and Superior, with the Island of Mackinac in their hydrographical centre, offer a delightful hot-weather asylum to all invalids who need an escape from the crowded cities, paludal exhalations, sultry climates and officious medication. Lake Erie lies too far south, and is bordered by too many swamps to be included in the salutiferous group.'

"'On reaching Mackinaw, an agreeable change of climate is at once experienced.' 'To his jaded sensibilities all around him is fresh and invigorating." Dr. Drake looked upon Mackinaw as one of the healthiest portions of the whole Northwest, and to which, in time, tens of thousands of persons, even from the furthest south, would resort to be reinvigorated in body, refreshed in mind, and delighted with the contemplation of the sublime and beautiful scenery in that region of expansive waters, of rocky coasts, of forest-bearing lands, and distant islands.

"Here the great currents, which are the natural lines of *movement* for the people, commerce, and productions of half North America, concentrate around a single point. No other place has the same advantage of *radial lines.* Quebec is relatively on the Atlantic. The upper end of Lake Superior is comparatively on an inhospitable land. Chicago is at a lateral point on the south end of Lake Michigan,—three hundred miles from the main channel of commerce. At Mackinaw concentrate all the radial lines of water navigation in the upper lakes. Which will be seen, if we take the following distances of direct navigation from this point to the principal points on the upper lakes:

"From Mackinaw to Fon du Lac (west end of Lake Superior), 550 miles; to Chicago, 350; to east end of Georgian Bay, 300; to Detroit, 300; to Buffalo, 700; to Gulf of St. Lawrence, 1,600.

"Here are two important points to be observed. Any city which, by competition, or the rivalry of production, or the power of wealth, can be supposed to interfere with the growth of Mackinaw, must arise on Lakes Michigan or Superior; for *there* only can be any commercial mart to receive and distribute the products around those immense bodies of water. But in consequence of the form and surface of those lakes, no lines of transit to the waters of the St. Lawrence can be made so short or cheap as the water transit through the Straits of Mackinaw. The concentration of products will, therefore, be ultimately made at Mackinaw, for all that immense district of country which lies around the upper lakes. Again, it will be seen that as the water transportation to that point is the best, so the radial line from that point to the Atlantic by water, is much the shortest. A steam propeller, leaving any one of the principal points on the upper lakes for either Buffalo or the Gulf of St. Lawrence, must, as compared with Mackinaw, pass over the following lines of transit, viz., From Fon du Lac (west end of Lake Superior) to Buffalo, 1,250 miles; Chicago, Ill., 1,000; Mackinaw, Michigan, 700; Fon du Lac to the Gulf of St. Lawrence, 2,150; Chicago to the Gulf of St. Lawrence, 1,900; Mackinaw to the Gulf of St. Lawrence, 1,600.

"It must be granted, at once, that for any water communication with the ports of the Atlantic, Macknaw has greatly the advantage over any commercial point in Minnesota, Wisconsin, Northern Illinois, Northern Michigan, or Northwest Canada. How great this advantage is, we shall see from the consideration of the surface drained by the water current of Mackinaw. An inspection of the map will show that from Long Lake, above latitude 50°, to the south end of Lake Michigan, below latitude, 40°, and from the Lake of the Woods, longitude 95°, to Saginaw Bay, longitude 83°, the country is entirely within the drainage of lakes and river whose currents concentrate at the Straits of Mackinaw. This surface comprehends a square of over six hundred miles on the side, or nearly four hundred thousand square miles. Deducting the surface of the lakes, it is enough to make eight States as large as Ohio. In that whole surface, there is not a single point which can rival Mackinaw as a point of *distribution for the products of that country.* That the advantage by water lines is in favor of Mackinaw, we have shown. That it will be equally so by railroad, is evident, from the fact that Mackinaw city to Port Huron, and thence to Buffalo, need not exceed four hundred miles, while that from Chicago to Buffalo, in a direct line is five hundred and fifteen miles.

"From any other point of Lakes Michigan or Superior, where a city can be built, it is further. Mackinaw is, therefore, the natural centre of drainage and distribution for a surface equal to that of eight large States, and whose products, whether of field, fruit, or mines, are superabundant in whatever creates commerce, sustains population, or affords the materials of industry.

"We are now considering Mackinaw in a state of nature, and must look to its natural products as the first and greatest elements of success. We have considered its climate, its water currents, its lines of navigation, and the surface drainage for its support. The latter within a space where there can be no competition, we have found to be but little less than 400,000 square miles. Vast as this is, it could not support a great commercial city, if that were a barren plain.

"Hence, we must now consider how far the products of the earth will sustain the city, which such lines of navigation, such means of commerce, and such an extensive surface leads us to anticipate.

"The soil is the first thing to be examined. The peninsula of Michigan—that of Wisconsin and the Copper region—of Minnesota and Canada, which make up the larger portion of surface drained by the currents of Mackinaw, has been supposed to be cold and wet. But is it more so than northwestern Ohio or northern Illinois, which, but twenty years since, were scarcely inhabited, but now are found to afford some of the richest lands in the country? On this point, we have numerous and competent witnesses, and whatever character they give to the country, we shall adopt as the true criterion of its producing resources.

"First of the Superior Country, the least agricultural portion of this district, we have the concurrent testimony of geologists, miners, settlers, and travelers, that it is one of the richest mining districts in the world. But in the midst of it are found some fertile sections. Of these, Mr. Ferris, in his account of the Great West, says: 'The surveyors report some good agricultural lands (of which many townships are specially enumerated), and these tracts of fertile land will become of great value, when the rivers shall have been opened and a mining population introduced, creating a sure and convenient home market for the productions of the farm.'

"*Disturnell,* an accurate authority, speaking of the Superior region, says: 'The traveler finds the whole district to within a few miles of Lake Superior, abounding in every resource which will make a country wealthy and prosperous. Clear, beautiful lakes are interspersed, and these have plenty of large trout and other fish. Water and water powers are everywhere to be found, and the timber is of the best kind—maple groves, beech, oak, pine, etc. No thing is now wanted but a few roads to open this rich country to the settler, and it will soon teem with villages, schools, mills, farming operations, and every industrial pursuit, which the more southern portion of our State now exhibits.'

"Turning to the immense territory north and northwest of Superior and the Straits, now constituting a portion of the British Dominions, and every part of which must be tributary to Mackinaw, we find that it affords, like Prussia and Poland, a fine agricultural region for all the breadstuffs and vegetables which are raised in the northern part of Europe. A writer in the *Toronto Globe*, exhibiting the value of a canal from Georgian Bay to Toronto—(a canal, the whole commerce of which coming from the northwest, must first have passed the Straits of Mackinaw) says: 'Westward we possess vast and fertile countries adapted to all the pursuits of agriculture life, countries susceptible to the highest cultivation and improvement. Between Lake Superior and the Lake of the Woods (above 49° of latitude), we possess a country of this description, in soil and character inferior to no part of Minnesota, and bordering upon this territory lies the valley of the Assinibone, or the Red River, as it is sometimes called. As a wheat growing country, it will rival Canada. It does so now in soil and climate.' The writer is here speaking of British possessions north of Lake Superior, and several degrees north of Mackinaw. He says they are as fertile and grain-growing as Canada, and Canada we know already produces not only its own breadstuffs, but large quantities for exportation. The valley of the Assinibone, referred to, and the whole region west of Superior to the Lake of the Woods and the Red River, can have no market outlet except through Lake Superior, and thence near the Straits of Mackinaw. The writer sees this, and says: 'The future products of these immense countries must seek the seaboard, and all the canals and railroads which can be constructed will scarce suffice to afford facilities for the products of the West.'

"Let us next examine the Southern Peninsula of Michigan. If the country far north of it is so productive, it can scarcely happen that this can be very deficient, although not ranked among the most fertile districts. On this point, we need only cite the same accurate authority to which we have referred. He says: 'The numerous streams which penetrate every portion of the peninsula, some of which are navigable for steamboats a considerable distance from the lake, being natural outlets for the products of the interior, render this whole region desirable for purposes of settlement and cultivation.' Even as far north as tho Straits of Mackinaw, the soil and climate, together with the valuable timber, offer great inducements to settlers; and if the proposed railroads under the recent grant of large portion of these lands by Congress, are constructed from and to the different points indicated, this extensive and heavily timbered region will speedily be reclaimed, and become one of the most substantial and prosperous agricultural portions of the West.' After speaking of the timber in that country, the same writer adds: 'But as the timber is exhausted, the soil is prepared for cultivation, and a large portion of the *northern part* of the southern peninsula of Michigan will be settled and cultivated, as it is *the most reliable wheat-growing portion of the Union.*'

The Detroit Daily Tribune of 1857, says: "Michigan is greatly undervalued because greatly unknown. The tide of emigration sweeps past us to Illinois, Wisconsin, Iowa and Minnesota, because the public do not know—what is but the sober truth—that Michigan possesses advantages unrivaled by any sister State in the Northwest, and an undeveloped wealth that will far exceed any one of those named. This is not a random statement, originating in State pride or self-interest, but the simple truth which is slowly being found out by the shrewd among men. We propose to speak of some of the advantages which we possess in the northern half of our lower peninsula, as yet almost uninhabited and unknown.

"'No other State can boast of such valuable forests of such perfect timber. Already our lumber trade exceeds in value and importance that in any other staple products, not excepting wheat, while if it were to increase in the ratio of the past five years, in five years more it would exceed all the other staples united, excepting only copper. But such a rate of increase would exhaust the pine timber to a great extent within ten years' time. Yet the demand for pine lumber is absolutely unlimited, and cannot be met.

"Look for a moment at the vast region depending upon the pineries of Michigan for its supply of lumber for building purposes of every kind—houses, fence and shelter of every description. The great States of Illinois, Iowa, and Missouri, and the Territory of Minnesota, depend almost solely upon Michigan, and must do so. The present season, lumber has been taken from the forest of southwestern New York and northern Pennsylvania, and sold in the market of St. Louis, so urgent is the demand and so entirely inadequate are the present or prospective rates of supply for that demand. We have before us the statistics of the lumber trade of the different

States and the principal markets in the country, but of what use is a parade of figures when a simple fact will show that the value of the pine forest of Michigan *must* be? Take the State Iowa alone. If every quarter section were to be enclosed with a common post and board fence, it would take every foot of pine on the soil of Michigan! Leave out of sight the great Territory of Minnesota, which can find but a mere drop of supply from the pineries of the Upper Mississippi. Leave out of sight the great State of Illinois, which depends upon us wholly. Forget entirely that villages are springing up like magic all along the lines of a dozen railroads running from Lake Michigan to the Mississippi; that cities are growing and spreading with unprecedented rapidity —and that every town and village, and city, and farm, must have its dwellings, and that the cheapest and best material for construction is pine. Leave all these out of the calculation, and remember only that one of these States would consume all our vast forests of pine in *fence boards alone,* and the dullest comprehension can perceive, with all these other demands of which we have spoken, in all those other regions, the value of the pine region is as certain as though it were a gold mine. And when we consider the pressing need for material whereof to build over all the western prairies, the wealth of northern Michigan cannot be put at any low amount. It must be immense—untold.

"After the timber shall have been removed in obedience to the pressing demands of a cash market and high prices, the value of northern Michigan will just begin to be developed. The soil possesses riches of which the heavy growth of timber is the outcropping. Rich as any prairie land, even more substantial in the elements of fertility, with a genial climate, southern Michigan, itself a garden, we predict will have to yield the palm of productive wealth to this portion of the State. Any one who will take the trouble to examine a map of this half of the State, projected on an extended scale, cannot fail to be struck with the superabundant water privileges that exist. It is literally covered with navigable rivers, and their tributaries, large streams, like the veins in the human system. These waters reach the remotest part and thread every portion, affording unfailing supplies and thousands of valuable sites for mills of every description and of all magnitudes. The State is divided near its geographical centre by a slight ridge, sufficient to divide the course of its streams. Two of the largest rivers of the State, the Manistee and the Eastern Au Sauble, rise within about three miles of each other, run parallel, southward, for twenty miles or more, approaching then within half a mile of each other, then turning abruptly almost due east and west, emptying into Lakes Michigan and Huron respectively on almost the same parallel of latitude.

"The Grand Traverse region, embracing the valley of the Manistee, is also one of the finest agricultural regions of the State; lying in the northerly portion, this region still has a mild climate, and the finest grains and fruits are raised at the settlements, as far north as the bay.

"Much might be said of other counties throughout this region. The whole slope of the peninsula embracing the courses of the Muskegon and Manistee Rivers, and from Grand River to Mackinaw, is a region of rich soil excellent timber of all kinds, good climate, and of easy access.

"The counties in the eastern part of the State, Alpena, Alcona, Iosco, Arrenac, and others north of Saginaw Bay, well situated, having a large extent of coast on Lake Huron, are not so well adapted for agricultural purposes, there is much good farming land in them all; but the forests of pine extending to within a few miles of the coast, render them very desirable. Alcona county, watered by Thunder Bay

River, with some smaller streams emptying into Lake Huron, is almost wholly a pine region. Some of the finest specimens of yellow, or Norway pine, in the whole State are found in this country. The white and yellow pine is nearly equally distributed in this region, extending also into the counties south, and reaching Rifle River in Saginaw and Arrenac counties, having an outlet on Saginaw Bay.

"This part of the State, upon whose advantages we have not space to particularize as we would like, will be very soon penetrated by railroads.

"There are *three* roads contemplated by the Act of Congress granting lands to this State at its last session. These, if built, will add more to the development of the natural wealth of Michigan than anything heretofore proposed in the way of public improvement.

"The different routes pass through some of the best counties in the State, and the opening of such thoroughfares will induce a tide of emigration, such as will soon render northern Michigan what it ought to be, one of the most important point in the West.

"The State of Michigan is in all respects more favorably situated than any of the Western States, being surrounded by the lakes and with railroads extending in every direction, affording the most extraordinary opportunities to reach markets of every class, great or small.

"With these natural advantages of transportation considered with the immense natural resources of this region (soil and timber) no one will doubt the very great value of Michigan lands.

"Fruit of all kinds is abundant in every part of this State. All our exchanges from the interior are acknowledging presents of luscious peaches, plums, pears, apples, etc., etc. This is as it should be. May they all, each succeeding year, be remembered in like manner.

"What is here said of the northern part of Michigan, is directly applicable to Wisconsin, the northern half of which must contribute directly to Mackinaw. Of the agricultural capacity of this new State, we need say no more, than that it has already attained half a million of inhabitants, and pours forth its surplus products though the ports of Lake Michigan.

"Of Minnesota, and its productiveness, less is known. As three-fourths of that rich and beautiful country, and the regions around the heads of the Mississippi, must contribute to the commercial importance of Mackinaw, let us glance at its agricultural capacity and prospects. Minnesota, of which we heard but yesterday, has now two hundred thousand inhabitants, produces this year two millions of bushels of wheat. St. Paul, its principal town has fourteen thousand inhabitants, and far to the northwest from St. Peters to the Red River, and Assinibone, the settlers are crowding in to till farms and create towns, where but recently the wild wolf and the wilder savage, alone possessed the face of the earth. In latitudes higher than that of Mackinaw, Michigan or Canada West, settlements are forming, and it requires no flight of imagination to see that beautiful land of lakes, rivers, forests, and prairies,—cold as it may be in winter—settled, tilled, and civilized. The fact of its rapid progress in population, is sufficient proof of its agricultural capacity ; but we shall again refer to the testimony of actual observers. Turning to Mr. Ferris's first description of the Northwest, we find his summing of the climate, and agricultural advantages of Upper Minnesota. 'Minnesota is detined to become a great agricultural, and grazing region. Its upland and lowland plains would support a dairy that would enrich an empire. All the principal grains, and roots thrive there in great vigor, as high toward the north as Pembina, below the dividing line between the United States and British America. Latitude does not always indicate the climate as has already been shown. The character of the soil has great influence upon the temperature of the air. A quick warm soil makes a warm atmosphere. The autumns of Minnesota are greatly lengthened out by the Indian summer, that smoky, dreary, balmy season, which protects the surface from frost, like a mantle flung upon the earth. The cold nips the vegetation, about as early along the Ohio, as along the St. Peters. The winters of Minnesota are cold; but then they are still and calm, and the icy air does not penetrate, as it does in a windy climate.'

"In the brief review of the agricultural advantages of that great northwestern region, whose centre of commerce must ever be at Mackinaw; we have arrived at the certain fact, that except small portions of the Superior country, where mining and mines absorb all other interests, no country in the northern part of America or Europe, has greater advantages. It is filled with inexhaustible springs, and streams; fertile in soil, rich in production, and only needs the cultivating hand of man, to render it capable of sustaining such dense populations as now inhabit the same isothermal parallel in Prussia and Poland.

"Let as now turn to its forests, mines, fisheries and resources, which though not bread, are those from which the implements, conveniences, and much of the wealth of civilization is derived. Of forests, furnishing almost illimitable quantities of timber and lumber—this is the very centre. Of this, we have evidence in the wharves of Chicago, Milwaukee, Detroit, and far down the lakes. The testimony of actual observers on this point, is so strong as to seem almost incredible. We shall cite but two or three unquestionable authorities. The peninsula, of Michigan is at the present moment, one of the greatest depositories of lumber in the world. Mr. Ferris says: 'On going toward the north, the lumber becomes more and more plentiful. Beeches begin to mingle with the oaks, and in a day or two beeches and maples will predominate over other varieties of timbers; large white-woods and bass-woods wlll be seen towering above the forest. The white ash, the shag bark, the black cherry, will have become abundant. The woods will seem to have been growing deeper and denser every mile of the way. Soon the traveler will doubt, whether Omnipotence himself could have planted the trees larger, taller, and thicker together, than they are.'

"Pressing still forward, the emigrant will enter the great pine woods of the north. For a while, however, before reaching them, he will have been wandering through groves of oak, and along the borders of natural meadows, and through clumps of beech and maple. But soon, as with a single step, the timber has become all pine—yellow pine, moaning overhead, darkening all the ground, shutting out the sun, shutting out the wind." The tall trunks support the dark green canopy full fifty feet above the earth. This belt of pine woods, stretches across the peninsula of Michigan from Saginaw Bay. After a while as you proceed further to the north, the pine grows thinner, and is succeeded by other timber. "The level lands again become covered with beech and maple, of a full and convenient growth, with here and there a gigantic Norway pine, six feet through without limb, till it begins to stretch up half its length above the surrounding trees.

In northern Wisconsin, we find another great pinery, in which, in one year, was sawed not less than two hundred millions of feet of pine timber. The same authority to which we have frequently referred, says: "Still further north and northwest, is one of the finest tracts of pine land in America, through which the streams tumbling down frequent falls, afford an incalculable amount of water-power, just where it is most needed for the manufacture of lumber. The Wisconsin forest of ever-greens is perfectly immense, covering one-third the State. The prairies of the Upper Wisconsin and its tributaries, are at the present most extensive, and those are distinguished still more for the fine quality, than for the inexhaustible quantities of the timber."

In the same manner, an immense forest extends over the upper part of Minnesota, while far to the northwest in the British possessions, extend deep forests of pine, spruce, and hemlock. It is evident, therefore, that on the great current of the Straits of Mackinaw, there will float for generations to come, all the timber and lumber, which are necessary for the markets of commerce, or the uses of a growing population.

Nor are the fisheries to be neglected, in any right estimate of the natural resources of that region. Not only do the one hundred thousand square miles of lakes and streams, furnish illimitable quantities of fish; but they furnish varieties, which are nowhere else to be found, and which an epicurean taste has long since pronounced among the richest luxuries of the palate. The lake trout, the Mackinaw trout, the Muskelunge, and the white fish, are celebrated throughout America. Good fishing grounds occur all along the north shore of Lake Superior, affording a bountiful supply. On the south shore, there are fisheries at White Fish Point, Grand Island near the Pitcairn's Rodes, Keweenaw Point, La Point, and Apostles' Islands, and at different stations on Isle Royal, where large quantities are taken and exported. Mackinac Island alone exports yearly a quarter million of dollars' worth.

The site of Old Mackinaw, now the county seat of Emmet county, and its surroundings, belonged to the Government of the United States until the year 1853, when Edgar Conkling, Esq., of Cincinnati, realizing its importance as a vast commercial centre, and one of the finest positions for a great city, formed a company consisting of seven persons, and entered at the Land Office in Ionia, Michigan, near one thousand eight hundred acres. In 1857 that portion embracing the ancient site of Old Mackinaw was surveyed and divided into lots. Mr. Conkling has, recently, become the sole proprietor of the city, and intends devoting his energies to its development. A pamphlet, published some time since, describes it as follows:

"The streets of the city are laid out eighty feet in width, and the avenues from a hundred to a hundred and fifty feet respectively. In the deed of dedication to the public, of these streets and avenues, provision is made for side-walks fifteen feet in width on each side, to be forever unobstructed by improvements of any kind, shade trees excepted, thus securing a spacious promenade worthy of a place destined to become a principal resort for health and pleasure. Provision is also made for the proper use of the streets and avenues by railroad companies adequate to the demands of the business of a city. The lots, with the exception of those in fractional blocks, are fifty by one hundred and fifty feet, thus affording ample room for permanent, convenient, and ornamental improvement.

The park, now laid off and dedicated to the city, embraces the grounds of Old Fort Mackinaw, sacred in the history of the country. These grounds, now in their natural condition, are unequaled for beauty of surface, location, soil, trees, etc., by any park in any city in the country, and when the skillful hand of the horticulturist has marked its outline and threaded it with avenues and paths, pruned its trees, and carpeted its surface with green, it will present the very perfection of all that makes a park delightful. The character of the soil, being a sandy loam, with sand and gravel underlying it, renders it capable of the easiest and most economical improvement, securing walks always dry, hard, and smooth. The park, with suitable blocks and lots for county and city purposes, such as public buildings, school-houses, etc., will be duly appropriated to those uses, whenever the proper authorities are prepared to select suitable sites; and lots for churches, institutions of learning, and charity, will be fully donated to parties contemplating early improvements. Thus the proprietor proposes to anticipate, by avoiding the errors of older cities, the wants of Mackinaw city in perpetuity, and free forever its citizens from taxation for any grounds required for the public good. He also designs to place it in the power of the General Government, to secure, by like donation at an early day, the grounds necessary for such fortifications as the wants of the country and commerce may require, on the simple condition of speedy improvement. This liberal policy will best promote the true interests of the city and country, and at the same time be productive of pecuniary profit to the proprietors and all who may make investments at that point.

The proprietor intends also to expend a large portion of the income from sales in providing for the public wants by the construction of docks at the most important points, and the establishment of ferries, for which he has purchased the land on the opposite side of the straits. He intends to make loans also, as his means will justify, to aid parties in the establishment of manufactories.

Building materials of great variety and in abundance are at hand. Lumber can be had for the mere cost of preparation, and the soil, at no distant point, is suitable for making bricks; while for immediate use, Milwaukee can furnish the articles of the best kind in any quantities. The shores of Lake Superior abound with exhaustless quantities of granite, sandstone and marble; the limestone and sand are on the spot.

Three fine harbors adjoin Mackinaw; the one on the east being the most spacious, and the best protected. The new United States charts show the depth of water sufficient for vessels of the largest size navigating the lakes. As many as thirty vessels have been at anchor in this harbor. The country in the rear of Mackinaw rises gradually until, at the distance of a mile or two, it rises into an elevation of high table land, from points of which there is a fine view of the straits and surrounding islands. A mountainous ridge extends up to within two miles of Mackinaw, covered with a dense forest of hard wood. The southern extremity of this range reaches to the head waters of the Grand and Saginaw rivers. From two to ten miles south of Mackinaw are several beautiful lakes, surrounded by a rich, warm soil of great fertility and covered with a heavy forest of hard wood, some of which has attained a gigantic growth. These lakes abound with fish of different varieties. Turtles have been taken from them, measuring from one and a half to two feet in diameter. Almost every kind of game can be found in the woods bordering upon these lakes, such as the black bear, raccoon, martin, fox, lynx, rabbit, ducks, partridges and pigeons.

CHAPTER XI.

The entrepot of a vast commerce—Surface drained—Superiority of Mackinaw over Chicago as a commercial point—Exports and imports—Michigan the greatest lumber-growing region in the world — Interminable forests of the choicest pine—Facilities for market—Annual product of the pineries—Lumbering, mining and fishing interests—Independent of financial crises—Mackinaw, the centre of a great railroad system—Lines terminating at this point—North and South National Line—Canada grants—Growth of northwestern cities—Future growth and prosperity of Mackinaw—Chicago—Legislative provisions for opening roads in Michigan—The Forty Acre Homestead Bill—Its provisions.

THE physical resources of this region are of such a nature and variety as to make Mackinaw city the entrepot of a vast commerce. This will appear, if we consider that it is the nearest point of that extensive district, including the entire north of the lakes inaccessible to Chicago. When all the lines of internal communication are completed, and the different points on the lakes settled down upon, then the real limits of Mackinaw will drain a geographical surface of three hundred thousand square miles; deducting the surface of the lakes from which, there will remain two hundred and eighty thousand square miles of country, with all the resources of agriculture and mining in the most extraordinary degree. It will be nearly three-fold that which can be drained by Chicago, and in point of territory, whether of quantity or quality, Mackinaw is vastly superior, as a commercial point. With the exception of a small portion of the mineral region, the agricultural advantages of Michigan, Upper Wisconsin, Minnesota, Canada West, and the Superior country, are at least equal, at the present time, to the district shipping at Chicago, while it is more extensive, and will have a large home market in a country affording diversity of employment. Nothing can be more obvious, than the superior advantages of Mackinaw, as a manufacturing point, over any other on the lake coast.

The value of exports and imports which flow through the Straits of Mackinaw and the Saut St. Mary was estimated a year or two since at over *one hundred millions of dollars.* But, who can estimate a commerce which every year increases in many fold? In 1856, there were sent through the

St. Mary Canal 11,000 tons of raw iron, 1,040 tons of blooms, and 10,452,000 lbs. of copper; and the commercial value of what passed through the canal amounted to upward $5,000,000. But perhaps the most correct idea of the rapid increase of commerce in Lake Superior may be taken from the arrivals at Superior City for the last three years, taken from the Superior Chronicle of January, 1857.

In 1854 there were two steamboats and five sail vessels. In 1855 there were twenty-three steamers, and ten sail vessels; and in 1856 forty steamers and sixteen sail vessels.

We thus see that in three years the increase was seven-fold. It is scarcely possible to imagine the limits of northwestern commerce on the lake, when a few years shall have filled up with inhabitants the surrounding territories.

According to the testimony of Senator Hatch, made on the floor of Congress on the 25th of Februry, 1859, there were over one thousand six hundred vessels navigating the northwestern lakes, of which the aggregate burden was over four hundred thousand tons. They were manned by over thirteen thousand seamen, navigating over five thousand miles of lake and river coast, and transporting over six hundred millions of exports and imports, being greater than the exports and imports of the United States.

The State of Michigan is the greatest lumber-growing region in the world, not only on account of its interminable forests of the choicest pine, but in the remarkable facilities for getting it to market. With a lake coast, on the lower peninsula alone, of over one thousand miles—with numberless water-courses debouching at convenient distances into her vast inland seas—she enjoys advantages which mighty empires might envy. Her white-winged carriers are sent to almost every point of the compass with the product of her forests, which, wherever it may go, is the sign of improvement and progress, while by the large expenditures involved in the manufacture, and the employment of thousands of hardy laborers, the general prosperity is materially enhanced, and a market opened within her own borders for a considerable share of the surplus production of her own soil.

The annual product of the pineries alone amount to the sum of *ten and a half millions of dollars.* The lumbering, mining, and fishing interest combine to furnish by far the best home market in the Union, and one which in seasons when a large surplus is not compelled to seek a market, can boast its independence of the "bulls" and "bears" of the great commercial metropolis. The dense forests in the interior of the State have not yet been reached, and when the contemplated roads are made, a field will be presented for the investment of capital of a most remunerative character

The government has already taken such steps as will soon make Mackinaw the centre of a great railroad system. We need only refer to the actual facts in order to make this clear. Congress, by an act passed in 1855–6, granted to the State of Michigan a large body of land for railroad purposes, designating four routes. 1. From Little Noquet Bay to Marquette, in the Superior country. 2. From Amboy, on the State-line of Ohio, throngh Lansing to or near Mackinaw. 3. From Grand Rapids to Mackinaw. 4. From Grand Haven to Port Huron. It will be seen that this plan is formed on the basis of a direct line from Lake Superior through the mineral regions to Lake Michigan. The law fortunately permitted the last two companies to make their lines at or *near* Traverse Bay, and as Mackinaw is but comparatively a short distance, both companies have wisely concluded to terminate their lines at Mackinaw. It is at once evident that the Michigan line, centering at Mackinaw, must be met *there*, by railroads penetrating various sections of the northern peninsula. This is evident, and we understand is already foreseen, and measures will be adopted to accomplish that end. In the mean time, let us examine the prospects and influence of the two long lines of Michigan railway terminating at Mackinaw. The whole amount of land granted to the Michigan railways is estimated to be about 3,880,000 acres. From this, however, there will be some deduction in consequence of lands already selected, and which may not be supplied by the quantity within the limited distance. The deficiency will not be great, and we understand that the amount estimated for the two Mackinaw roads will scarcely be less than *two millions of acres.* Of the quantity and value of these lands, we give the estimate made by these roads, as well as the cost of construction. The estimate made by the *Grand Rapids and Indiana Railroad* is as follows:

"The proximity to lake navigation; having several navigable rivers passing through them, the abundance of hydraulic power, the healthfulness of the climate, the fertility of the soil; and lying immediately on the line of this road, are facts which contribute to enhance the value of these lands.

"The length of this road from the Straits of Mackinaw to Fort Wayne, will be about three hundred and fifty miles. If the company meet with as good success as the merits of the enterprise deserve, the entire cost of the road should not be over $25,000 per mile, which makes an aggregate sum of $8-759,000."

On the supposition that the minimum amount of land is obtained and sold, at half the price above stated, there will yet be broad enough basis to secure the construction of the work.

The Amboy and Lansing Company are equally confident of success. They have also located a large quantity of land, and expect their value to be equivalent to the construction of their road. Accordingly, they have put a portion of their road under contract, and have obtained large local subscriptions.

Both these lines of railroad will terminate at Mackinaw, on the north, and Cincinnati on the south; hence they will be carried south till they terminate at Norfolk, Charleston, Savannah, and Pensacola, thus forming the grandest and most extensive system of railroads on the continent. Nothing in America equals it—nothing in Europe can compare with it! When all the links shall have been completed, it will stand out the greatest monument to human labor and genius which the world presents.

The single line from Mackinaw to Pensacola has been looked upon as one of the most important undertakings of the age. We extract from the "Expositon of its Plan and Prospects," by E. D. Mansfield, Esq., some of the facts, which exhibit its importance, and bearing, and influence on Mackinaw City.

"To illustrate," says the Exposition, "the value of this North and South National Line, by its power of producing commerce, mark, in a tabular form, the natural products of each degree of latitude, thus:—

States.	*Latitude.*	*Productions.*
Florida, - -	31 deg. - -	Oranges.
" - -	31 " - -	Sugar.
" - -	31 " - -	Cotton.
Alabama, -	32 " - -	"
" - -	33 " - -	"
" - -	34 " - -	Cotton, Corn.
Tennessee, -	35 " - -	" "
" -	36 " - -	Cotton, corn, tobac., iron.
Kentucky, -	37 " - -	Corn, tobac., coal, iron.
" - -	38 " - -	Corn, wh't, cat. tob. h'mp.
Ohio, - - -	39 " - -	Corn, wh't. cat. h'gs, wine.

States.	*Latitude.*	*Productions.*
" - - -	40 " - -	Wh't, c'rn, h'gs, cat., flax.
" - - -	41 " - -	Wheat, corn, cattle.
Michigan, -	42 " - -	Wheat, cattle, hay, wool.
" - - -	43 " - -	Pine, cedar, coal.
" - - -	44 " - -	Pine, cedar, coal.
" - - -	45 " - -	Pine, hemlock, cedar.
" - - -	46 " - -	Pine, copper, lead, fish.

This statement is enough to show an extraordinary stimulus to commerce, on a line of railway. The length of the entire line will be less than half that which is proposed to be made from Cincinnati and other cities to San Francisco; yet, will pass through varieties of production, which that line cannot have. In two days, every inhabitant on that line may be supplied, from their native source, with sugar, cotton, corn, wheat, tobacco, iron, coal, lead, copper, pine, cedar, with wool, flour, hemp, and fruits of every description; with fish of the sea and fish of the lakes; with bread, and oil, and wine; in fine, with everything that supports, clothes, or houses man; with everything that supplies his wants, or contributes to his material happiness."

It is obvious, that such a line of railroad as this—peculiar in its resources, vast in its comprehensions, and embracing in its grasp all the products of tropic or of temperate climes—must, of itself, rear, at its *termini*, commercial towns of great importance. But, this is not all. The road from Grand Haven to Port Huron will intersect the Amboy and Lansing line about mid-way, and then a railroad will at once be made in the direction of the Canada lines and Buffalo—completing the *radii* from the far northwest through Mackinaw, to the eastern Atlantic. The natural point of termini for the Northern Pacific and Canada Railroads is also at the Straits of Mackinaw. The one giving financial strength and business to the other, connecting Portland with the mouth of Columbia by the nearest possible route.

Canada has already granted four million acres of land to railroads running to Saut St. Mary. Those having the management of the Northern Pacific railroad will do well to consider the propriety of co-operating and uniting with the Canada and Pacific Railroad at the Straits.

The following from the New York Daily News is valuable in this connection. It is from the pen of E. Conkling, Esq.:—

"You will please excuse me for calling your attention, not to the importance of a Pacific railroad, for that is conceded, and our country is suffering from want of it, but to the mode of getting the means to construct the Northern Pacific railroad. I don't remember to have noticed as yet any allusion to this method, or any other practical one, aud I trust you will consider the suggestions, and add thereto any other methods.

"The railroads now provided for and made to St. Paul, and Crow Wing from Chicago and Milwaukee will have exhausted local means, State aid and available land grants. However desirable it may be to sustain those roads by a business beyond that, and to the country beyond that, by extending the Northern Pacific Railroad, yet for want of means it cannot be done, unless foreign capitalists can be induced by land grants, at least to invest sufficient to make the road finally, and be made to see that their present large unproductive investments in Canada railroads can be made productive in the use of more of their capital.

Canada railroads lie *too far North* to receive any benefit in business from railroads terminating from the northwest as far south as Chicago, and but little from the railroads terminating at Milwaukee, as the cost of transhipment and delay to cross by steam ferry eight months yearly at Milwaukee with eighty-five miles ferriage, must divert the trade and travel either to the north or south end of Lake Michigan, and every year will render that delay and cost more unpopular. And yet to get that trade the Great Western Railroad of Canada have permanently invested $750,000, in the Detroit and Milwaukee Railroad, and recently loaned a half a million more, demonstrating the idea I shall advance, that to make good present investments more means can be had. The State of Michigan itself will furnish a good trade to roads through it and to roads east of it.

"The Straits of Mackinaw is the great natural ferry of about four miles wide for roads of Michigan and Canada to centre, the point necessarily for the passage of lake commerce, and for a large population north of it to cross, naturally attracting and combining elements of great importance to railroads.

"Land grants are now made to the straits from the south. The Grand Trunk and Great Western Railroads of Canada can go to the Straits of Mackinaw, aided by those grants. The Ottawa and Huron Railroad to Saut St. Mary, may also go to the Straits, aided by land grants from Saut St. Mary. From there the three Canadian railroads, aided by land grants yet to be made, can go to Crow Wing or near there, and there form a junction with the Chicago roads—thence to the Pacific, aided by land grants.

"By affording the Canada interest a chance for a

portion of the Pacific trade, and thus making present Canada investments profitable, it is made the interest of foreign capitalists to make our Northern Pacific railroad.

"This protective interest to Canada railroads is the greatest inducement to be offered them.

"They will not invest in the road beyond Crow Wing, simply for the sake of grants of lands, made valuable only by the outlay of their money; even should the lands finally redeem the previous outlay for the road, that is no object, because the road will not pay more than cost of running and sustaining it, and if it should some beyond that, it will be frittered away by bad management and stealing. At least it is fair to suppose so, and hence they must be assured of enough of land grants to finally make the road, which of itself will pay nothing, only in the way of affording the roads east of Crow Wing, owned by them, fair dividends. This consideration will of itself induce them to furnish capital to the Pacific, and it is in the power of the government thus to interest them. No other proposed route can claim foreign aid because of such good reasons. Our government can aid only in lands; in valueless lands she is or may be wealthy. No bill can pass Congress, only by affording equal aid in lands to the Northern,

Central and Southern routes, each standing on their commercial merits before capitalists.

"The chance for us thus to enlist them, is but for a limited time. Soon they will become committed to the North Canada Pacific Road, north of Lake Superior, when they will not help ours, and thus protract ours for want of means and competing road. At present, two of the most important Canada roads can be enlisted in the above views, because if the Canada road north of Lake Superior is made, it will divert the trade from them, they being too far south to be benefited. But by going to the Straits of Mackinaw, they secure a division of the Western trade—among the three roads. The road through the mineral regions will develop that country and afford a good market for the produce of the country west of it.

"Chicago is no more on the direct route from the East to Iowa, than is Mackinaw city on the direct route to the northwest from New York.

"Lake Michigan naturally forces such a division of the Western and Northwestern trade, and the Strait of Mackinaw is most favorably situated for crossing. Cars can be transferred by ferry boat from point to point, without delay or cost of transhipment.

That country is nearer to market than any other Western State; cheaper lands and good soil, and healthy climate, and a superior wheat country, affording employment in lumbering, fishing, mining, manufacturing, &c., offering great inducements to foreigners, and of interest to New York, to be settled."

The history of the West has presented some remarkable facts, contrary to the ordinary experience of human progress. It is assumed, as an historical fact, in European or Asiatic progress, that the growth of towns and states must be slow. It requires generations to bring them to maturity, and even imperial power has failed to create cities, without the aid of time and gradual increase. But, this has been reversed in America. We cannot take it for granted that because the natural site of a town is now clothed with the forest, and remote from habitations, that it will not become a prosperous city, within a half-dozen years. For, we know that in the Northwest, cities have arisen on a substantial basis, to a numerous population, in a space so brief that history has no record of their existence, and the school maps no name for the place of their being.

Chicago which commenced its growth in 1834, had a population in 1857, of 100,000, Milwaukee in twenty-one years rose to 50,000, St. Paul in fifteen years to 15,000; Keokuk in eighteen years to 15,000, Grand Rapids in twelve years to 8000; Saginaw city in twenty-two year 4000, and Superior city in the short space of two years to 4000.

We thus see, that, in the Northwest, cities do grow up, in the midst of the wilderness, and the wilderness itself soon blooms as the rose. To say, then, that a point affording every natural and commercial advantage for the growth of a large city is not *now* a city, is to say nothing against its position or prospects. Within the memory of a generation the five great States, (which have heretofore been termed the Northwest,) contained less then a half a million of people, and Cleveland, Toledo, Chicago, Milwaukee, and St. Paul, were not even dots on the map of States. A mission or a military fort was all they could boast. These States now contain six millions of inhabitants, and the towns on the lake shore two hundred and fifty thousand. But to present the point of growth, in the clearest point of view, let us consider it dependent wholly on that of the surrounding country. This we can tell almost precisely. We know the rate of growth in Michigan, Wisconsin, Minnesota and Canada West.

Canada West in 1840, had a population of 640,000,

in 1850, of 982,000, and in 1857, 1,100,000, Michigan in 1840, was 212,000, in 1850, 397,000, and in 1857, 700,000. The population of Wisconsin in 1840, was 30,000, in 1850, it was 305,991, and in 1857, it was 600,000. The increase in Minnesota in seventeen years was 200,000.

The annual *increment* from 1840 to 1850, was 50,000 per annum, or about six per cent. The annual increment from 1850 to 1857, was 172,000, or about twelve per cent. The *ratio* of increase is, therefore, increasing, and we may assume it will not be less than *ten* per cent. per annum till 1860. This will give 3,380,000 for 1860, or *fourfold the population* of 1840! At a diminishing ratio the territory round Mackinaw will contain 5,400,000 in 1870, and (8,000,000) *eight millions* in 1880. The principal city of the district (wherever it may be) must then contain about *one hundred thousand inhabitants.*

Of the cities and towns we have above enumerated, the greatest and most rapid in its development is Chicago, whose first warehouse lot was sold in 1834, and which, in 1857, is said to contain near one hundred thousand inhabitants. Let us, for a moment, compare the *material advantages and resources* of that place, with those of Mackinaw city. Dean Swift said, that a large city must combine the resources of agriculture, commerce and manufactures. Cities have risen, however, to large size almost exclusively on commerce. Witness Tyre and Palmyra. But commerce, we concede, when left to itself, is so fluctuating, that the cities it builds, like Tyre and Palmyra, may, in the decay of commerce, be left to ruin and desolation. Cities may, likewise, be built up almost exclusively on manufactures, such as Birmingham and Sheffield; and it is quite remarkable that the oldest and most stable cities have depended largely on manufactures. Damascus, the oldest historical city—which has resisted all the destructive influences of time and revolution—has always been a manufacturing town. Paris, Lyons, Lisle, the great interior towns of France, depend very largely on the manufacture of fine and fashionable articles, distributed throughout Europe and America, Of the great elements of civic success, we consider manufactures the most important; but, to make a city of the first magnitude, it is obviously necessary to have all the resources of food, industry and commerce. Chicago is remarkable chiefly as a grain city—like Odessa, on the Baltic. But, whence is the grain derived? By the construction of railroads, at that point, from Indiana, Illinois. Missouri, Wisconsin and Iowa, the whole mass of surplus grain in that region—amounting to more than twenty millions of bushels per annum—has been exported from Chicago. But, this is the drainage of three hundred thousand square miles, two-thirds of which will not export through Chicago when railroads extend directly east to Milwaukee, Superior and Mackinaw, from Wisconsin and Iowa, and connect, from the south, at Cairo, with Missouri and Illinois. Reduced to its own proper limits, the agricultural resources of Chicago must be confined to half the surface of Illinois, Missouri and Iowa, or about one hundred thousand square miles. This is but little over one-third the surface drained of agricultural products toward the Straits of Mackinaw. Will it be said that this new region of the Northwest is less productive in agriculture? The contrary, for the great element of breadstuffs, is likely to be true. Attentive observers of agricultural production have remarked, that the different grains *produced most on the northern edge of the belt,* in which *they will grow at all.* Is it not so in Europe? The *isothermal line* of Mackinaw passes in the midst of those countries which alone produce the surplus grain of Europe, viz., Prussia, Pomerania, Poland, Southern Russia. As if to place this beyond a doubt, the crops of Canada West have, in fact, failed much less frequently than those of

Ohio, Indiana and Illinois. In regard to agricultural production, it will be difficult to show that the country drained by Chicago, has any advantage over that which will be drained by the Straits of Mackinaw.

In regard to commerce—the natural position of Mackinaw is far superior to Chicago. Mackinaw is at the *head* of Lake Michigan—Chicago, at the *foot.* Mackinaw is at the junction of *three* great lakes; Chicago at the foot of *one.* Mackinaw will concentrate the navigation of *eighty thousand* square miles of water *surface;* Chicago of *twenty-four thousand.* Mackinaw is three hundred and fifty miles nearer the Atlantic by water; three hundred miles nearer the upper extremity of the lakes, and as much nearer any of the Eastern Lake ports which are points of distribution. The comparison need be made no further, for whoever looks upon the map will see, that, while Chicago touches one end of a single lake, a world of waters gather round Mackinaw. For an internal water commerce, it has no equal.

It will be said, that railroads now carry commerce. This is true, but, railroads do not carry commerce over the surface of lakes, and the multiplication of vessels on the lakes proves that *that* commerce will ever be great and increasing. But what railroad commerce can be greater than that which will concentrate at Mackinaw, when it connects, in a direct line, not only with the cities of the Ohio Valley, but with those of the far South. To Cincinnati, to Louisville, to Charleston, Savannah, and Pensacola, will the cars move, laden with the people and products of the North. Lastly, neither Chicago nor any other point can be superior to Mackinaw in the elements necessary to support manufactures, the great support of cities, these elements we have already exhibited in detail. Copper, iron, lead, coal, wood, timber, bread, in fine, everything which can feed machinery, give material for its work, or feed the people who gather in the great workshops of industry, and distribute the products of labor. Here materials all lie near enough for the purposes of either work or distribution. Birmingham, Manchester, Lyons, and Cincinnati, have their materials no nearer. There, if anywhere, is a site peculiarly proper for a manufacturing town.

But, neither agriculture, commerce, nor manufactures are the only things necessary to build up a large city. Healthiness is more important than either. Here again, Mackinaw has more advantage over Chicago. Mackinaw has been proved by two hundred years experience to be one of the healthiest points in America. Chicago is generally healthy, but is subject to more severe epidemics. The cholera visited it in in 1832 and in 1849, with fearful force; while its very low position and muddy streets expose its inhabitants to those diseases which arise from damps.

The Legislature of Michigan, recently passed a bill to provide for the drainage and reclamation of the swamp lands of the State by a system of State roads, accompanied by a lengthy and able report. The bill provides among others, a road from Ionia north to the straits, and thence to Saut St. Mary.

They also passed a bill entitled the "Forty Acre Homestead Act." This act requires the commissioners of the State Land office to issue a certificate of purchase to every settler on the swamp lands belonging to the State, for forty acres of said lands, whenever such settler shall have resided upon it for five continuous years, and when he has drained the same so as to comply with the provisions of the Act of Congress making this grant to the State. Before the settler can acquire the right thus to occupy and drain any of the swamp lands, he is required to file with the commissioner his application, accompanied by an oath of his intention to settle upon and drain it for the purpose of obtaining a title thereto. And he must also make oath that he is not already the owner of forty acres of land in any State of the United States. It is also expressly provided that he shall not cut or carry away any timber from said land, unless it be to clear it for cultivation, under such penalties as are now prescribed for trespassing upon State lands. It will be seen, therefore, that the object of the law is to provide homes for the homeless, and at the same time promote the actual, *permanent* settlement of the northern portion of the State. No man who possesses forty acres of land either in Michigan or anywhere else, is entitled to the benefits of the act. It is emphatically a law for the poor man. To all such it secures a *home,* without money and without price. All it requires of him is to settle upon and cultivate it. How many are there in Detroit and other portions of the State, who will avail themselves of this beneficent republican measure?"

CHAPTER XII.

The Great Western Valley—Its growth and population—Comparison of Atlantic with interior cities—Relative growth of river and lake cities—Centre of population—Lake tonnage—Progress of the principal centres of population.

THE following chapter on the population and growth of the Great Western Valley is taken from De Bow's Review:—

The westward movement of the Caucasian branch of the human family from the high plains of Asia, first over Europe, and thence, with swelling tide, pouring its multitudes into the New World, is the grandest phenomenon in history. What American can contemplate its results, as displayed before him, and as promised in the proximate future, without an emotion of pride and exultation?

Our nation has the great middle region of the best continent of the world, and our people are descendants from the most vigorous races. Western Europe, over-peopled, sends us her most energetic sons and daughters, in numbers augmenting with each succeeding decade. Asia is beginning to send forth a portion of her surplus population to our shores. Though of inferior race, the Eastern Asiatics are industrious and ingenious cultivators and artisans. A large influx of these laborers, though it may lower the average character of our people, will, it is hoped. in a greater degree elevate theirs; and thus, while adding to the wealth and power of a nation, do something toward the general amelioration of the race. While, then, we contemplate with patriotic pride the position which, as a nation, we hold in the world's affairs, may we not indulge in pleasant anticipations of the near approach of the time, when the commercial and social heart of our empire will occupy its natural place as the heart of the continent, near the centre of its natural capabilities?

New York has long been, and for some decades of years it will continue to be, the necessary chief focal point of our nation. But, in all respects, it is not the true heart. In its composition and dealings, it is almost as much foreign as American. Located on our eastern border, fronting the most commercial and the richest transatlantic nations, and of easy access to extensive portions of our Atlantic coast, it is the best point of exchange between foreign lands and our own, and for the cities of the sea border of our Republic. As Tyre, Alexandria, Genoa, Venice, Lisbon, and Amsterdam, in their best days, flourished as factors between foreigners and the people of the interior regions, whose industries were represented in their markets, so New York grows rich as the chief agent in the exchange-commerce between the ocean shores and the interior regions of our continent. As our numbers have swelled, since we became a nation, from three and a half millions to thirty millions, so New York, including Brooklyn and other suburbs, has increased in population and wealth still more rapidly, to wit, from twenty-five thousand to more than one million. While the nation has increased less than tenfold, New York has grown more than four times tenfold. In 1790 the city of New York contained thirty-three thousand, and the State of New York three hundred and forty thousand—the city having less than one-tenth of the people of the State.

Believing that this most prosperous of the Atlantic cities will be eclipsed in its greatness and glory by one or more of the interior cities of the great plain, we have selected it as the champion of the

Atlantic border, to hold up its progress during the thirty years from 1830 to 1860, the most prosperous years of its existence, in comparison with the progress, during the same period, of the aggregate cities and towns of the plain. The result of our investigation, the summing up, will be found in the following table. It will be seen that many of the items are put down in round numbers—no document being accessible or in existence to furnish the exact number of many of the new towns, in 1830. The estimate for 1860 may, in some instances, be above the figures which the census will furnish, but the over-estimate for 1830 is believed to be in a larger proportion to actual numbers at that time. Making a liberal allowance for errors, the result of the aggregate cannot be materially varied from that at which our figures bring us:

	1830.	1860 Est.	Increase.
New York, including Brooklyn and other suburbs	234,438	1,170,000	5 times.
Cities and chief towns of the great plain	270,094	2,706,300	10 " nearly

Leaving out the exterior cities of the plain, to wit, New Orleans, Mobile, Galveston, Quebec and Montreal, the comparison between New York and suburbs, and the interior cities of the plain will be shown by the following figures:

	1830.	1860 Est.	Increase.
New York and accessories	234,448	1,170,000	5 fold
Interior cities and town of the plain	172,000	2,346,000	13 "

The five largest cities of the Atlantic border exhibit a growth, as compared with the five largest cities of the plain, as follows:

		1830.	1860 Est.
New York and dependencies		235,000	1,170,000
Philadelphia	"	170,000	700,000
Baltimore	"	83,000	250,000
Boston	"	80,000	200,000
Charleston	"	31,000	60,000
		599,000	2,380,000

Cincinnati and suburbs		28,000	250,000
New Orleans	"	47,000	170,000
St. Louis	"	6,000	170,000
Chicago	"	100	150,000
Pittsburg	"	17,000	145,000
		98,000	885,000

This table shows the five Atlantic cities to have quadrupled, and the five cities of the interior plain have increased nine times. Is this relative rate of increase of the exterior and interior cities to be changed, and, if it is to be changed, when is the change to commence? We can foresee no cause adequate to that effect, or tending toward it. On the contrary, it seems to us certain as any future event, that the rate of growth of the interior cities, compared with those on the Atlantic border, will be increased.

The proportion which their present numbers bear to the numbers of the rural population does not exceed one to six, whereas the urban population of the Atlantic border is not less than one to three of the rural. This disproportion of city and rural population will hereafter change more rapidly in favor of the interior than the Atlantic cities, because of the greater fertility of soil producing more food from an equal amount of labor; and also, by reason of the more rapid growth of the general population, of which an increasing proportion will prefer city to country life. Will it not be so? Will not the general increase of population be greater in the interior States? Will not the productions of the soil increase faster? And can there be a doubt that the large disproportion in the distribution of the population between city and country, in the interior, will be lessened, so that, instead of being, as now, only one to five or six, they will rapidly approach the proportion of one to two or three? Here, then, are the sources of superior increase so obviously true, as to need only to be stated to insure conviction.

Let us now compare the growth, for the thirty years since 1830, of the five largest Atlantic cities, with the five largest cities of the plain, and, by its side, extend the comparison to 10, 15, and 20 of the largest city of each section:

		1830.	1860 Est.
New York and	accessories	235,000	1,170,000
Philadelphia	"	170,000	700,000
Baltimore	"	83,000	250,000
Charleston	"	31,000	60,000
		599,000	2,380,000
			Increase 4 times.

		1830.	1860 Est.
Cincinnati and	suburbs	28,000	250,000
New Orleans	"	47,000	270,000
St. Louis	"	6,000	170,000
Chicago	"	100	150,000
Pittsburg	"	17,000	145,000
		98,000	2,885,000
			Increase 9 times.

Let us now compare the *ten* largest of each section.

Atlantic.

	1830.	1860 Est.
The aggregate of the five largest as above	579,000	2,370,000
Providence	17,000	55,000
Lowell	6,500	40,000
Washington	19,000	60,000
Albany	24,000	65,000
Richmond	16,000	35,000
	661,000	2,625,000

Increase 4 times.

Interior.

	1839.	1860 Est.
Aggregate as above	98,000	885,000
Buffalo	9,000	100,000
Louisville	10,500	80,000
Milwaukee	50	75,000
Detroit	2,000	80,000
Cleveland	1,000	70,000
	120,550	1,290,000

Increase 10 7-10.

Aggregate of the ten, with five more of each section added, added, to wit:

	1830.	1860 Est.
Aggregate as above	661,000	2,625,000
Troy	11,500	35,000
Portland	12,500	30,000
Salem	14,000	25,000
New Haven	10,000	30,000
Savannah	7,500	15,500
	716,500	2,760,500

Increase 3 8-10 times.

	1830.	1860 Est.
Aggregate as above	120,550....	1,290,000
Toronto	1,700....	65,000
Rochester	9,000....	50,000
Mobile	3,000....	30,000
Memphis	1,500....	25,000
Hamilton	1,500....	25,000
	137,000....	1,485,000

Increase 16 7-10 times.

Aggregate of the fifteen, with five more added in each section:

	1830.	1860 Est.
Aggregate as above	716,500....	2,760,500
Springfield, Mass.	7,000....	24,000
Worcester, "	4,500....	24,000
Bangor, Me.	3,000....	23,000
Patterson, N. J.	5,000....	22,000
Manchester, N. H.	50....	22,000
	736,500....	2,875,500

Increase 3 8-10 times.

	1830.	1860 Est.
Aggregate as above	137,250....	1,485,000
Dayton	3,000....	24,000
Indianapolis	1,500....	22,000
Toledo	30....	20,000
Oswego	3,200....	20,000
Quincy	1,500....	20,000
	149,700....	1,591,000

Increase 10 6-10 times.

From the above tables, we see that the city of

New York, with its neighboring dependencies, will have made in growth in thirty years, between 1830 and 1860, increasing its population 5 times. During the same period,

The 5 largest Atlantic cities and suburbs, including New York, increased.............	4 1-10	times.
The 10 largest Atlantic cities and suburbs, including New York, increased.............	4	"
The 15 largest Atlantic cities and suburbs, including New York, increased.............	3 8-10	"
The 20 largest Atlantic cities and suburbs, including New York, increased.............	3 8-10	"
And that the 5 largest cities of the great plain, during the same period, increased.........	9	"
And the 10 largest cities of the great plain, during the same period, increased........	10 7-10	"
And the 15 largest cities of the great plain, during the same period, increased.........	10 7-10	"
And the 20 largest cities of the great plain, during the same period, increased.........	10 6-10	"

If the number of cities and towns of each section were increased to twenty-five, thirty, and thirty-five of each section, the disparity would increase in favor of the interior cities, most of these to be brought into comparison, having come into existence since 1830.

We commend the comparison between the old and the new cities so far back as 1830, to give the former a better chance for a fair showing. If a later census should be chosen for a starting point, the advantages would be more decidedly with the interior cities.

In the article on the great plain, in the May number of this Review, we gave prominence to the two great external gateways of commerce offered to its people in their intercourse with the rest of the world: that is to say, the Mississippi river entrance into the Gulf of Mexico, and the outlet of the lakes through St. Lawrence and Hudson rivers. These constitute the present great routes of commerce of the people of the plain, and draw to the cities on the borders of the great lakes and rivers the trade of the surrounding country. Between the cities of the great rivers and lakes there has of late sprung up a friendly rivalry, each having some peculiar advantages, and all, in some degree, drawing business into their laps for the benefit of their rivals. That is to say: river cities gather in productions from the surrounding districts which seek an eastern market through lake harbors; and lake cities perform the same office for the chief river cities. Each year increases, to a marked extent, the intercourse which these two classes of cities hold with each other; and it may be safely anticipated that no long period will elapse before this intercourse will become more important to them than all their commerce with the world beside.

In comparing the interior cities of the great plain, situated on the navigable rivers, with those located on the borders of the lakes, two considerations bearing on their relative growth should be kept in view. The river cities were of earlier growth, the settement from the Atlantic States having taken the Ohio river as the high-road to their new homes, many years before the upper lakes were resorted to as a channel of active emigration.

This gave an earlier development to country bordering the central rivers, the Ohio, Wabash, Illinois, and Lower Missouri. The States of Kentucky and Tennessee, also, had been pretty well settled, in their more inviting portions, before any considerable inroad had been made on the wilderness bordering on the upper lakes. Owing to these and other circumstances, the river cities, Pittsburg, Cincinnati, Louisville, and others of less note, were well advanced in growth, before the towns on the lakes had begun, in any considerable degree, to be developed. Another advantage the river cities possessed in their early stage, and which they still hold; that of manufacturing for the planting States bordering the great rivers.

For many years, in a great variety of articles of necessity, they possessed almost a monopoly of this business. Of late, transportation has become so cheap, that the planters avail themselves of a greater range of choice for the purchase of manufactured articles, and the lake cities have commenced a direct trade with the plantation States, which will doubtless increase with the usual rapidity of industrial development in the fertile West.

If we claim for the upper lake country some superiority of climate for city growth over the great river region, we do not doubt that the future will justify the claim. More labor will be performed for the same compensation, in a cool, bracing atmosphere, such as distinguishes the upper lake region, than on the more sultry banks of the central affluents of the Mississippi, where are the best positions for the chief river cities.

Refraining from further comment, let us bring the actual development of the interior cities—on the navigable rivers and on the lakes—into juxtaposition for easy comparison. As our comparison of Atlantic cities with the cities of the plain has been made for thirty years, from 1830 to 1860, we continue it here for the same period, between the river cities and lake cities. We select twenty cities, now the largest of each region, and put down the population in round numbers as nearly accurate as practicable. That for 1860, is of course, an estimate only, but it is certainly near enough to the truth to illustrate the growth, positive and comparative, of our interior cities.

This table exhibits a growth of the interior cities on the navigable waters of the Mississippi and its affluents, which brings their population, in 1870, up to 11 4–10 that of 1830. This is, unquestionably, much beyond the expectation of their most sanguine inhabitants, at the commencement of that period, being three times that of the chief cities of the Atlantic border. Yet even this rapid development is seen, by our figures, to fall far behind that which has characterized the cities created by lake commerce during the same period.

Interior River Cities		1830.	1860.
Cincinnati and dependencies		25,500	250,000
Pittsburg,	"	15,500	155,000
St. Louis,	"	6,000	180,000
Louisville,	"	11,000	80,000
Memphis,	"	2,500	25,000
Wheeling,	"	6,000	20,000
New Albany	"	1,500	20,000
Quincy,	"	1,000	19,000
Peoria,	"	800	18,000
Galena,	"	2,000	18,500
Keokuk,	"	50	16,000

Dubuque,	"	100	16,000
Nashville,	"	6,000	15,000
St. Paul,	"		15,000
Madison, Ind.,	"	2,500	13,000
Burlington, Ind.,	"		12,000
La Fayette, Ind.	"	300	13,000
Rock Island,	"		8,000
Jeffersonville,	"	800	8,000
		81,550	914,000

Lake Cities.		1830.	1860.
Chicago and dependencies		100	150,000
Buffalo,	"	8,663	100,000
Detroit,	"	2,222	80,000
Milwaukee,	"	50	75,000
Cleveland,	"	1,047	70,000
Toronto, C. W.	"	1,667	65,000
Rochester,	"	9,269	50,000
Hamilton, C. W.	"	5,500	25.000
Kingston, C. W.	"	2,500	20,500
Oswego,	"	3,200	20,500
Toledo,	"	30	20,000
Sandusky City,	"	350	14,000
Erie,	"	1,000	10,000
G. Rapids, Mich.,	"	300	10,000
Kenosha,	"		10,000
Racine,	"		10,000
St. Catharine's, C.W.	"	400	10,000
Waukegan,	"		8,000
Port Huron,	"	100	8,000
Fon du Lac,	"	20	8,000
		32,408	764,000

These, according to the table, exhibit a growth which makes them, in 1860, more than *twenty-three* times as populous as they were in 1830. This is double the progress of the river cities, and more than five times that of the cities of the Atlantic coast. In the face of these facts, how can intelligent men continue to hold the opinion that New York is to continue long to be, as now, the focal point of North American commerce and influence? Yet well informed men *do* continue to express the opinion that New York will *ever* hold the position of the chief city of the continent. Every one at all familiar with the location and movement of our population, knows that the central point of its numbers is moving in a constant and almost unvarying direction west by north. An able investigator, now Professor of Law in the University of Michigan, Thomas M. Cooley, five years ago, entered into an elaborate calculation to ascertain where the centre of population of the United States and Canadas was, at that time. The result showed it to be very near Pittsburg. It is generally conceded that it travels in a direction about west by north, at a rate averaging not less than seven miles a year. In 1860, it will have crossed the Ohio River, and commenced its march through the State of Ohio. As our internal commerce is more than ten times as great as our foreign commerce, and is increasing more rapidly, it is plain that it will have the chief agency in building the future and permanent capital city of the continent. If the centre of population were, likewise the centre of wealth and industrial power, other things being equal, it would be the position of the chief city, as it would be the most convenient place of exchange for dealers from all quarters of the country. But this centre of wealth and industrial power does not keep up, in its western movement, with the centre of population! nor, if its movement were coincident, would it be at or near the right point for the concentration of our domestic and foreign trade, while traversing the interior of Ohio. If we suppose our foreign commerce equal to one fifteenth of the domestic, we should add to the thirty-three millions of the States and Canadas, upward of two millions of foreigners, to represent our foreign commerce. These should be thrown into the scale represented by New York. This, with the larger proportion to population of industrial power remaining in the old States, would render it certain that the centre of industrial power of our nation has not traveled westward so far as to endanger, for the present, the supremacy of the cities central to the commerce of our Atlantic coast. Until the centre of industrial power approaches a good harbor on the lakes, New York will continue the best located city of the continent for the great operations of its commerce. That the centre of wealth and consequent industrial power is moving westward at a rate not materially slower than the centre of population, might be easily proved; but, as those who read this article with interest must be cognizant of the great flow of capital from the old world and the old States to the New States, and the rapid increase of capital on the fertile soil of the new States, no special proof seems to us to be called for. The centre of power, numerical, political, economical, and social, is then, indubitably, on its steady march from the Atlantic border toward the interior of the continent. That it will find a resting place somewhere, in its broad interior plain, seems as inevitable as the continued movement of the earth on its axis. The figures we have submitted of the growth of the principal lake cities plainly show great power in lake commerce, so great as to carry conviction to our mind that the *principal city of the continent will find its proper home and resting-place on the lake border, and become the most populous capital of the earth.* A full knowledge of the geography of North America will tend to confirm this conviction in the mind of the fair inquirer. The lakes penetrate the continent to its productive centre. They afford, during eight or nine months of the year, pleasant and safe navigation for steam-propelled vessels. Their waters are pure and beautifully transparent, and the air which passes over them exceedingly invigorating to the human system. Their borders are replete with materials for the exercise of human industry and skill. The soil is fertile and very productive in grains and grasses. Coal in exhaustless abundance crops out on or near their waters, to the extent of nearly one thousand miles of coast. The richest mines of iron and copper, convenient to water transport, exist, in aggregate amount, beyond the power of calculation. Stone of lime, granite, sand, and various other kinds suitable for the architect and the artist, are found almost everywhere convenient to navigation. Gypsum of the best quality crops out on the shores of three of the great lakes, and salt springs of great strength are worked to advantage, near lakes Ontario and Michigan. Timber trees in great variety and of valuable sorts, give a rich border to the shores for thousands of miles. Of these, the white oak, burr oak, white pine, whitewood or tulip tree, white ash, hickory and black walnut, are the most valuable. They are of noble dimensions, and clothe millions of acres with their rich foliage. No-where else on the continent are to be seen such abundance of magnificent oak, and the immense groves of white pine are not excelled. Heretofore little esteemed, the great tracts of timber convenient to lake navigation and to the wide treeless prairies of the plain, are destined soon to take an important place in the commercial operations of the interior. Already, oak timber, for ship-building and other purposes, finds a profitable market ln New York and Boston. The great Russian steamship "General Admiral," was built in part from the timber of the lake border. A great trade is growing up, based on the products of the forest. Whitewood (Diriodendron tulipifera) oak staves, black and white walnut plank, and other indigenous timber, are shipped, not only to the Atlantic cities, but to foreign ports. The lumber yards of Albany, New York, Philadelphia, as well as those of Chicago, Milwaukee, Detroit, Toledo, Cleveland and Buffalo, receive large supplies from the pineries bordering the great lakes. Cincinnati and other Ohio river cities, receive an increasing proportion of pine lumber from the same source. These great waters are also, as is well known, stocked with fish in great variety, whose fine gastronomic qualities have a world-wide reputation.

As before stated, these lakes penetrate the continent toward the northwest as far as its productive centre. They now have unobstructed connection with the Atlantic vessels of nine feet draft and three hundred tons burden, by the aid of sixty-three miles of canals overcoming the falls of the St. Mary, Niagara and St. Lawrence Rivers, with a lockage of less than six hundred feet. By enlarging some of the locks and deepening the canals, at a cost of a very few millions, navigation for propellers of from one thousand to two thousand tons may be secured with the whole world of waters. The cost is much within the power of the Canadas and the States bordering the lakes, and will be but a light matter to these communities when, within the next fifteen years, they shall have doubled their population and trebled their wealth. The increase of the commerce of the lakes, during the last fifteen years, is believed to be beyond any example furnished by the history of navigation. A proportionate increase the next fifteen years, would give for the yearly value of its transported articles, thousands of millions. According to the best authorities it is now over four hundred millions. In 1855, that portion of the tonnage belonging to the United States was one fifteenth of the entire tonnage of the Union. During the same year the clearances of vessels from ports of the United States to the Canadas, and the entrance of vessels from the Canadas to ports of the United States, as exhibited in the following table, show a greater amount of tonnage entered and cleared than between the United States and any other foreign country :

Clearances from ports in the United States to ports in Canada in 1855 :

Number of American vessels	2,369
" Canadian "	6,638
Whole number	9,067
Tonnage American	890,017
" Canadian	903,502
Total cleared from the States,	1,793,519

The registered tonnage of all the States, the same year, was 2,676,864; and the registered and enrolled together, 5,212,000.

The value of lake tonnage was, in 1855, $14,835,-000. The total value of the commerce of the lakes, the same year, was estimated, by high authority, (including exports and imports) at twelve hundred and sixteen millions ($1,216,000,000.) This seems to us an exaggerated estimate, though based principally on official reports of collectors of customs. Eight hundred millions would, probably, be near to the true amount. It will surprise many persons to learn that the trade between the United States and Canadas, carried on chiefly by the lakes and their connecting waters, ranks third in value and first in tonnage, in the table of our foreign commerce; being, in value, only below that of England and the French Empire, and in tonnage above the British Empire.

American goods to Canada - -	$9,950,764
Foreign goods - - - -	8,769,580
	$18,720,344
Canadian goods to the States, - -	12,182,314
	$30,902,658

We here append a table showing the progress, from decade to decade, of the principal centres of population of the plain since 1820. It has been made with all the accuracy which our sources of information enable us to attain. There are in it, no doubt, many errors, but it will be found, in the main, and for general argument, substantially correct. For future reference, it will be valuable to persons who take an interest in the development of our new urban communities. Included in each city are its outlying dependencies—such as Newport and Covington with Cincinnati, and Lafayette with New Orleans.

	1830.	1840.	1850.	1860.
New Orleans......	46,310	90,000	130,565	180,000
Cincinnati.........	21,831	47,000	130,739	250,000
St Louis...........	5,852	16,469	82,000	180,000
Chicago............	100	4,650	29,963	150,000
Pittsburg..........	12,568	25,000	71,595	125,000
Buffalo............	8,653	18,213	42,265	100,000
Montreal...........	30,000	40,000	55,000	90,000
Louisville..........	10,341	21,210	43,194	89,000
Detroit............	2,222	9,162	21,019	80,000
Milwaukee..........	50	1,730	20,061	75,000
Cleveland..........	1,047	6,071	19,377	70,000
Toronto............	1,677	13,500	27,500	70,000
Rochester..........	9,269	20,191	36,409	50,000
Quebec............	26,250	32,500	41,200	55,000
Columbus, O.......	2,450	6,671	17,882	40,000
Mobile.............	3,194	12,672	20,515	35,000
Hamilton, C. W....	1.500	4,200	13,000	25,000
Memphis...........	1,500	3,500	8,839	25,000
Nashville	5,566	6,929	10,478	25,000
Dayton	2,954	6,067	10,977	25,000
Indianapolis........	1,000	2,692	8,034	22,000
Wheeling, Va.......	5,221	7,885	11,435	20,000
Kingston, C. W....	2,500	5,500	10,000	20,000
Lockport, N. Y.....	3,800	6,500	12,323	20,000
Oswego............	3,200	4,665	12,205	20,000
Toledo.............	30	1,229	3,829	20,000
Zanesville..........	3,000 est.	6,000 est.	12,355	20,000
New Albany.......	1,500 est.	4,000 est.	9,895	20,000

	1830.	1840.	1850.	1860.
Peoria...............	800 est.	2,000 est.	5,095	20,000
Quincy, Ill.........	1,000	3,000	6,902	20,000
Galena..............	2,000	4,000	6,004	20,000
Dubuque............	200	1,500	3,108	16,000
Keokuk.............	...	1,000	2,478	16,000
Davenport..........	...	500	2,478	12,000
Burlington, Ia.......	...	1,000	1,848	12,000
Columbus, Ga.......	1,000	4,000	5,052	10,000
Alton, Ill...........	250	2,500	3,585	10,000
Steubenville.........	2,964	5,203	6,140	9,000
Chillicothe..........	2,840	3,977	7,100	9,000
Grand Rapids, Mich.	300	1,500	3,148	9,000
Huntsville. Ala.....	1,200	1,500	2,863	6,000
Adrian, Mich........	200	1,800	3,006	9,000
Ann Arbor.........	200	2,000	4,868	9,000
Sandusky City.......	350	2,000	8,500	13,000
Fort Wayne, Ia......	100	1,600	4,282	13,000
Madison, Ia.........	2,500	4,500	8,508	13,000
St. Paul............	...	...	1,012	15,000
Lafayette, Ia........	200	2,000	6,129	13,000
Maysville, Ky.......	1,800	2,741	4,256	9,000
Terre Haute, Ia.....	600	2,000	4,900	9,000
Evansville, Ia.......	300	1,500	3,235	9,000
Jeffersonville, Ia.....	500	2,000	3,487	9,000
Portsmouth, Ohio....	1,000	2,000	4,011	9,000
Marietta, O.........	1,200	1,815	5,254	9,000
Springfield, Ill.......	800	2,579	4,553	9,000
Rock Island City....	...	400	1,711	8,000
Chattanooga, Ten....	500	1,000	3,500	8,000
Bytown, or Ottawa, C. W. ...	500	2,000	5,000	10,000
London, C. W.......	500	2,000	5,000	10,000
St. Catherines, do....	200	800	4,000	10,000
Galveston, Texas.....	1,200	2,000	4,177	10,000

	1830.	1840.	1850.	1860.
Houston, "	...	500	3,000	10,000
Erie, Pa.............	1,260	3,500	5,858	10,000
Lexington, Ky......	4,500	6,997	9,180	10,000
Ogdensburg.........	1,500	3,000	6,500	10,000
Natchez, Miss.......	2,000	3,000	4,434	9,000
Three Rivers, C. E.	800	2,000	4,000	8,000
Racine, Wis..........	...	1,000	5,111	9,000
Waukesha............	...	200	2,313	8,000
Marshall, Mich.......	200	1,200	2,822	8,000
Pontiac, "	150	1,300	2,820	8,000
P't Huron "	100	400	2,313	8,000
Jackson "	150	1,000	3,051	6,000
Kalamazoo "	150	900	2,363	6,000
Mineral Pt., Wis.....	500	800	2,584	6,000
Kenosha "	...	500	3,055	8,000
Fon du Lac, "	...	1,000	3,451	6,000
Janesville "	...	1,200	2,782	7,000
Beloit "	...	500	2,732	6,000
Madison "	...	100	1,500	7,000
Elgin "	...	100	2,359	5,000
Oshkosh, "	...	...	2,500	6,000
Monroe, Mich........	400	2,000	2,813	5,000
Lansing "	...	100	1,229	5,000
Columbus, Miss......	800	1,500	2,611	5,000
Jacksonville, Ill......	800	1,500	2,745	5,000
Waukegan "	...	800	2,949	6,000
Lasalle "	50	1,000	3,201	6,000
Joliet "	...	1,000	2,659	6,000
Jefferson City, Mo...	1,000	2,000	3,000	5,000
St. Joseph "	...	1,000	2,557	5,000
Independence "	...	500	3,500	6,000
Iowa City, Iowa......	...	...	1,582	5,000
Muscatine "	...	400	2,540	6,000
Springfield, Ohio.....	1,080	2,094	5,108	8,000
Newark "	1,000	2,705	3,654	7,000

	1830.	1840.	1850.	1860.
Hamilton "	800	1,409	3,210	7,000
Lancaster "	1,000	2,120	3,483	5,000
Akron "	800	1,664	3,266	6,000
Mt, Vernon "	800	2,363	3,711	7,000
Tiffin "	...	728	2,718	7,000
Urbana "	400	1,070	3,414	6,000
Massillon "	600	1,300	2,697	5,000
Lawrenceburg, Ia.....	600	2,000	3,487	6,000
Richmond, Ia.......	500	1,000	1,443	5,000
Knoxville, Tenn.....	1,800	....	2,076	6,000

The preceding table is instructive, showing, as it does, the steady and rapidly increasing tendency of the people of the plain to seek a home in cities and villages, notwithstanding the great temptation which fertile, cheap, and easily-improved lands hold out to become tillers of the soil and growers of cattle. Stock farming is largely remunerative, but our western people—wild and uncultivated as they are supposed to be by those unacquainted with their true character—prefer homes where the advantages of education and social intercourse is a constant enjoyment. Nowhere in the world are educational establishments on a better footing or more universally accessible than in some of the new States of the centre, as in Ohio, Michigan, Wisconsin and other States."

CHAPTER XII.

Michigan Agricultural Reports for 1854—Professor Thomas's Report—Report of J. S. Dixon—Products of States—Climate —Army Meteorological Reports.

FROM the Agricultural Reports of the State of Michigan we take the following:—

"From old *Fort Mackinaw* to the *Manistee River*, the land immediately upon the lake shore, and not unfrequently extending back for many miles, is considerably elevated, and occasionally rises very abruptly to the height of from one hundred to three or four hundred feet. The country (more particularly the northern portion) continues to rise as we proceed into the interior, until it attains an elevation equal to any other portion of the peninsula.

"This is more particularly the case in the rear of Traverse Bay, where this elevation continues for many miles into the interior, giving to the landscape a very picturesque appearance when viewed from some of the small lakes, which abound in this as well as in the more southern portion of the State.

"The tract of country under consideration is based on limestone, sandstone, and shales, which are covered, excepting at a few points, with a deposit of red clay and sand, varying in thickness from a few inches to more than four hundred feet. The interior of the northern portion of the peninsula, west of the meridian, is generally more rolling than that on the east. It is interspersed with some extensive cedar swamps and marshes, on the *alluvial* lands, and in the vicinity of heads of streams and some of the lakes. The upland is generally rolling, has a soil of clay, loam and sand, and is clad with evergreen timber, intermixed with tracts of beech and maple, varying in extent from a few acres to several townships. Several of the most extensive of these tracts are in the vicinity of the Cheboygan and Tahweegon rivers, their lakes and tributary streams. There are also large tracts of beech and maple timber lying between the head of Grand Traverse Bay, and the Manistee and Muskeegon rivers.

"The elevated portion of land on the shore of Lake Michigan, known as the 'Sleeping Bear' as well as Manitou Island, (see latitude 45) which, when viewed from a distance, has the appearance of sand, is found to be composed of alternate layers of highly marly clay and sand. The clay is of a deep red color, and in many places its strata are much contorted.

"The hilly region, to which allusions have been made, is mostly heavily timbered with beech, maple, bass, oak, ash, elm, birch, etc., interspersed with an occasional cedar swamp. In the vicinity of Grand Traverse Bay, this character of country extends into the interior for many miles, bordering on a series of small and beautiful lakes, which vary in length from two to eighteen miles, and are generally free from marsh and swamp. This country, as also that in the interior from Little Traverse Bay, is well adapted to the purposes of agriculture.

"Passing south of this rolling district, the country becomes less elevated and more variable, the soil assuming a more sandy character, and being generally clad with evergreen timber. There are, however, exceptions to this in some fine tracts of beech and maple near the lake coast, also, in the vicinity of some of the streams in the interior.

"It is nevertheless true, that there are many extensive swamps and marshes in this part of the peninsula, but it is doubted whether, upon the whole, they exceed the quantity or extent of those of the more southern part of the State.

"In point of soil and timber, this portion of the

State is not inferior to the more southern—and such are the advantages it offers to the settler, that the day is not distant when it will be sought as a place of residence by the agriculturist.

"The beauty of its lakes and streams is not anywhere surpassed. Such is the transparency of their waters as to permit objects to be distinctly seen at the depth of more that thirty feet.

"That part of the peninsula situate north of Grand River is usually regarded by many of the inhabitants of the more southern part of the State, as being either an impenetrable swamp, or a sandy barren waste, and as possessing too rigorous a climate to admit of its successful application to purposes of agriculture.

"This is an erroneous opinion, and one which will most certainly be corrected, as the facts with regard to this part of our State come more fully to be known. The inhabitants of Flat, Royale, Muskegon and White Rivers, and the Ottawa Indians, living on the Grand and Little Traverse Bays, and on the Manistee River, have extensive cultivated fields, which uniformly produce abundant crops.

"The country on Flat and Royale Rivers is generally rolling, interspersed with level and knobby tracts; but none is so rough as to prevent it from being successfully cultivated. The timber in the vicinity of the streams consists of black, white, and burr oak, which is scattering, and forms what is denominated openings and plains; small tracts of pine barrens, beech, maple and oak lands, interspersed with tracts of white pine.

"Settlements are rapidly advancing in this part of our State, and much of the land under cultivation produces excellent crops of wheat, oats, corn, potatoes, etc., and so far as experience has been brought to the test, is not inferior to, or more subject to early frosts in the fall, than more southern counties of the State.

"The soil varies from a light sand to a stiff clay loam.

"The country on the Muskegon is rolling, and may be considered as divided into beech and maple land, pine lands, pine barrens, oak openings, plains and prairies. Small tracts of the latter are situated near the forks of the river, about forty-five miles from its mouth, and between thirty and forty-five miles north of the Grand River.

"Crops of corn, oats, wheat, etc., were here as flourishing as those of the more southern part of State. The soil of the prairies and openings is sandy, while that of the beech and maple lands is a sand and clay loam.

"The Indians on Grand and Little Traverse Bays and vicinity, also obtain good crops of corn, potatoes, squashes, etc. Some of the most intelligent Indians informed me that they were seldom injured by frosts in the fall or spring. They also have many apple trees which produce fruit in considerable quantities.

"The soil is strictly a warm one, and, exposed as the whole country, bordering on Lake Michigan, is to the influence of the southern winds during summer and parts of spring and fall, it seldom fails to be productive."

Professor Thomas, Geologist, has placed in our hands the following report of the Geology of Mackinaw, Michigan:

"From the site of old Fort Mackinaw, at the very extremity of the peninsula, south to the Manistee River, a direct distance of about one hundred and forty miles, the immediate shores of the lake are almost invariably considerably elevated, sometimes rising abruptly to a height of from three to four hundred feet.

"The soil of the vicinity, in consequence of the large amount of calcareous matter which enters into its composition, possesses a fertility that a superficial observer would scarcely ascribe to it.

"The limestone chiefly consists of an irregular assemblage of angular fragments united by a tufaceous cement. These fragments usually appear at first sight to have a compact structure, but a more minute examination shows them to contain *minute* cells, sufficiently large to admit water, which, by the action of frost, subjects the rock to rapid disintegration. Portions of the rock may, nevertheless, be selected partially free from this difficulty, and which are possessed of sufficient compactness to render them of value as a coarse building stone; horn-stone, striped jasper (imperfect); hog-toothed spar, calcareous spar, and fluor spar, are imbedded in the rock, although the latter is of rare occurrence.

"Lime rock again occurs at the Straits of Mackinaw, and in the vicinity, it appears upon the Island of Mackinac, together with the Bois Blanc, Round, and St. Martin's Islands, as also upon the northern peninsula north from Mackinaw.

"Gypsum occurs on the St. Martin's group of islands, and also upon the northern peninsula between Green Bay and Mackinac.

"MACKINAW LIMESTONE.—The rock is of a light color, and the fragments of which it is composed frequently contain numberless minute cells. These were undoubtedly once filled with spar, which has been washed out of the exposed part of the rock by the action of water. The upper part is unfit for building purposes, but the lower is more compact, and has marks of regular stratification.

"COAL.—The coal is highly bituminous, a character in common with all that has been seen in the State, and it may safely be said, that none other may be looked for in the peninsula.

"From the facts now before me, I am led to hope that coal will be found in the elevated hills of the northern part of the peninsula, easterly from Little Traverse Bay, a circumstance which, should it prove to be the case, will add much to the value of that portion of the State."—*Houghton' Geological Reports of Michigan.*

"Foster and Whitney, United States Geologists, in their Reports to the Government, laid down the Onondago Salt Group of rocks as extending over a portion of the southern part of the northern peninsula of Michigan, not a great distance from Mackinaw, and also as existing on the St. Martin's and Mackinaw Islands.

"ONONDAGA SALT GROUP.—As a whole, it is an immense mass of argillo-calcareous shaly rocks, inclosing veins and beds of gypsum; hence this has been designated by some as the 'gypseous shales.'

"Four divisions have been distinguished in the description of the Onondaga Salt Group, though the lines of separation are by no means well defined.

"1. Red and greenish shales below.

"2. Green and red marl, shale, and shaly limestone with some veins of gypsum.

"Shaly, compact, impure limestone, with shale and marl, embracing two ranges of plaster beds with hopper-shaped cavities between.

"4. Drab-colored, impure limestone with fibrous cavities; the 'magnesian deposit of Vanuxem.' Of these, the third is the only one that has yielded gypsum in profitable quantities. The included masses of gypsum, though, for the most part, even-bedded at their base, are usually very irregular at their upper surface, often conical. The plaster beds are supposed to be separations by molecular attraction from the marl.

"This third division contains not only the gypseous beds, but is most probably the source of all the salt so extensively manufactured at Onondaga, Cayuga, and Madison; at least Vanuxem informs us that, except in these gypseous beds, there is no evidence of salt existing in the solid state in any of the other divisions of the Onondaga Salt Group.

"The fourth division is remarkable for a fine columnar structure, or needle-formed cavities, dispersed through the mass.

"In the middle counties of New York, the entire thickness of the Onondaga Salt Group must be from six hundred to a thousand feet. Notwithstanding its great thickness, this formation is very barren in fossils. The corals and shells of the Niagara group suddenly ceased to exist, perhaps, as Hall suggests, being overwhelmed by a sudden outbreak of a buried vulcano at the bottom of the ocean, by which the waters became surcharged not only with argillaceous sediment, but became contaminated, either with free sulphuric acid, or sulphate of magnesia and soda.

"The country through which the Onondaga Salt Group extends, is usually marked by a series of low, gravelly hills, and clayey valleys, on which a stunted growth of timber prevails, known by the name of 'Oak Openings.' Small portions of sulphate of strontia, galena, and blende, with rhomb spar, occur in the upper portion of the group. Gypsum and salt are, however, the only minerals of economical value: of the former many thousand tons are excavated. Several acidulous springs issuing from these deposits, have been found to contain free sulphuric acid."—*D. D. Owen's Review of the N. Y. Geological Reports.*

Jules Marcou, in his Geology of the United States, places the northern portion of the southern peninsula of Michigan in the Terrain Devonian.

Report of J. S. Dixon and others, on Grand Traverse Bay, p. 523, in Michigan Agricultural Reports for 1834, says:

"The atmosphere is moist and wholesome—no disease, and healthy as any portion of country. It is a well established fact, that water cools first on the surface, then sinks while the warm water rises, and consequently ice never forms till the whole body of water has been cooled to thirty degrees. Now, from this fact, the philosopher will at once deduce the climate of this region. Traverse Bay is from one hundred to nine hundred feet deep and the water never cools to thirty-two degrees till the middle of February, and in Lake Michigan in the middle never, and so long as the water in these continuous reservoirs is warmer than the air, the former must obviously warm the latter.

"It is accordingly well known that in England, on the east side of the Atlantic 7° or 8° farther north than Traverse Bay, the climate, as it regards cold in winter, is about equal to that of Washington City, and so it is on the east side of the Pacific ocean, in Oregon. Hence it is evident that the seasons on the east side of Lake Michigan must be uniform.

"Around Traverse Bay the frost seldom kills vegetables till in November, and seldom occurs in spring later than the 1st of May. In November it gets cold enough to freeze. The vapors arising from the lake and bay fall in snow and cover the ground before the frost has penetrated it at all; it accumulates several months till it is two feet deep, sometimes deeper, and remains till April; and when it goes off, cattle find enough to eat in the woods. This region is much more sunny between the middle of March and December than southern Michigan, and every vegetable physiologist will at once state that the influence of this on vegetation must be very great, and accordingly spring crops grow with such rapidity that corn is fit to be cut by the 1st of September. From December to March, as above, the atmosphere is hazy, cloudy, and frosty, though the thermometer never sinks so low as in the south of Michigan by ten or twelve degrees (8 or 10 degrees below zero, being the lowest yet known), and a winter thaw is unknown here. Hence we never have mud in winter, and but little at any season.

"With the very defective cultivation hitherto used here, yield of crops are as follows:—Potatoes, free of rot, 150 to 300 bushels to the acre; oats 25 to 60; corn 25 to 50; wheat (spring) the largest yet raised 27 bushels. Wheat raised here is much more plump than in southern Michigan, and there is no instance of its being smothered or injured by snow, because the snow never thaws and alternately freezes into a hard crust, or ice, so as to exclude the air from the wheat, as in other places.

"We confidently predict that this will become the most prolific wheat region in the west; rust and insects are unknown. All experience goes to prove that this will be a great fruit country. The Indian apple and peach trees, although few in number bear well every year; and as to wild blackberries and raspberries, both as to size and flavor, there is absolutely no end. They serve all the inhabitants and millions of pigeons for several months."

United States census, 1850, shows products of States.

	Average per acre of Wheat.		Oats	Corn.	Potatoes.
Michigan	10	Bushels	26	32	140
Illinois	11	"	29	33	105
Indiana	12	"	20	33	100
Iowa	14	"	36	32	100

	Average per acre of Wheat.		Oats	Corn.	Potatoes.
Ohio................	12	"	21	36	
Wisconsin...........	14	"	35	30	
Pennsylvania........	15	"		20	
New York...........	12	"	25	27	

CLIMATE.—Council Bluffs is in latitude 41½°, Dubuque 42¾°, Green Bay 43½°, and Mackinaw City about 46°. By reference to the following tables of temperature, it will be seen that these points are about on the same isothermal line, practically removing, by these tables, the prejudices generally existing against the climate of northern Michigan—see Blodgett's Climatology and Army Meteorological Reports of United States.

Quebec, Canada, average in	January	above	zero,	13°
Montreal, "	"	"	"	16
Hampden, Maine............	"	"	"	17
Portland, "	"	"	"	21
Cannel, "	"	"	"	15
Burlington, Vt.	"	"	"	19
Deerfield, Mass.	"	"	"	21
Granville, N. Y............	"	"	"	22
Potsdam, "	"	"	"	18
Plattsburgh "	"	"	"	20
Gouverneur, "	"	"	"	20
Lowville, "	"	"	"	22
Oneida, "	"	"	"	22
Buffalo, "	"	"	"	23
Silver Lake, Pa.	"	"	"	22
Concord, N. H.	"	"	"	22

Boston, Mass.	average in January above zero,			28°
Albany, N. Y.	"	"	"	24
Chicago, Illinois	"	"	"	24
Ottawa, "	"	"	"	23
Muscatine, Iowa	"	"	"	20
Detroit, Michigan............	"	"	"	27
Pittsburgh, Pa.	"	"	"	29
Philadelphia, "	"	"	"	32
Cincinnati, Ohio	"	"	"	30
Green Bay, Wis.	"	"	"	19
Dubuque, Iowa, ...	"	"	"	20
Council Bluffs	"	"	"	19
Mackinaw City	"	"	"	19

These extremes of latitude of Philadelphia and Mackinaw include the principal agricultural, mining, manufacturing, and commercial interests of America, elements naturally pertaining to Michigan, and second in their variety and extent to no State of the Union.

Archangel, Russia, in January,	averages above zero			6.60°
St. Petersburg, "	"	"	"	15.70
Christiana, Norway,......	"	"	"	21.30
St. Bernard, Switzerland,..	"	"	"	14.40
Moscow, Russia,..........	"	"	"	13.60
Erzeroum, Turkey,.......	"	"	"	18.
Taganwa, Sea of Azof,....	"	"	"	20.70
Astracan, Caspian Sea,...	"	"	"	21.30
Kasow (Volga) Russia,....	"	"	"	3.50
Stockholm, Sweden,......	"	"	"	24.30
Cracow, Poland,.........	"	"	"	23.40
Pekin, China,............	"	"	"	26.00
Odessa, S. Russia,........	"	"	"	25.20
Berlin, Prussia,..........	"	"	"	27.70

Extremes below zero, 1835.

Bangor, Maine................	January 4,	below 40°
Bath "	"	" 40
Portland, "	"	" 21
Boston, Mass.	"	" 15
Salem, "	"	" 17
Chicago, Ill.	February 8,	" 22
St. Louis, Mo.	"	" 22
Cincinnati, O.	"	" 18
Lexington, Ky................	"	" 20
Nashville, Tenn.	"	' 10
Huntsville, Ala..............	"	· 9
Philadelphia, Pa.............	"	" 6
Lancaster, Pa.	"	" 22
Washington City	"	" 16
Clarksville, Geo.	"	" 15

Army Meteorological Reports for 1854.

	January. Mean.	Range. Max'm.	min'm.	above mean.	below mean.
Fort Hamilton, N. Y.	31.49°	50.	12.	18.5	19.5
Fort Niagara, "	25.04	48.	6.	23.	19.
Alleghany, Pa.........	29.08	64.	5.	34.9	24.1
Fort Delaware, Md.....	32.38	54.	10.	21.6	17.4
Cincinnati, Ohio.......	31.78	54.	1.	22.2	32.8
Fort Snelling, Min.....	1.30	45.	36.	43.7	37.3
" Leavenworth, Kan.	24.68	67.	8.	32.3	32.7
" Mackinaw, Mich.	13.09	34.	15.	10.9	28.1

Blodgett's and Army Rain Charts, showing rain and snow in inches for a series of years.

	Jan.	Feb.	M'ch.	Dec.	Total in year.
Mack'w Island, Mich.	1.25	.82	1.14	1.24	23.87
Fort Kent, Maine...	3.73	2.60	1.77	3.36	36.46
Portland, " ...	3.37	3.39	2.92	4.17	45.25

	Jan.	Feb.	M'ch.	Dec.	Total in year.
Charleston, Mass....	2.66	2.22	4.08	2.27	35.83
Montreal, Canada..	2.84	1.84	2.69	2.58	47.28
Fayetteville, Vt.....	3.93	3.91	4.07	3.55	53.99
Cincinnati, Ohio,...	3.35	3.51	3.93	4.29	46.89
Green Bay, Wis....	1.19	0.87	1.70	1.30	34.65
Detroit, Mich......	2.18	1.38	2.86	1.30	30.07
St. Louis, Mo......	1.93	3.37	3.82	1.99	41.95
Fort Hamilton, N.Y.	2.98	3.67	3.65	3.84	43.65
Pittsburgh, Pa.....	2.18	2.17	2.70	3.13	34.96
Philadelphia, Pa....	3.09	2.94	3.43	4.03	43.56

CHAPTER XIII.

Agricultural interest—Means of transportation—Railways and vessels—Lumber—Vessels cleared—Lake cities and Atlantic ports—Home-market—Breadstuffs—Michigan flour—Monetary panics—Wheat—Importations — Provisions — Fruit — Live stock—Wool—Shipping business — Railroads — Lake Superior trade—Pine lumber trade—Copper interest—Iron interest—Fisheries— Coal mines—Salt—Plaster beds.

We copy from the Detroit Tribune of 1860, a somewhat elaborate and lengthy article containing recent and highly important information in regard to the industrial interests of Michigan. Though there are portions of this article which we have to some extent anticipated in some of our previous chapters, we consider it highly important to extract largely from it, because of its more recent date. To all interested in the development and future growth of the Northwest, it will prove most valuable. The writer, Mr. Kay Haddock, commercial editor of the Tribune, says:—

"We know of no similar extent of country on the globe so highly favored by nature as our own State, which but twenty-three years since emerged from the chrysalis condition of a territory, but which to day, by the quickening influence brought to bear upon her natural advantages by an enterprising and enlightened people, possesses elements of wealth and greatness that might well be coveted by empires. The characteristics for which she is pre-eminent are neither few in number nor ordinary in character. She occupies the very front rank in respect to important minerals, as well as in the extent and quality of her forest products, while her fisheries are altogether unrivaled, and, like her mines and forests, are the source of exhaustless wealth. With regard to the extent and diversity of her natural resources, it would indeed seem difficult to over-estimate them. Predictions that seem visionary to-day, are to-morrow exceeded by the reality, as some new treasure is revealed. A glance at the map is of itself the most eloquent commentary that could be presented with reference to her geographical position. As nature does nothing in vain, the shipping facilities afforded by the noble inland seas that clasp our shores, are a sign and promise of the commercial greatness that awaits us in the future. We may well be proud of the condition of our agricultural interest—that great interest which underlies every other; which alike gives to the wealthy his opulence and the beggar his crust. Our farmers have unmistakably indicated their determination to accept of no secondary position in the quality of their wheat, and their wool is not only rapidly gaining the first rank as respect the amount produced, but is sought for with avidity for its superior quality by all the principal manufacturers of the country. Pomona, too, has thrown her influence in the scale. The region that has thus far been devoted to the culture of fruit, in proportion to its extent, cannot be surpassed in the Union, if indeed it can be equaled. Such is a faint picture of the 'Peninsular State.'

"The snail-like progress hitherto made in the settlement of a large share of the State, is an enigma to those not versed in our early history. While occupying the position of a dependent of the central power at Washington, we were so unfortunate in some instances as to have men placed over us with whom personal interests were paramount to the great interests of the territory, which, at the critical period when the seeds of prosperity should have been planted, was fatal to our advancement. Next came the era of Utopian projects of internal improvement, by which our people were saddled with an onerous load of debt. In the mean time immigrants were misled by false reports concerning the character of the soil in the interior of the State, and there were no roads by means of which they could satisfy themselves of the true character of the country. They therefore passed on to find homes upon what then seemed the most attractive prairies of the far West. But there is at last a great change in the tide of affairs. The value of our timber is justly regarded as greatly overbalancing the doubtful advantage of settling upon prairie land, and the active demand that has recently sprung up for it must constantly make a still greater difference in our favor. Lands long held in the iron grasp of speculators are rapidly coming into the possession of actual settlers. Our State is being intersected by a system of roads, which will ere long demonstrate the necessity of an extension of the system. Our course is indeed onward and upward.

"Having seen a statement, given upon the authority of some gazeteer, to the effect that about six million dollars were invested in this State in manufacturing, which we felt assured was a libel upon the State, we have taken steps to procure statistics of the more important industrial establishments throughout the entire State. We find that in the manufacture of pine lumber alone, there are about seven million dollars invested, exclusive of the standing timber of proprietors, which perhaps might properly be included as part of the capital.

Such indications of thrift, enterprise, and prosperity in a region that twenty-four years ago was a howling wilderness, it may be safely said, is without a parallel. The other counties, we are tolerably safe in estimating, will swell the amount to $10,000,000, making, with the lumber manufactories, and the $2,148,500, invested in the iron manufacture, more than twenty million dollars!

The apathy of the citizens of Detroit in availing themselves of the magnificent advantages possessed by the city for prosecuting manufacturing upon an extensive scale, is wholly inexplicable. There is a mine of unproductive wealth in our midst that might at once be placed at compound interest. It now lies dormant in the sinewy arms of men and the nimble fingers of women and children. There is thus a moral aspect in this question that addresses itself with peculiar earnestness to the philanthropic. But it were a philanthropy that would lay up treasures on earth. Daily, almost hourly, raw material takes its departure from our city destined to be received at eastern manufactories, there to be worked up and returned to us for our consumption, by which we are taxed with the freight both ways, in addition to losing the profit of the manufacture. Every property holder has a direct interest at stake. If a liberal sum were to be subscribed to-morrow for investment in this important branch of enterprise, the direct benefit that would accrue to the real estate of the city would be at least double the amount invested.

The Western States look with deep interest to the Grand Trunk Railway, and are hopeful that it may prove a great benefit to them in enabling producers to reach the markets of European consumers at a cheap rate for carriage. Unquestionably great benefits will grow out of the opening up of the great thoroughfare. At the same time there are questions of grave importance to shippers which will soon have to be met, and nothing can be lost, while something may be gained, by meeting them at the outset.

We set out, then, with the proposition that the bulky products of the West must be carried by water and not by rail, and will state a few facts that in our humble opinion will place this proposition beyond all cavil. So far as figures can be obtained, and correct calculations made, it has been demonstrated that freight cannot be moved on American railroads for less than one cent per ton per mile. This is actually the *first cost,* even in the coal regions of Pennsylvania. It is therefore fair to presume that the Grand Trunk, with conceded advantages of superior and economical management, cannot move freight at a less cost, and that the figure named will yield nothing to the stockholders in the shape of dividend. It is true that freight has been carried at an actual loss, and, as we are about to show, the same thing will to some extent be done again, but if persevered in this can only result in ruin, and no one will assert that it ought to be taken as a legitimate basis for future calculations. It follows, then, that $8,80 is the lowest sum for which a ton can be moved from Detroit to Portland, the distance between the two cities being eight hundred and eighty miles. This showing may not be relished by those most immediately interested in the Grand Trunk Railway, nor may it be palatable to the producers of the West, who have built high hopes on this road as an outlet to the Atlantic, but it is useless to attempt to shut our eyes to obvious facts. The West has for years possessed shorter and consequently cheaper routes to the seaboard, and in winter the cost of reaching the Atlantic cities has always been and now is from 100 to

200 per cent. greater by rail than during the navigation season by the cheaper mode. This is easily proved. Let us look at the distance by the old route by the way of Suspension Bridge:

Detroit to Suspension Bridge, is 232 miles; the Bridge to Albany, 300; Albany to Boston 200; total 732.

Thus we see that the whole distance from Detroit to Boston is seven hundred and thirty-two miles, or one hundred and forty-eight *less* than from Detroit to Portland. As regards shipments from Detroit to Boston, via the Grand Trunk, the matter is worse, for we have to add one hundred and three miles from Portland to Boston, making the old route two hundred and fifty-three miles shorter to that point than by the newly opened road. It is evident therefore, that the West is not likely to gain anything permanently by the new route, except in so far as it may open up some local trade, which, inconsiderable at first, may eventually assume considerable importance. Of course, what is true regarding Detroit, is also true with respect to every point west of us.

Every one conversant with trade must admit that goods can be carried as cheap from any port in Europe to New York as to Portland. The distance from New York to Detroit, *via* Albany and Suspension Bridge, is six hundred and eighty-two miles, or one hundred and ninety-eight miles less than from Portland to Detroit. Goods ought certainly to be carried cheaper from New York to Detroit than by a route near two hundred miles further.

We learn that the New York Central Railroad Company are now perfecting a plan for ticketing passengers and goods from any point in the Western, Southern, and Southwestern States, and *vice versa.* Thus at least one important advantage to the West is already apparent, growing out of the comprehensive action of the Grand Trunk managers, while the action of the New York Central is the sure precursor of a momentous era in railroad annals. The present year is likely to witness the first battle in a war for the European and domestic trade of the West, that may in the end turn the entire current into other channels. It will be a strife of giants, and the prize the most magnificent ever battled for, either in the tented field or in the nobler contests of nations for commercial supremacy. That prize is the carrying trade of an empire fast rising into manly vigor, and destined to attain to a point during the present generation that will dazzle the world with its vastness and grandeur. On one side will be arrayed the Grand Trunk Railway, with its sixty million dollars of capital, backed by the government of Canada, and sustained by every merchant of the British North American colonies, aided by powerful friends in Europe—men of character, standing and capital, who will strain every nerve to supply their darling road with business, in which they will have the sympathy of the whole English people—for in both England and Canada the Grand Trunk is looked upon as a great triumph of national engineering skill, while at the same time it gratifies the national pride, as it gives the world one more convincing proof of that indomitable pluck that is the chief secret of the great celebrity attained by the merchants of the "fast anchored isle" for commercial enterprise.

On the other side will be marshaled the forces of the "Grand Trunk" lines of railroad leading to the Western States from the Atlantic sea-board. The most prominent on the list is the New York Central Railroad, with her natural allies, the Great Western of Canada, the Hudson River Railroad, and the Western Railroad of Massachusetts. Next in order, as parties in the struggle, are the New York and Erie, the Pennsylvania Central, and the Baltimore and Ohio Railroad, not to speak of the local roads in Ohio, Indiana, and Michigan, that will be affected more or less in the contest for supremacy.

The Grand Trunk will fight under one banner, and that banner will carry on its broad folds the commercial prestige of the British Empire, and will have the sympathy of the British people. This, which will probably carry with it, as a coincident, plenty of the "sinews of war," will be decidedly a vantage ground to stand upon.

The American interests will come into the field under different leaders, having no unity of action, and hating and fearing each other; who have never had confidence in each others' words or actions; who have never displayed any generosity toward each other; whose dealings with each other have been marked by cheating and bad faith, as the breaking of all convention treaties has proved. Under such a load of demoralization, all of them combined are perhaps not more than a match for the Grand Trunk. One of the American roads will have to stand in the van and sustain the first onset, and the elected one will be the NEW YORK CENTRAL. In every point of view it is the one best able to do so. It is managed and controlled by men of large experience and iron will—men who do not know what defeat is, and who, come what may, will show that their metal has the true ring.

The result of such a contest none can foresee; albeit after the smoke of the battle is cleared away, the wreck will only show that it has been a costly and useless fight for the stockholders, and the conviction that God's highways are superior to man's will gain strength, insomuch as to assume far more practical importance than it has hitherto attained. The only method of carrying on a successful trade between the Western States and the seaports of Europe, is by water, and to this conclusion all must come, in the end, on both sides of the Atlantic.

In order to make the trade productive of substantial benefit to all interested in it, the West must have free course down the St. Lawrence, and an enlargement of the Canadian canals, so that vessels of say eighteen hundred tons can pass down to the ports of Montreal and Quebec without unloading, and continue on their way to Europe without breaking bulk. A depth of fourteen feet water, with locks of corresponding capacity on the canals would accomplish this important end. The multifarious and rapidly increasing products of the Great West, her timber, flour, wheat, corn, oats, rye, barley, pork, beef, butter, lard, cheese, meal, and every description of agricultural produce could then be laid down in the ports of England so cheaply that it would greatly reduce the cost of the necessaries of life, and give a new impetus to the manufacturing interest of Great Britain. At the same time it would directly tend to cheapen every article that the West requires to import, thus proving of double advantage to our producers. In both cases the producer and consumer would be brought face to face, to the obvious advantage of all concerned. The manufacturing prosperity of England depends upon an unlimited supply of cheap labor, and that supply cannot be had unless she can supply such laborers with an unlimited supply of cheap food. The West has the capacity not only to furnish an inexhaustible quantity of cheap food, but it can purchase and consume a larger amount of the productions of English skill and labor than any other section of the world. Why, then, cannot both parties hit on some scheme that will bring them more closely into the fellowship of trade? It can be done, if both will unite to obtain an unimpeded outlet via the St. Lawrence for vessels and steamers of heavy burden.

So far as Quebec and Montreal are concerned, it is very difficult to say whether the consummation of the proposed enlargement would redound most to their benefit, or to that of our Western lake cities. In both cases the gain would be beyond computation. The two important Canadian cities named would become at once important seaports. They would become two of the depots for the vast commerce of two continents, and would derive great benefits from the opening up of a local traffic with the West, which at present amounts to but very little, so far as they are concerned. Our lake cities would all become large commercial centres, and would supply the population of the region tributary to them, respectively, with dry goods, crockery, hardware, paints, oils, and all kinds of imported merchandise, at a cheaper rate by a considerable per centage, than they could be purchased at New York, or any city on the Atlantic. Detroit would be much nearer Liverpool than Buffalo now is by the usual route, and Chicago and Milwaukee would be almost as near, practically.

A few figures will show the decided advantage of water over rail as a medium of transporting the bulky products of the West to market.

It has already been shown that a ton of any kind of freight cannot be laid down at Portland from Detroit, by rail, under $8.80, without a loss to the stockholders, nor to Boston under $9.65, except with the same result; nor at New York *via* the Great Western, New York Central, and Hudson River roads under $6.82, without actual loss to those roads, so that the case would stand thus:—Detroit to Portland, per ton, *via* G. T. R., $8.80; Detroit to Boston, do. do., $9.85; Detroit to New York, $6.82. Add $4,00 per ton for ocean freights, and we have in each case respectively, $12.80, $13.85, and $10.82 per ton to Liverpool.

Now we maintain that a screw steamer of 1800 tons burden, costing, when completed, $150,000, can carry much cheaper than a road like the Grand Trunk, costing $60,000,000, or the New York Central and its connections. A steamer of that capacity would carry 1,500 tons of freight; 600 tons of coal would run her across the Atlantic, and she could coal from Chicago or Detroit to Newfoundland, and from the latter point to Liverpool. By doing this, she could carry 300 tons more freight than if she coaled for the entire voyage from Chicago to Liverpool. All the principal exports and imports of Michigan, Indiana, Western Ohio, Kentucky, &c., would find their way to Detroit, and this point would of necessity become the great centre of the direct trade between Europe and the States above mentioned.

Two steamers per week could be run with profit on the route during the season of navigation; each steamer would make two round trips and a half per season of seven months' navigation, allowing two months for each round trip. At this rate sixteen ocean steamers would be required to make up a semi-weekly line, and were the Canadian canals enlarged and ready for use by the middle of next April, there would be at once sufficient trade to sustain them, at much cheaper rates for freight and passage than is now charged by any route or combination of routes in existence, as the following will show conclusively:

Each round trip would give the following sums for freight and passage:—1500 tons of freight at $6 per ton, $9,000; 40 cabin passengers at $50 each, $2,000; 50 steerage do. do. $25 each, $1,250. Total for the trip out, $12,250. Inward bound:—600 tons feight at $6, $3,600; 75 cabin passengers at $60, $4,500; 300 steerage do. do., $30, $9.000—$17,100. Add outward receipts, $12,250. Total, $29,350. The total cost of the trip, including insurance, would not exceed $14,000. Total net profits, $15,250.

It will be seen by the above figures that our staple products can be carried to England in the right kind of vessels, at one half the cost that railroads and connecting steamers can perform the same service, even when the latter carry at a rate that brings no profit to the shareholders, while the former would pay large dividends. At the rates named for passage (but little more than one-half the present cost of going from Detroit to England) crowds of the European settlers in this country would flock to the mother country to see dear friends and relatives, and tens of thousands of the American people would embrace the opportunity to behold the tombs and temples and wonders of the land from whence their ancestors came. A feeling of friendship of the true stamp would spring up spontaneously between the Anglo-Saxon races on each side of the Atlantic that never could be severed, and which would alternately shed the blessings of Christianity and civilization to every corner of the world. Such free intercourse would show that to be appreciated by each other they only need to be better acquainted. And it is our firm belief, that the day that beholds the commencement of direct trade between the old world and in the inland seas of the Great West, by vessels of the class named, will see a day of glory and promise brighter and greater than has ever yet dawned on any efforts put forth to subdue the world by human means, to peace and universal brotherhood.

Our readers are aware that a trade of great importance has sprung up within two or three years between Detroit and other lake ports, and the leading seaports of Europe. The particulars of its inauguration are already familiar to the public. Of the vessels which cleared hence in this trade in 1858, one was owned and sent out by a merchant of this city; another was loaded by a Cleveland house; the others were all owned or chartered by Capt. D. C. Pierce, the enterprising pioneer of the trade. His first venture on the *Kershaw*, notwithstanding some few incidental circumstances that worked to his disadvantage, was productive of some direct profit, but a much greater profit inured to himself, and those who followed him in this important commerce, by his becoming well versed in the European trade, insomuch as to be enabled to avail himself of the peculiar advantages offered by each market, as well as in determining the character of freight most profitable to carry. The cheapest, best and safest means of transporting the diversified products of the West, and particularly the region of which Detroit is the centre, to the European markets, reurning with foreign fabrics in exchange, had long challenged the attention of capitalists, who saw in it the germ of a mighty commerce, but seemed to lack the practical knowledge and tact to put the ball in motion. Last year twenty-one vessels cleared from the different lake ports, mostly from Detroit.

Another important point which is now in a fair way to be gained, is the making of European consumers acquainted with the fact that their wants can be supplied to any desired extent. When this information becomes general the consumption must be vastly stimulated, affording one of the most inviting fields for enterprise known in the commercial annals of the world. The resources of the State are amply sufficient to afford employment for half a century to a tenfold larger number of vessels than have yet engaged in it. By a carefully compiled estimate, it has been ascertained that in prosperous times the annual product of our *pineries* is hard upon TEN MILLION DOLLARS. Large as this sum is, it is the opinion of those who are well qualified to form an estimate, that it may easily be surpassed by the product of our hard timber. Take for example the region around Saginaw Bay, which is perhaps the most remarkable locality in the world as respects the quality and variety of hard wood timber. Here, for near a hundred miles in extent, upon streams debouching into the bay, are dense forests of the choicest oak, with a profusion of hickory, black walnut, white ash, whitewood, and other desirable varieties. The manufacture of agricultural implements, as well as many other articles that afford employment to the toiling millions of the old world, must receive a new impetus when it is found that wood admirably adapted to their construction can be had direct from our forests at the moderate rate at which it will bear transportation. So of birds-eye maple for cabinet ware, red elm for carriage hubs, and other varieties applicable to specific uses. We have designated only such as abound in great plenty. The profusion of the growth is in fact equaled only by its accessibility, the whole country being so permeated by streams that it can be floated off with very little trouble.

The Saginaw District, important and extensive as it is, comprises but a small portion of our hard-wood lumber region. In addition to numerous almost interminable forests in the north, equally accessible and almost equally valuable, there are extensive regions in the interior where timber abounds of such choice quality as to abundantly warrant railroad transportation hither. Although some of the shipments last season were of the far-famed Canada oak, shippers all concur in assuring us that the Michigan timber was held in as high estimation, if not higher, than any other offered in the foreign market. A most significant fact, coming right to the point, came under our observation a few months since. In the summer of 1858, five passenger cars for the Michigan Southern Road were built at Adrian, which unprejudiced judges pronounced the finest ever built in the United States. Every foot of timber in them —as well as every pound of iron—was of Michigan production. Last spring, after being in use some twenty months, these cars were for the first time overhauled for repairs, along with a number of eastern cars which had been in use for a like period of time, when it was found that the latter, owing to the inferior quality of timber, cost for repairs nearly as many dollars as the Michigan cars did cents! We have the authority of gentlemen of the highest respectablity for stating this as a literal fact.

The following is a complete list of the vessels which cleared for European ports the past year, together with the character of their cargoes, respectively, and the port to which they sailed:—

Bark D. C. Pierce,	Staves,	Liverpool.
" Allies,	Lumber and staves,	Cork.
" W. S. Pierson,	Lumber and staves,	Greenock.

Bark Massillon,	Lumber and staves,	Liverpool.
Brig J. G. Deshler,	Staves,	Glasgow.
" Caroline,	Lumber and staves,	Liverpool.
" Black Hawk,	Staves,	London.
Schr R. H. Harmon,	Staves,	Liverpool.
" J. F. Warner,	Staves,	Liverpool.
" Gold Hunter,	Staves,	Cork.
" Dousman,	Staves,	London,
" Valeria,	Lumber and staves,	Liverpool.
" Vanguard,	Staves,	Liverpool.
" Grand Turk,	Lumber,	Hamburg.
" St. Helena,	Lumber and staves,	Cork.
" Chieftain,	Lumber and staves,	London,
" C. H. Walker,	Lumber and staves,	Liverpool.
" M. S. Scott,	Lumber,	Hamburg,
" E. Bates,	Lumber and staves,	Liverpool
" H. Barclay,	Staves,	London.
" Republican,	Lumber and staves,	Cadiz.
" Messenger,	Staves, &c.	Calais.

Of the above, Messenger cleared from Buffalo; the Pierson and Republican hailed from Milan, Ohio; the Massillon and Valeria from Cleveland; the Scott loaded at St. Joseph, and was sent out by a Milwaukee house; all the others either loaded at this port, or were owned or chartered here. Eight of the number were chartered by Messrs. Aspinwall & Son, and two of the others were owned here.

The following is the aggregate amount of lumber and staves shipped to Europe the past year, exclusive of the cargoes from Cleveland, Milan, and Buffalo:—

West India staves No........................692,057
Standard pipe staves, No......................142,662
Lumber, feet..................................474,693

[A Quebec standard pipe is equal to four West India staves.]

The Lily of Kingston, was the first vessel that ever passed down from the lakes to the ocean, bound to an European port. Her destination was Liverpool. This was about the year 1847. She afterward sailed in the Quebec and Liverpool trade, but was lost, we believe, on her third ocean voyage.

As collateral to this trade, an important commerce has sprung up between the lake cities and the Atlantic ports which promise to increase rapidly, Prior to 1857, the passage of vessels from the Welland Canal to the ocean was of very rare occurrence. As a matter of curiosity, we present a complete statement of the vessels which have passed through the canal bound for Atlantic or European ports, with the year of sailing, avoiding a repetition of the list above given. The Dean Richmond, and those clearing in 1857 and 1858, all sailed for Europe. Those designated in this list as having sailed in 1859, all cleared for Atlantic ports:

1847...American steam revenue cutter Dallis.
" ...Canadian barque Arabia.
1848...American barque Eureka.
1850...Canadian schooner Scotia.

1854...Canadian schooner Cherokee.
1855...Canadian bark Reindeer.
1856...American schooner Dean Richmond.
1857...American bark C. J. Kershaw.
" ...English schooner Madeira Pet.
1858...American brig Black Hawk.
" ...American schooner R. H. Harmon.
" ...American schooner Col. Cook.
" ...American schooner Correspondent.
" ...American bark D. C. Pierce,
" ...American schooner D. B. Sexton.
" ...American schooner John E. Warner.
" ...American bark H. E. Warner.
" ...American bark C, J. Kershaw,
" ...American schooner C. Reeve.
" ...American schooner Harvest.
" ...American bark Parmelia Flood.
1859...American bark Magenta
" ...American brig Sultan.
" ...American brig Indus.
" ...American brig Kate L. Bruce.
" ...Canadian schooner Union.
" ...American schooner Kyle Spangler.
" ...American schooner Muskingum.
" ...American schooner Adda.
" ...American schooner Clifton.
" ...American schooner Metropolis.
" ...American schooner Energy.
" ...American schooner W. B. Castle.
" ...American schooner Alida.
" ...American tug Uncle Ben.
" ...American tug Cushman,
" ...American schooner Typhoon.
" ...American schooner Sarah Hibbert.

Presuming that those who may hereafter become interested in this commerce, would like the benefit of the experience of those who have already embarked it, we have procured some valuable information for their benefit. First, as to the kind of timber most profitable to ship: Although black walnut appears to be growing in favor, and where once it has been used is again inquired for, yet a decided preference is given to oak, with the qualities of which all are entirely familiar. Choice, selected oak commands more money for cabinet purposes in all the foreign markets than the same quality of black walnut. Contrary to previous expectation, it is not likely that the latter can ever be brought into general use in Great Britain. It is the greatest mahogany market in the world, and that wood is in universal use, particularly the common or cheap kind. If ever so common, it is not liable to warp, which cannot be said of black walnut, although, as we have before intimated, those who have worked it, praise it very highly. Beech, elm and ash, are used for a great many purposes, and are in good demand, but oak commands more money than either of them, and is therefore the most profitable to ship at present.

The fact is notg enerally known, but the information has been purchased at a dear rate, that the purchase of lumber for the foreign market by board-measure, instead of cubic, involves a heavy loss. In European markets all lumber is sold by the cubic foot, so that the cost of sawing is completely thrown away. Black walnut, for example, cannot be laid down in Detroit, or any lake port, under $18 to $20 per M., while the lumber can be obtained for $125 to $150 per M. cubic feet, 1,000 feet cubic measure being equal to 12,000 feet board measure. Thus in purchasing by cubic measure, the buyer pays only $125 to $150 for an amount that by board measure would cost $216 to $240, making a clear difference of *ninety dollars* upon only one thousand cubic feet, equal to $900 upon a cargo of some of the vessels engaged in the trade last year. The same rule would apply substantially to other kinds of lumber. Independent of this, a decided preference is given to lumber in the log, owing to the good condition in which it can be delivered. There is one more point which manufacturers as well as shippers should bear in mind. The value of much of the lumber sent out was greatly impaired by being attached to the heart, which is the most porous part of the tree, and therefore most liable to crack. To obviate this objection the saw should pass upon each side of the heart, thus leaving the whole of it attached to a single piece of timber, instead of one or more pieces, and thereby making only one cull. By observing this rule a difference will be made in the market of thirty or forty per cent.

Are staves or lumber the more profitable to ship? This depends upon circumstances. Last year it was very dull for both. For staves especially the season could not, for various reasons, have been more unfavorable. In the first place, the grape crop was a very short one, not only in France, but in all the vine countries, including the Canaries. This, of course, greatly lessened the demand for staves, and there were consequently very few taken from England to France, although French vessels are in the habit of taking them for ballast at a merely nominal rate, owing to the difficulty they experience in procuring return freights from England. The short crops in Canada and the great scarcity of money, forced an unusual number of laborers in that country into the stave and lumber business. Under advices that heavy shipments were in prospect, coupled with the general check upon business on account of the war, prices became depressed. Notwithstanding all this, the shipments hence, being early in the market, sold to advantage, and may therefore be considered as a signal success, under the circumstances. The smallest vessel going out from here netted a freight of $3,500.

The most striking feature with regard to Detroit, in a commercial point of view, is her admirable location, which constitutes her the metropolis of a vast region, than which no city off the sea-board can boast one equally grand or important. The region embraces a circuit of some three thousand miles, composed of land and water, which both seem to vie with each other in contributing to the material prosperity of our city, while every interest involved is benefited in some degree by her. In the far north, where the rugged coast of the upper peninsula is lashed by the waters of the monarch of lakes, Detroit enterprise assists in redeeming the hidden treasures of the earth from their state of profitless inertion. There is not a hardy delver in the mines who is not familiar with the skill of Detroit machinists, nor an echo in all the majestic wilds skirting that noble expanse of waters, that has not been awakened by Detroit steamers. Further down upon the limpid waters of Lake Huron, where the army or rather the navy of fishermen set their nets for the capture of the finny tribes, here, too, our city possesses an interest almost as direct as if the canvas of their tiny crafts were spread within sight of her spires, the product comprising one of the most important staples in her multiform commerce. Last, but not least, is the great lumber region with which the prosperity of Michigan is so largely identified. The population of this region, as well as of the others we have referred to, raise almost literally nothing for their own consumption, their respective pursuits being inconsistent with that of tillers of the soil, so that in addition to the usual stores required by farmers, they have to purchase their breadstuffs and similar supplies. The bulk of these are bought of our dealers, this being not only the most convenient, but the cheapest and best market, as is amply proven by experience.

Under the appropriate head will be found a complete and authentic statement of the commerce of the Saut St. Mary Canal, by which it will be seen that the aggregate value of the upward-bound freight is estimated at $5,298,640. The up-freight nearly all carried by steamers, of which the number running the entire season was seven, three from Detroit, one from Chicago, and three from Cleveland. The Detroit boats have generally been loaded to their utmost capacity, while we have the word of the Cleveland captains to the effect that two-thirds of their cargoes are usually taken on at this port. We must therefore be clearly within bounds in claiming that three-fourths of the above amount is part and parcel of the commerce of our city which would show our Lake Superior exports to be $3,960,000. In seasons in which the crops of our Canadian neighbors partially fail—a common occurrence within the past few years, but which we hope may never occur again—they naturally become our customers; and since the partial destruction of the wheat crop in Ohio last summer by frost, there have been considerable shipments of breadstuffs to Cleveland, Toledo, Sandusky, etc., which may very properly be included in the home traffic.

The shipments of flour and grain for the supply of our home trade by lake craft, from the opening of navigation for the year 1859, as appears by the books of our Custom House, are as follows:

	Flour.	Wheat.	Corn.
Port Huron	10,885	253	6,916
Saginaw	3,790	30	..
Cleveland	6,155	28,057	1,146
Thunder Bay	106	..	..
Green Bay	175	..	..
Northport	175	..	..
Sandusky	705	..	..
Huron, O.	660	..	..
Toledo	665	616	..
Lake Superior	11,321	..	..

	Flour.	Wheat.	Corn.
Other Amrican ports...........	245....	.. ....	..
Malden	1,289....	160....	14,548
Chatham	3,671....	1,736....	..
Wallaceburg	705....	.. ....	..
Goderich	.. ....	318....	1,274
Saugeen	168....	.. ....	..
Bayfield	.. ....	200....	..
Other Canadian ports...........	1,330....	95....	749

There were also 7,446 bushels oats to Port Huron, and 588 bushels do. to other ports, beside 3,400 bushels corn, and 11,962 bushels oats which were included in the heavy shipments to Lake Superior. We give the places for which vessels cleared; many of the shipments were for intermediate ports. Besides the flour and grain there were large shipments of pork, butter, lard, meal, etc., etc.

The above were all by water. There were in addition large local shipments to various points on the Great Western, the Detroit and Milwaukee, and other roads, that may with equal propriety be regarded as pertaining to the home trade.

The article of corn is one to secure customers, for in Canada it is not essential there should be short crops there. Large amounts are taken for the supply of the numerous distilleries on that side. A single house in our city has sold the past year 100,000 bushels for that purpose.

During the year commodities have been interchanged by lake craft between Detroit and no fewer than sixty-three lake and river ports, to say nothing of the hundreds of towns and cities on the various railroads that are daily trading with us. We have not included those ports to which the bulk of our surplus produce is forwarded, but only such as come strictly within the scope of our subject. There are few places where trade develops statistics of similar character, or anything approximating thereto, while there are plenty of cities of no inconsiderable pretensions, and even great advantages, that would think themselves made if they possessed one-fourth the commercial facilities we enjoy.

Within the past year, by the opening up of new and most important channels of railway communication, our position with respect to the great railway system of the continent, is rendered all that could be desired. In that regard it is indeed difficult to point out how any improvement could be made. With respect to our local advantages, however, admirable as they are, there is yet much in store for us. The signs are far more favorable than at any former period for the rapid settlement of the State, as well as for the more adequate development of her resources. We are constantly receiving intelligence that some new source of wealth has been revealed within our borders, or that one previously discovered is likely to surpass the expectations at first entertained. These events must not only tend directly to hasten the settlement of the State, but also add in a still greater ratio to her commercial importance and her wealth.

If we were to fail to refer, in this connection, to the law passed by our legislature last winter, providing for the reclamation of the "swamp lands," technically so called, and inaugurating an admirable system of State roads throughout all the upper portions of the State, we should be ignoring decidedly the most pregnant of the signs of promise. In adopting so well-timed and beneficent a measure, our law-givers have proved themselves worthy guardians of a commonwealth whose interests so plainly bespeak a much greater degree of wise legislation than has heretofore been wielded for her benefit. Next in importance to these wholesome measures, is the law providing for the appointment of Commissioners of Emigration—one resident here, and the other stationed in New York. Those seeking homes in the West have only to be made aware of the unequaled inducements presented by our State, to secure immense accessions to our population.

Detroit does not alone reap the benefit of her advantageous position. It is shared by all interests, but perhaps by none others to so great an extent as the tillers of the soil. It is a most significant fact that breadstuffs and provisions not unfrequently bring as high prices here as in New York, giving producers all the advantages at home of a sea-board market, and virtually putting the cost of shipment into their pockets. Thus a farmer whose land possesses a nominal value of ten or twenty dollars per acre, can enjoy all the pecuniary advantages of a location near one of the largest eastern cities, where farms are valued at one to two hundred dollars per acre. This fact alone should go very far toward transforming our northern wilderness into cultivated fields.

As a matter of interest, and to some extent of curiosity, we present a comparative statement exhibiting the ruling prices of extra Michigan flour twice a month throughout the year, in Detroit, New York and Liverpool, and also the prices in the latter market, for the corresponding dates in the year 1858:

	Liverpool, '58.	Liv'l., '59.	N. York, '59.	Detroit, '59.
Jan. 1st.	5 76a6 74	4 80a5 04	4 95a5 15	5 00a5 12
" 15th.	5 76a6 24	4 80a5 04	5 60a5 85	5 00a5 12
Feb. 1st.	5 76a6 24	4 80a5 04	5 90a6 40	5 75a6 00
" 15th.	5 52a6 00	4 80a5 04	5 90a6 25	6 25a6 50
Mar'h 1st.	5 52a6 24	4 80a5 04	6 30a6 50	6 25a6 50
" 15th.	5 52a6 24	4 80a5 04	6 50a6 75	6 50a6 75
April 1st.	5 28a5 52	4 80a5 04	6 30a6 75	a6 75
" 15th.	5 28a5 76	4 80a5 04	6 00a6 60	a6 50
May 1st.	5 28a5 52	5 04a5 28	6 25a6 75	a6 50
" 15th.	5 28a5 52	6 00a6 24	7 30a7 85	a8 00
June 1st.	5 04a5 28	a5 76	7 00a7 40	a7 50
" 15th.	5 04a5 28	a5 76	6 70a7 05	7 12a7 25
July 1st.	5 04a5 28	a	6 00a6 50	a7 25
" 15th.	5 08a5 40	5 04a5 28	5 45a6 00	7 00a7 12
Aug. 1st.	5 28a5 40	4 80a5 52	4 90a5 50	4 75a4 87
" 15th.	5 04a5 28	5 04a5 52	4 30a4 65	4 50a4 75
Sept. 1st.	5 16a5 40	5 04a5 52	4 40a5 00	4 62a4 75
" 15th.	5 16a5 40	4 80a5 52	4 65a4 85	4 25a4 50
Oct. 1st.	5 04a5 28	5 28a5 76	4 75a5 10	4 62a4 75
" 15th.	5 04a5 28	5 28a5 76	4 80a5 20	a4 75
Nov. 1st.	5 04a5 28	5 52a6 00	5 00a5 30	a5 00
" 15th.	4 80a5 04	5 76a6 24	5 24a5 45	a5 12
Dec. 1st.	4 80a5 04	6 76a7 00	5 45a5 65	a5 12
" 15th.	4 80a5 04	6 76a7 00	5 48a5 65	a5 12

The Detroit mills manufacture excellent flour, and it is to be regretted that they are not capable of making a much larger quantity of their well-known brands. There are six flouring mills of different capacities in the city, and although they are generally at full work such is the demand for flour they make, that they are very often not able to supply their customers. These mills ought to be enlarged, or others built. Detroit, the commercial metropolis of a great wheat-growing State, should be capable of manufacturing an immense quantity of flour. The increased expenditure of money, in the purchase of wheat, would be very beneficial to the trade of the city.

For the last fifteen years, the exports of bread-stuffs from the United States have fluctuated very much. In 1846 they amounted to nearly twenty-eight millions of dollars, and rose in 1847 to sixty-nine millions. In 1848 they fell to thirty-seven, and in 1852 to twenty-six millions. In 1853 they amounted to nearly thirty-three millions, and in 1854 they rose to about sixty-millions, but fell in 1855 to about thirty-nine millions, and again rose in 1857 to seventy-seven millions. In 1858 they again declined to about fifty millions. We cannot accurately detail the exports of 1859, but they have been very light on account of fall in the European market, after the termination of the war in Italy. During these years there were various causes for the remarkable fluctuations which we have noted; namely, famine in Ireland, the Crimean war, and the failures of the harvest at home and abroad, nor have these exportations been regularly divided or spread over the various months of each year. They have increased or diminished according to the European demand, governed by the supply at home and regulated by advices from the other side of the Atlantic. It is likely that the export of breadstuffs in 1860 will be very considerable.

Michigan possesses many advantages over her sister States, and these enable her to bear up against monetary panics better than they. Her immense length of lake coast is indented with excellent harbors, which invite commerce from every quarter, and furnish excellent outlets for her surplus produce or mineral wealth. The great and diversified resources of the State support her in the evil day, and bring her through a commercial crisis in safety. From the ushering in of the year to the close, there is not a day in which the marts of commerce are not enlivened by the contributions of grain or live stock from our fields, fish from our lakes, lumber from our forests, or ores of various kinds from our inexhaustible mines.

According to the census returns of 1840, the State of Michigan produced 2,157,108 bushels of wheat, there were 190 flouring mills at work, employing 491 hands, and producing 202,880 barrels of flour annually. In 1853 this State produced

7,275,032 bushels of wheat, there were 245 flouring mills at work, employing 604 persons, and manufacturing 1,000,000 barrels of flour in a year. It will be seen that the flouring mills have increased greatly both in number and capacity since 1840, and that very large quantities of flour are now manufactured in the interior of the State, a circumstance which partly accounts for the comparatively small quantity of wheat that is now exported. The number of flouring mills have doubtless increased since 1853, and as steam power has been applied in many instances their manufacturing capacity must now be very great. Farmers are beginning to understand the importance of disposing of their produce near home, and having the surplus exported in a manufactured state, instead of sending away the raw material; the bran and "shorts" being very valuable for mixing with the food of horses, cattle, and swine. A flouring mill is a great benefit in a rural district, it furnishes the farmer with a home market, and when he receives the price of his produce, there are many domestic wants which must be supplied, and on this account we always see stores and mechanics' shops clustering around a mill, and villages springing up in places where the solitude of the forest was, until lately, unbroken by a sound.

It is evident that the mill power of Michigan is increasing rapidly, and that in future the greater part of the surplus grain crop will be exported in a manufactured state.

In former years the prices of grain in the United States were controlled by the European markets, and consequently the grain trade of the Western States was governed by the produce merchants in the Atlantic ports, but lately the whole order of things seems to have been reversed, as breadstuffs of every kind were dearer in the Western than in the Eastern markets. There were several reasons for this anomaly. On account of the ravages of insects, and other causes which we have alluded to, farmers were induced to place very little reliance on the wheat crop, and many were driven into other branches of husbandry, and in some places wheat became scarce. Add to this the rapid increase of the population which created a local demand for all kinds of food, and caused immense quantities of breadstuffs to be required in places where a few years before there was no market for anything. The rapid and extraordinary growth of Detroit and all the Western cities, and the formation of new settlements, created a home market for Western produce, for the population of cities being consumers of the fruits of the land, instead of producers, have always a wonderful effect on the markets of their localities, and the pioneers in the forest or prairie must for a time depend on the older settlements for subsistence.

From a defective system of agriculture the soil of the old States has been deteriorating for several years. In Massachusetts the hay crop declined twelve per cent. from 1840 to 1850, notwithstanding the addition of 90,000 acres of mowing lands and the grain crop depreciated 6000 bushels, although no less than 6000 acres had been added to the tillage lands of that State.

In 1840 the wheat crop of New York was about twelve and a quarter millions of bushels, and only nine millions in 1850, a decrease of 25 per cent., while the Indian corn in the same State increased during the same period from about ten to twenty millions of bushels. The harvest of 1859, found several parts of the country entirely destitute of flour, and the farmers with a fixed and firm determination never again to allow themselves to run out of the staff of life.

The number and capacity of the flouring mills have increased considerably since 1853, so that it is probable that there are at present more than three hundred of them at work in the State, and the number of hands employed by them cannot be much less than twelve hundred. It is probable that they are now capable of manufacturing 1,25,000 barrels of flour annually, and this quantity would require 5,625,000 bushels of wheat. Add to this the large quantity of seed required for sowing an increased breadth of land, and the portion of the crop kept for domestic use, and the result will be sufficient to explain the reason why so little wheat has been exported from Michigan this season. There are about 50,000 families in this State who depend on agriculture for subsistence; all of these had suffered more or less inconvenience form failure of the wheat crop, and the high price of flour for the last few years, and it is no wonder that they should endeavor to secure a full supply of wheat or flour of the produce of the late harvest, and a very large portion of the crop was disposed of in this way.

Since the Reciprocity Treaty came into operation, thre has been considerable exportation of flour from Detroit to Canada on account of the repeated failures of the wheat crop in that country, and thus a new market for Michigan produce has been opened near home.

Some of these sources of demand are trifling when

standing alone, but the aggregate makes a very large amount. It is considered that about half the produce of the wheat crop still remains in the hands of the farmers and may be expected to reach the market gradually.

Michigan wants woolen and cotton, and various other factories to provide employment for the over-crowded population of her cities and villages, and to open a market for all her produce. The farmers of Great Britain and Ireland could not pay the high rents and taxes which are imposed on them, were it not far their proximity to the great manufacturing cities of England. The cotton factories of Manchester, the woolen factories of Leeds and Huddersfield, the hardware works of Birmingham and Sheffield, and the potteries of Staffordshire, employ hundreds of thousands of men, women, and children, who consume the fruits of the soil, and create a steady demand for the farmer's stock and grain. All these manufactures were fostered by protective laws until they had attained a magnitude and importance which enabled them to protect themselves by the wealth of their proprietors and the excellence of their products. Large cities always afford a market for farm produce, and on this account exert a very beneficial influence on agriculture. The population of

London is about two and a half millions, and they are possessed of so much wealth, and are so fastidious in their requirements, that almost every part of the world contributes to supply them with the necessaries or luxuries of life. The rapid growth of the cities of Michigan afford a home market for the fruits of the the soil. A great deal of land in the old settlements of this State has been exhausted by a too frequent repetition of the wheat crop, and is now being employed as pasture for sheep and cattle. After remaining in grass for a few years, this land will be in excellent condition for producing wheat, especially when fertilized with that plentiful supply of barn-yard dung which the raising of stock always produces.

There are some varieties of wheat which are much better suited to the climate and soil of Michigan than others, as they are in a great measure able to withstand the combined attacks of wheat insects and the various diseases to which the plant is liable. These are now fast supplanting the worn out grain, and as every malady has its cure or preventive, it is probable that the introduction of the best kind of seeds, the alternation between grass and tillage, and the supply of rich manure which the raising of stock creates will have a very great tendency to improve the wheat crop of this State.

It is a remarkable fact that although the wheat crop has rather declined in the majority of States, the corn crop has steadily increased in all of them. Thus in 1840, the entire corn crop of the United States amounted to 400,000,000 of bushels; in 1850 it was nearly 600,000,000 of bushels. The crop of 1855 was between 7 and 800,000,000, and that of 1858 was fully 800,000,000 of bushels. Taking into consideration the large breadth of land planted in 1859 and the damage by the frost, we might with safety set down the crop as amounting to 800,000,000 bushels.

Last year our importations from Indiana were large, but since the new crop came in, that State has been shipping largely toward the Ohio River, and we get comparatively little. The immense distilleries of Cincinnati consume a very large quantity of corn annually, and Indiana is beginning to find a good market in that quarter. The demand for Michigan corn is always active on account of its excellent milling qualities, and on this account it generally sells from wagons as high, or a shade higher than the outside figure for Western corn from store. The corn crop of Illinois has been much injured by the frosts of June and July, and on this account the receipts in Chicago up to this date have been much lighter than usual. The European potato crop has been greatly damaged by rot, and it is probable that a large export of corn will take place from this country in order to supply a deficiency occasioned by this failure. It is said that several New York capitalists have gone west and purchased corn and provisions, storing them up until next spring, anticipating at that time a considerable advance in price. The generality of farmers have sorted their corn carefully this year and used up the unripe and inferior part for feeding hogs and cattle: there is a large quantity of very good corn in the country, which will no doubt command a good price in the spring.

Indian corn is one of the staple productions of Michigan, and can be raised with success in any suitable soil in the lower peninsula. According to the statistics of 1850 this State produced nearly 6,000,000 of bushels that year. It is probable that the census of the present year will show a vast increase in the amount. In 1850 the value of this crop in all the States amounted to nearly $300,000-000, being about equal to the united values of the wheat, hay, and cotton crops, and it has perhaps doubled since that date. In fact the value of the corn crop to Michigan and all the other States cannot be estimated, as it is much used for the food of man and all the domestic animals, and to it the American farmer is indebted for much of his prosperity, for without it he would not be able to bring his cattle and hogs into the market at the right time and in proper condition.

Heretofore the amount of pork packed has always been insufficient to meet the demand, and the deficiency has been supplied by importations from other cities, chiefly from Cincinnati. This season not only has there been a considerable increase in the number packed, but the market opens a great deal duller than last year, when the Canada trade and the building of the Detroit and Port Huron link of the Grand Trunk Railway induced a fair demand.

Cincinnati is the greatest provision maket on the continent or in the world. At that place speculation has been quite rife for the past two or three years, operators obtaining a controlling interest in the stock for the purpose of putting up prices. Last year the plan did not work well, owing to various causes, one of which was the small number of works in progress, such as railroads, etc., the supply of the laborers upon such works, being the life of the provision trade. Heavy losses were sustained, but it is said that the sufferers were a different class from that regularly engaged in the trade. This season the speculative fever has again prevailed. The issue has yet to be revealed.

Last year nearly 1,000 head of cattle were slaughtered here, all of which were forwarded to Lake Superior as soon as packed. The price of mess beef has ranged from $8.50 to $12.00. About the first of July prices reached their highest point. During the fall the range has been from $8.50 to $10.00.

When the marshy lands, skirting our water-courses in St. Clair, Macomb, Wayne, and Monroe counties, shall have been drained, (which will, no doubt, be consummated at no distant day,) a large tract will be rendered available for grazing, which will prove equal for that purpose to any in the Union. Butter and cheese will then become a leading article in our commerce.

Potatoes constitute another of our staple products, and, in seasons of scarcity elsewhere, large purchases are made for shipment, but being generally based on present demand, they can hardly be called speculative. The crop of 1857 was rather meagre, and last spring and summer prices ruled high, going up to $1.20 for a short time in June. Last year we had an abundant crop, since which, under a limited export demand, prices have ruled low. The receipts at this point, from all sources, did not vary greatly from 175,000 bushels, of which 80,500 bushels were exported, chiefly to Ohio and the upper country.

It is claimed, that southern Michigan produces more fine fruit than any other locality of the same extent in the United States, if not on the globe. At the same time almost every quarter of the State is constantly improving both in quality and quantity. This fact is creditable to the sagacity of our agriculturists, for probably in nothing else can an equal amount of profit be realized with the same outlay.

Our market is not an important one for live stock, much of the greater share of the receipts by rail being through freight. Our wholesale market is mainly governed by that at the East, buyers for shipment are always on the look-out, and whenever anything can be purchased that affords even a moderate margin, it is promptly taken. Extra cattle are always sought for by our butchers, and command full rates. A spirit of emulation on the subject of fine stock is pervading the minds of our farmers, and, as a consequence, its quality is rapidly improving. At the last State Fair, the display of cattle was such as to elicit the admiration of good judges from abroad.

There are so many interests claiming the attention of our agriculturists, that the idea of becoming famous as to *quantity*, is perhaps precluded; if so, they may well rest content in the attainment of high rank in point of *quality*.

The raising of fine sheep is constantly attracting more and more attention, and from the progress already made by our State, she bids fair at no distant day to take a position in advance of all her sister States,

The year 1859 opened with rather flattering prospects for wool-growers. The last year's stock was nearly exhausted before the new clip came into the market. Prices of woolen fabrics were advancing, and bid fair to rule high. On the eve of the wool season prices declined in the Eastern markets, although there was no particular reason for this unfavorable turn. It was considered at the time, that the fall in prices was occasioned by a regular combination among buyers to break down the market. The news of the passage of the Ticino by the Austrians, and the actual commencement of hostilities in Italy, arrived in this country before the wool was brought into the market, and this circumstance was seized on as a pretext for lowering the price of the new clip. Buyers were very industrious in circulating reports that a general European war was commencing, and, as it was not known how affairs would terminate, it would be unsafe for American buyers to make investments in the wool trade, except at prices that would leave a large margin for profit. It was fortunate that farmers did not take the same view of transatlantic complications, for they refused to sell except at remunerating prices, a decision which caused some of the Eastern buyers to retire from the market in disgust. Almost the entire press of Michigan supported the views of the farmers on this occasion, and declared that they could see no reason why the war in Italy should affect the prices of wool in America, especially as all the domestic clip, and a very large quantity of foreign wool would be manufactured in this country. Michigan produces excellent wool. There are numerous flocks of French, Spanish, and Saxon Merinos in this State, which have been selected or bred with the greatest care, and the wool produced by them cannot be surpassed in any of the Western States. There are also flocks of coarse-wooled sheep which produce heavy fleeces, and when fattened for the butcher make excellent mutton. In 1840 the wool clip of this State was about 150,000 lbs., in 1850 something over 2,000,000 lbs., and 1859 it amounted to nearly 4,000,000 lbs. It will be seen by these figures that it has nearly doubled during the last nine years. There are but few woolen manufactories in Michigan, and the most of the wool clip of this State is purchased by Eastern manufacturers. A considerable portion of it goes to Boston and other parts of Massachusetts. We want a large woolen factory in Detroit, where everything that is necessary for its operation can be easily procured. We want more manufactories of every kind in Michigan.

Our city is largely interested in the shipping business, and its trade gives employment to a larger number of side-wheel steamboat lines than any other three cities on the entire chain of lakes. During the last season, the following regular lines of steamers were in successful operation:

Detroit and Cleveland,	Detroit, G. Bay and Buffalo,
Detroit and Toledo.	Detroit, and Lake Superior.
Detroit and Sandusky.	Detroit and Port Huron.
Detroit and Saginaw.	Detroit and Chatham.
Detroit and New Baltimore.	Detroit and Wallaceburg.
Detroit and Malden.	Detroit and Gibraltar.

Two of the above routes sustain opposition lines, and to the list might be added the line of lake steamers to Buffalo, and the line to Goderich, which though not run last year, will probably be in successful operation the coming season, making in all sixteen lines. It is significant that the late financial revulsion, which fell with such crushing weight upon the shipping interest all over the country did not occasion the withdrawal of any of our steamboat lines, save one. As a still more striking fact, we may state that until last season none of the cities located in the vast region between the foot of Lake Michigan and the foot of Lake Erie, has for many years past supported a single line of steamers that did not make Detroit a terminus. Last year a line was put in successful operation between Buffalo and Cleveland, and another between the latter place and Toledo, but it ought to be added that both of these were established by Detroit enterprise.

In addition to the line above enumerated, we have daily lines of propellers to Ogdensburg, Buffalo, Dunkirk and to the Upper Lakes, which do an immense freighting business.

We are indebted to Captain J. H. Hall, the public-spirited proprietor of the Detroit shipping-office for following statement of the number of vessels that passed Detroit in 1859:

Number of Vessels passing Detroit, 1859.

	No. Times.		No. Times.
Steamers passed up,	194	Steamers passed down,	195
Propellers, "	492	Propellers, "	503
Barks, "	273	Barks, "	284
Brigs "	295	Brigs, "	314
Schooners, "	1,811	Schooners, "	1,825
Total number up,	3,065	Total number down,	3,121

Greatest number passed up in one day, eighty-five; greatest number down, seventy-three.

The number of entries and clearances reported at the Custom House during the year is as follows:

	Arrived.	Cl'd.		Arrived.	Cl'd.
Jan	48	70	July	403	597
Feb	49	71	Aug	461	519
March	161	288	Sept	316	481
April	334	375	Oct	288	319
May	438	586	Nov	294	316
June	458	568	Dec	45	71

During the past year the amount of total losses has been light, not greater, probably, than the number of vessels built, so that although the classification is slightly changed, there is no material change so far as concerns the aggregate tonnage. Detroit owns, therefore, *nearly one-sixth of the entire tonnage of the lakes.*

As a matter of some interest we present a comparative statement showing the tonnage, steam, and total, of a number of the more important maritime places in the country, taken from the report of the Register of the Treasury on Commerce and Navigation:

	Steam tonnage.	Total tonnage.
New York	118,638	1,432,705
New Orleans	70,072	210,411
Philadelphia	22,892	219,851
Baltimore	18,821	194,488
Pittsburg	42,474	56,824
Cincinnati	23,136	26,541
Chicago	8,151	67,001
St. Louis	55,515	61,266
Boston	9,452	448,896
Buffalo	42,640	73,478
Detroit	35,266	62,485
Charleston, S. C.	8,230	60,196

The following exhibits the number and tonnage of vessels owned in this district—nearly all of them in this city—on the 31st of December, 1859:

	Number	Tons.	95ths
Steamers	73	29,175	02
Propellers	32	6,090	81
Barks	4	1,337	08
Brigs	7	1,877	75
Schooners	131	19,671	56
Scows and all others	136	4,322	68
Total	383	62,485	05
In 1857	301	52,991	50
Increase in two years	82	9,493	50

The following was the aggregate tonnage of the lakes in December 1858:

	AMERICAN.		
69	Side-wheel steamers register tons		44,562
110	Propellers	do.	45,562
70	Tugs (propellers)	do.	6,880
46	Barks	do.	18,788
79	Brigs	do.	22,558
711	Schooners	do.	166,725
109	Scows	do.	11,848
1194	Total		316,923

	CANADIAN.		
67	Side-wheel steamers, register tons		25,966
16	Propellers	do.	4,631
4	Tugs (propellers)	do.	388
19	Barks	do.	5,697
16	Brigs	do.	2,988
186	Schooners	do.	19,311
13	Scows	do.	609
321	Total		59,580

The Michigan Central was the first railroad built in the State, and since its completion has been known as one of the best managed in the West. Its beneficial effects to the region of country through which it passes, is incalculable. On its line, have sprung up a number of beautiful towns and villages as if by magic, while many of those that had an existence prior to its construction have grown into flourishing cities. Ypsilanti, Ann Arbor, Jackson, Marshall,

Battle Creek, Albion, Kalamazoo, Niles, and others that might properly be included, all located upon this road, are beautiful places, noted for their thrift and enterprise as well as for their rapid advances in all that pertains to well-regulated cities. Their commerce is rapidly increasing and the country along the entire route will vie with that traversed by the great throughfares of any of the older States along the seaboard.

The Central was commenced and partially built by the State, but in 1844, passed into the possession of the company now owning it, who completed it to Chicago. A telegraph line has been in use for some years past along the entire line of the road, with an office at each station, by which means the exact position of each train may be at all times known at each and every point. To this admirable system may be attributed in a very great degree the extraordinary exemption of the road from serious accidents, while its advantages are very great in every point of view respecting the general management. The eastern terminus of the road being at Detroit, it has the full advantages of the numerous connections at this point, the Great Western and Grand Trunk Railways, the important steamboat route from Cleveland, the lines of Detroit and Buffalo propellers with their immense freight traffic, as well as the numerous other steamboat routes of which our city is the nucleus. At Chicago it has the advantages of connection with all the roads radiating from that flourishing city. Freight is now taken from Chicago to Portland without breaking bulk but once. An important "feeder" is the Joliet Cut-off, by means of which it has a direct connection with St. Louis, via the Chicago, Alton, and St. Louis Railroad. An important arrangement was consummated last summer with the latter road, for the direct transmission of freight between this city and St. Louis. Fifty cars have been diverted to this route, under the name of the "Detroit and St. Louis Through Freight Line." The time between the two cities is thirty-eight hours. The advantages of this line to shippers are very considerable, and the arrangement is adding, and will continue to add, materially to the commerce of our city.

A commendable progressive spirit has latterly been evinced by the managers generally, of our railroads, in the transmission of freight, especially live stock and grain. The improvement is a most grateful one to shippers, who have ordinarily quite enough anxiety and vexation to suffer in the fluctuations of the market and subjection to unlooked for and onerous charges, without having superadded unreasonable exposure and deterioration of their property while en route to market. In this movement the management of the Central has fully sympathized. Their stock and grain cars have received high commendations from those for whose benefit they were intended. The entire equipment of the road is such as to comport with them; the safety, comfort and convenience of the public, being constantly kept in view, regardless of the cost incurred.

The three staunch and magnificent steamers belonging to the company, the Plymouth Rock, Western World and Mississippi, owing to the hard times have been laid up at their dock since the fall of 1857, to the great regret of the public generally, as well as to the detriment of the business interest of our city. With the return of a more prosperous era they will doubtless be again placed in commission. The line formed by these boats is the most pleasant and expeditious medium of communication between the East and the West and Southwest, and cannot fail to be well patronized, especially now that the Dayton and Michigan Railroad is completed, which will bring a large amount of both freight and passenger traffic by way of Detroit that formerly sought other routes.

The rolling stock now on the road consists of ninty-eight engines, seventy first class passenger cars, twelve second class cars; twenty-nine baggage cars, and two thousand seven hundred and seventy-eight freight cars, making a total of two thousand eight hundred and eighty-nine cars and all of which were built in the company's own shops.

This road is one hundred and eighty-eight miles long, and has been in operation throughout its whole extent since November, 1858. It is deserving of the distinctive appellation of the *Back Bone Road of Michigan*, having been of incalculable value in developing the resources of the region through which it is located, decidely one of the richest and most important in the West. The principal towns and cities upon its line are Pontiac, Fentonville, St. Johns, Ionia, Grand Rapids and Grand Haven. The growth of these places has received a great impetus since its completion, while numerous villages have also sprung into being as if by magic at various points along the line. These changes are plainly visible in the improved trade of our city, and the increase from the same cause, must continue to be strongly marked. Last season over one-fourth of the wheat and wool received here was by this new route, and a number of vessels loaded at the company's noble and spacious wharf for European ports direct.

Within the year past, the company have completed one of the finest railway wharves in the world. It is 1,500 feet long by 90 broad, the west end of which is occupied by the freight house, the dimensions of which are 450 by 132 feet.

One of the most important events to Detroit and the entire West, that has transpired for many years, is the completion of this great thoroughfare. The link from Port Huron to this city was opened to traffic on the 21st of November, since which date the businesss crowding upon it has fully equaled its capacity. It is the Minerva of railways, having reached at a single bound a condition of prosperity outrivaling many of the oldest established roads on the continent.

It possesses important advantages over any other road both for freight and passenger traffic. Being of uniform guage, no change of cars will be necessary from Sarnia to Portland; and being also under the management of one corporation, it affords better facilities for the protection of passengers and the preservation of their baggage than where they are required to pass over lines under the control of different and perhaps conflicting corporations. Having only one set of officers quartered upon its exchequer, it can afford to do business at lower proportionate rates, than a number of shorter lines, each having a different set to salary, while the delay and vexation which not unfrequently arise from short routes, being compelled to wait upon each other's movements, will all be avoided, which is certainly no small consideration both to passengers and shippers.

The harbor of Portland is one of the finest and most eligible in the world, and our immediate connection with a point of such importance is of itself a matter deserving particular mention. Portland district, as appears by the official statement of the tonnage of the United States, made to June, 1857, then owned 145,242 tons of shipping, being the ninth port in the Union in point of tonnage; she is very largely interested in the West India trade, her annual imports of molasses exceeding those of any port in the United States. She offers, therefore, to the Western States, peculiar facilities for procuring at a cheap rate the products of the West Indies. The harbor is without any bar, and so easy of access that no pilots are required, and strangers, with the sailing directions given in the American Coast Pilot, have brought their ships into it with safety.

There are no port charges, harbor dues, or lighthouse fees, excepting the official custom house fees.

The Grand Trunk Railway is likely to become the avenue through which an immense tide of immigration will pour into Michigan. It will be a favorite route for emigrants, who will thus avoid the rascally impositions of the swindlers and Peter Funks of New York, who have given that city an unenviable notoriety throughout the world. It is predicted that more immigrants will hereafter come by the new route than by all others put together. There is no valid reason why this prediction should not prove strictly true. This is therefore a matter likely to be of vast importance to our State, with a large share of her territory as yet an unbroken wild, offering tempting inducements to the hardy settler.

The completion of this stupendous bond of connection between the Eastern and Western States, Canada and Europe, will render markets available which were before difficult of access, and enable far-distant countries to exchange their products at all seasons. The Grand Trunk may be called the first section of the PACIFIC RAILROAD, as it already communicates with the Mississippi through Michigan, Illinois and Wisconsin Railroads, and we expect to see the line completed from the Mississippi to California. It is not easy to form an estimate of the amount of traffic and intercourse that the 1,150 miles of Grand Trunk Railway will bring to Michigan and the neighboring States. A junction has been already formed with that model of western lines the Michigan Central by which freight and passengers reach Chicago and the numerous lines which diverge from that great commercial city. It is probable that another junction will be made with the Detroit and Milwaukee Railway by means of a branch from Port Huron to Owasso. In this case there will be a direct line across Michigan connecting with the Milwaukee railroads by the ferry across the lake, and penetrating into Iowa, Minnesota, Nebraska, and Oregon by lines which have not yet been traced on the railway maps of the United States.

The ostensible western terminus of this road is at Windsor, opposite our city, but it is practically as much a Detroit road as any that can be named. The connections with the other routes centering here is made by a number of ferry boats of the most staunch and powerful description. The receipts by this route of general merchandise consigned to the cities and points westward of us is immense, and it enjoys a large and growing local traffic

The main line of the Southern Michigan and Northern Indiana Railroad, which taps a rich and important portion of Michigan, is 461 miles in length. The business on this line has recently shown a decided improvement.

The D. and T. Road, which is 65 miles in length, was opened to traffic in January 1857. It was built by the "Detroit, Monroe, and Toledo Railroad Company," who leased it to the Michigan Southern Road. It is now an important link in the great railway system extending from the East to the Great Southwest, of which system, Detroit, from its favorable position, has become the centre and soul. Since the opening of the Grand Trunk, in November, a large amount of freight has passed through, billed for Liverpool direct, a species of freight which must steadily increase.

L. P. Knight is agent at Detroit. The office is in the depot building of the Detroit and Milwaukee Railway.

The Dayton and Michigan Railroad was completed last fall, placing us within a few hours' ride of the Queen City of the West. This is justly regarded as a most important route to our city, and will develop new features to some of our leading business interests. The consumer of our State will have the benefit of lower prices for the products of Kentucky, Tennessee, Louisiana, and the West Indies. The want of direct communication between Detroit and New Orleans has long been felt. Sugars and molasses can now be laid down here for fifty cents per 100 lbs., including all charges from New Orleans, *via* the Mississippi and Ohio Rivers, and D. and M. Railway, giving us, in a word, the benefits of as low freights in winter as in summer. With the cost of transportation thus reduced to a merely nominal standard, prices of Southern products will be upon an average no higher here than in Louisville. It is more than probable, nay, quite certain, that the advantages which must ultimately accrue to the State from our connection with Cincinnati *per se*, if not so general, will be even more marked and important than those to which we have above referred. The prices of provisions will be equalized, giving our lumbermen and miners the benefit of reduced rates throughout most of the year, and when speculation is rampant, and the price of pork, the great staple of our neighbors, reaches an extreme figure—as has been the case for two successive seasons, and will be the case again—our farmers will reap the benefit of the movement. The growth of Cincinnati is altogether without parallel in the world, taking into account the character of that growth—its *quality*, so to speak. All its great interests, particularly its manufactures, have kept pace with its numerical increase. It is indeed difficult to determine whether manufactures or commerce is most intimately identified with its prosperity. The connection with her will give us new and desirable customers for some of our surplus products, particularly our choice lumber.

The entire line of the Flint and Pere Marquette Railroad, as located, is 172½ miles; track laid and completed, 7¾ miles; additional length graded 24½ miles, the ties for which have all been delivered.

It is thought that hereafter twenty miles per year will be completed without difficulty until the whole is completed. This road will be important in developing the resources of a very rich tract of country.

On the line of Amboy, Lansing, and Grand Traverse Railroad, the entire distance from Owasso to Lansing, twenty-six miles, is ready for the iron, except three miles. On the division from Lansing to to Albion, thirty-six miles, the work of grading and furnishing ties is progressing, and some one hundred men at work. Between Owasso and Saginaw, thirty-three miles, arrangements are nearly completed to start the work. The work of grading and preparing for the iron is done by local subscriptions, of which $3,000 per mile has been subscribed and is being paid.

The existence of copper on the shores of Lake Superior appears to have been known to the earliest travelers, but it has been only a few years since it has entered largely into Western commerce. But the country had long been a favorite resort for fur traders, and as long ago as 1809, and perhaps still further back, the Northwest Company (British) owned vessels on Lake Superior. This organization was at that period the great trading company of the region in question, the operations of the Hudson's Bay Company being confined chiefly to the region further north. At the period of which we speak, the bulk of the trading was done by means of birch canoes, some of them large enough to carry two or three tons. With these, the traders passed up to the Indian settlements in the fall, with goods, provisions, and trinkets, usually returning to the trading posts during the month of June with the furs which they had procured in exchange. Mackinac and the Saut were trading posts at an early day. At a somewhat later period, the Northwest Company had an agency on an island in Lake Huron, not far from the mouth of Saut river. The formation of the

American Fur Company was of more recent date, that company dating its origin during the war of 1812, or soon after.

Prior to the building of the canal, a number of steamers had been taken over the portage to Lake Superior, but so far as our knowledge extends, only one or two craft larger than a canoe were ever taken over the rapids, one of which was the schooner Mink. She was built of red cedar, on Lake Superior, about the year 1816, and was of some forty tons burden. She became the property of Mack & Conant, who had her brought down the rapids. In making the descent she suffered some injury by striking against a rock, but, notwithstanding this mishap, she lived long enough to ride out many a stormy sea, running for several years in the trade between Buffalo and the City of the Straits. Shubael Conant, Esq., at this day an honored citizen of Detroit, was one of the firm that purchased the Mink.

In the spring of 1845, the fleet on Lake Superior consisted of the schooner White Fish, belonging to the Hudson's Bay Company, the Siscowit, belonging to the American Fur Company, and the Algonquin, owned by a Mr. Mendenhall. The same year the schooners Napoleon, Swallow, Uncle Tom, Merchant, Chippewa, Ocean, and Fur Trader, were all added. In 1845, the propeller Independence, the first steamer that ever floated on Lake Superior, was taken across the portage, and the next year the Julia Palmer followed her, she being the first side-wheel steamer. In the winter of 1848–9, the schooner Napoleon was converted into a propeller. In 1850, the propeller Manhattan was hauled over by the Messrs. Turner, and the Monticello in 1851, by Col. McKnight. The latter was lost the same fall, and Col. McK. supplied her place the next winter with the Baltimore. In 1853 or 1854, E. B. Ward took over the Sam Ward, and Col. McKnight took the propeller Peninsula over in the winter of 1852 or 1853.

In the spring of 1855, the Saut Canal was completed, since which date the trade with that important region has rapidly grown into commanding importance. It will be seen by the table below that the importations of machinery, provisions, supplies, and merchandise, for the past year amounted to $5,298,-640, while the exports of copper, iron, fur and fish amount to $3,071,069.

The following are the names of the steam craft now regularly employed in this trade:

S. B. Illinois.	Prop. Mineral Rock.
S. B. Lady Elgin.	Prop. Montgomery.

S. B. North Star.	Prop. Northern Light.
Prop. Marquette.	Prop. Iron City.

A number of other steam-craft made occasional trips last year, and next season it is expected that another line will be placed on the route permanently. The Detroit shipping-office has published the names of ninety-six sail vessels that have been engaged in the iron trade the past year.

Rapid as this trade has increased, it is destined, no doubt, to yet undergo a still greater transformation. The latent resources of the Upper Peninsula are of a character and magnitude that defy all estimates of their future greatness. With regard to the importance of the trade to our city, and the steps to be taken to retain it, ample comments have already appeared in the *Tribune*, both editorially and in the form of communications, to which we can add nothing.

The aggregate amount of tolls collected in May, July, August and September, was $10,374.18, a large increase over the corresponding months last year. Including the probable amount for the months not reported, and we have at the lowest not less probably than $16,000, as the tolls for 1859.

Number of passengers: May, 2,493; June, 1,764; July, 2,116; August, 2,617; September, 1,588; October, 1,015.

It is *now* almost universally admitted that the State of Michigan possesses in her soil and timber the material source of immense wealth. While in years past it has been difficult to obtain satisfactory information concerning the real condition and natural resources of a large portion of the surface of the Lower Peninsula, the re-survey of portions of the government land, the exploration of the country by parties in search of pine, the developments made by the exploring and surveying parties along the lines of the Land Grant Railroads, and the more recent examinations by the different commissions for laying out the several State roads under the Acts passed by the last Legislature, have removed every doubt in reference to the subject. The universal testimony from all the sources above mentioned, seems to be that in all the natural elements of wealth the whole of the northern part of the Peninsula abounds.

The pine lands of the State, which are a reliable source of present and future wealth, are so located and distributed as to bring almost every portion of the State, sooner or later in connection with the commerce of the lakes. The pine timber of Michigan is generally interspersed with other varieties of timber, such as beech, maple, white-ash, oak, cherry, etc., and in most cases the soil is suited to agricul tural purposes. This is particularly the case on the western slope of the Peninsula, on the waters of Lake Michigan and along the central portion of the State. On the east and near Lake Huron, the pine districts are more extensively covered with pine timber, and generally not so desirable for farming purposes. There are good farming lands, however, all along the coast of Lake Huron and extending back into the interior.

A large proportion of the pine lands of the State are in the hands of the Canal Company, and individuals who are holding them as an investment, and it is no detriment to this great interest, that the whole State has been thus explored and the choicest of the lands secured. The developments which have thus been made of the quality and extent of the pine districts, have given stability and confidence to the lumbering interest. And these lands are not held at exorbitant prices, but are sold upon fair and reasonable terms, such as practical business men and lumber men will not usually object to.

It is a remarkable fact that almost every stream of water in the State, north of Grand River, penetrates a district of pine lands, and the mouths of nearly all these streams are already occupied with lumbering establishments of greater or less magni tude. Those lumber colonies are the pioneers, and generally attract around them others who engage in agriculture, and thus almost impreceptibly the agricultural interests of the State are spreading and developing in every direction. The want of suitable means of access alone prevents the rapid settlement of large and fertile districts of our State, which are not unknown to the more enterprising and persevering pioneers, who have led the way through the wilderness, and are now engaged almost single-handed in their labors, not shrinking from the privations and sufferings which are sure to surround these first settlements in our new districts.

The Grand Traverse region, with its excellent soil, comparatively mild climate, and abundance of timber of every description, is attracting much attention, and extensive settlements have already commenced in many localities in that region. The coast of Lake Michigan, from Grand River north, for upward of one hundred miles to Manistee River, presents generally a barren, sandy appearance, the sand hills of that coast almost invariably shutting out from the view the surrounding country.

North of the Manistee, however, this characteristic of the coast changes, and the hard timber comes out to the lake and presents a fine region of country extending from Lake Michigan to Grand Traverse Bay and beyond, embracing the head waters of the Manistee River. This large tract of agricultural land is one of the richest portions of the State, and having throughout its whole extent extensive groves of excellent pine timber interspersed, it is one of the most desirable portions of the Peninsula. Grand Traverse Bay, the Manistee and the River Aux Becs Scies are the outlets for the pine timber, and afford ample means of communication between the interior and the lake for such purposes. The proposed State roads will, if built, do much toward the settlement of this region.

A natural harbor, which is being improved by private enterprise, is found at the mouth of the River Aux Becs Scies, and a new settlement and town has been started at this point. This is a natural outlet for a consideration portion of the region just described.

The lands here, as in other localities in the new portions of the State, are such as must induce a rapid settlement whenever the means of communication shall be opened.

The valley of the Muskegon embraces every variety of soil and timber, and is one of the most attractive portions of the Peninsula. The pine lands upon this river are scattered all along the valley in groups or tracts containing several thousand acres each, interspersed with hard timber and surrounded by fine agricultural lands.

The Pere Marquette River and White River, large streams emptying into Lake Michigan, pass through a region possessing much the same characteristics. This whole region is underlaid with lime rocks, a rich soil, well watered with living springs, resembling in many features the Grand River Valley. Beds of gypsum have been discovered on the head waters of the Pere Marquette.

The unsettled counties in the northern portion of the State, the northern portion of Montcalm and Gratiot, Isabella, Gladwin, Clare and a portion of Midland, are not inferior to any other portion. There is a magnificent body of pine stretching from the head of Flat River in Moncalm county to the upper waters of the Tettibiwassee, and growing upon a fine soil well adapted to agriculture.

This embraces a portion of the Saginaw Valley, and covers the high ground dividing the waters of Lakes Huron and Michigan. The eastern slope of the Peninsula embraces a variety of soil and timber somewhat different in its general features from other portions of the State. The pine lands of this region are near the coast of the lake, and lie in large tracts but with good agricultural land adjoining. There are in the Lower Peninsula, in round numbers, about 24,000,000 acres of land.

Taking Houghton Lake, near the centre of the State, as a point of view, the general surface may be comprehended as follows: The Muskegon Valley to the southwest following the Muskegon River in its course to lake Michigan. The western slope of the Peninsula directly west, embracing the pine and agriculture districts along the valleys of several large streams emptying into Lake Michigan. The large and beautiful region to the northwest embracing the valley of the Manistee and the undulating lands around the Grand Traverse Bay. Northward, the region embraces the head-waters of the Manistee and Au Sauble, with the large tracts of excellent pine in that locality, and beyond, the agricultural region extending to Little Traverse Bay and the Straights of Mackinaw. To the northeast, the valley of the Au Sauble, and the pine region of Thunder Bay. To the east, the pine and hard timber ex tending to Saginaw Bay. To the southeast, the Saginaw Valley; and to the south, the high lands before described in the central counties.

That portion of the State south of Saginaw and

the Grand River Valley is so well known that a description here would be unnecessary.

Thus we have yet undeveloped over half the surface of this Peninsula, embracing, certainly, 12,000,000 to 15,000,000 of acres, possessing stores of wealth in the timber upon its surface, reserving soil for the benefit of those, who, as the means of communication are opened, will come in and possess it, and thus introduce industry and prosperity into our waste places.

We have not the figures at hand, but it is probable that at least one-tenth of the area north of the Grand River is embraced in the pine region. The swamp lands granted to the State will probably cover nearly double the area of the pine lands proper The remainder for the most part is covered with a magnificent growth of hard timber suited to the necessities of our growing population and commerce.

The statistics herein furnished will give some idea of the importance and value of the lumber traffic in this States. The trade in pine timber, lumber, shingles and other varieties of lumber, with the traffic in staves form one of the most important branches of manufacture and commerce in our own State, and this trade alone is now accomplishing more for the development and settlement of the country than all other causes in operation.

The lumber manufactories in Detroit and its suburbs are eleven in number. The following are the names of the proprietors and the amount cut last year by each:

	FT. LUMBER.	PCS. LATH.
H. A. & S. G. Wight	6,500,000	2,220,000
Samuel Pills	3,500,000	482,000
— Moffat (est)	1,500,000	
H. B. Benson	3,254,029	
W. Warner & Co	194,370	
Brooks & Adams	3,800,000	
Baughman, Hubbard & Co	3,378,080	1,043,300
Kibbee, Fox & Co	3,000,000	800,000
N. Reeve	800,000	20,000
Davis & David	2,000,000	
Copeland	1,000,000	
Total	29,426,479	4,745,300

The aggregate of capital employed by these mills is $1,440,000. The above amount is no criterion of their capacity. The same mills cut 46,000,000 feet in 1856, and nearly the same in 1857, and their probable capacity is 54,000,000. Warner & Co., run their mill only about five weeks last year, and are now about retiring from business. One of the others sustained a temporary loss of business by fire. The product will in the aggregate be doubled next season.

The logs sawed in Detroit are procured from St.

Clair River, Black River, Mill Creek and, Belle River. As a large share of that sold here has been on contract, there has been no great fluctuation in the market at this point. On the first of July the rates by the cargo were $25a$26 for clear and $19a20 for second clear; on the first of October, $24 for clear, and $18 for second clear.

Last winter and spring were very unfavorable for lumbering. Owing to the small quantity of snow, but few logs were got out, and many of them being on small streams, owing to the failure of the usual spring freshets, were not sawed, so that upon the whole the mills of the State turned out only about half the amount of their capacity.

The market opened in the spring with flattering prospects. Buyers from a number of important points in the Eastern States, previously deriving their supplies from Maine, visited our State, anxious to secure contracts for choice lumber, and the opinion prevailed that the demand would exceed the supply. The prospect encouraged manufacturers to make unwonted exertions in turning out all the stock that could be rendered available, which involved increased expense. In some places, as was the case at Saginaw, a very large amount was got out in the early part of the summer. About the close of June, the market experienced a sudden and unlooked-for depression, after which prices tended speedily downward, falling to such a low point before the close of the season that manufacturers on the west coast generally suspended their shipments. Those on the east coast continued to ship, but their shipments to a very great extent still remain unsold. We are cognizant of 7,000,000 feet held in that way by only four manufacturers.

The accounts this winter are very favorable, but the idea that obtains, fixing the amount at a very high figure, is vague and erroneous. The true state of the case is, that manufactures, as a general thing, in view of the depressed condition of the trade, have been making calculations to do a light business, and got out their logs sooner than they expected, and will on the whole do rather more than they had anticipated, having gone into the woods lighthanded. The most experienced judges concur in fixing the amount of logs got out this winter on River St. Clair, at Port Huron and Saginaw Bay, but not including the rivers above, at 175,000,000 feet. In the Saginaws, it is ascertained that about 100,000,000 will be got out. Taking the entire east coast, it is thought the logs this winter would exceed those of last by fifteen to twenty per cent.

By Custom House statements of shipments, added to actual receipts at one of the receiving points—Chicago—it will be seen below that for 1859 a little over 269,000,000 feet is the amount of shipments arrived at. These figures, taken in connection with the estimates of those competent to judge, render it certain that the actual amount shipped out of the State did not vary materially from 400,000,000 feet. There being no penalty involved in the failure of masters of vessels to report, there is great carelessness in the matter. The Cleveland, Toledo and Sandusky shipments, are at the outside, not more than half reported. Those reported to Buffalo, Oswego etc., are a little nearer the truth, but they fall, considerably below the mark.

The amount made in 1859, did not vary materially from that shipped. In the district embracing the River St. Clair, Port Huron and the Lake Shore, 6,000,000 feet more were wintered over last year than this. On the west coast it was different generally, so that the variation in the aggregate cannot be much either way. The capacity of the mills in the pine lumber region is 900,000,000 feet, or possibly a little more.

As regards the amount of shingles made, even dealers are much in the dark. To add 50 per cent. to the Custom House returns would certainly be within bounds for the eastern coast. This would give 120,000,000 as the amount. For the west coast, if we take the amount received at Chicago, say 165,-000,000, with an additional twenty-five per cent. for that received at Milwaukee, and then estimate that two-thirds of the whole amount were from the west coast of Michigan, which is doubtless true, we have 137,500,000 as the amount shipped by the coast, making 267,500,000 for the whole State.

The improved demand for staves has greatly stimulated the production, and in localities where the production of pine lumber is decreasing, that of staves is taking its place. At Saginaw 2,500,000 were got out last year, and this year there will be full as much, or more. The greatest activity prevails, and dressing by machinery has been started. At Lakeport, Burchville, Lexington, Port Sanilac, Forester, Point aux Barque, and Foresterville, 850,000 were got out last year; from Port Huron and St. Clair 750,000. The amount turned out in the whole State could not have been short of 20,000,000.

An immense amount of lath were turned out. A mill that can turn out three millions of lumber, generally makes one million of lath. On this basis about 133,000,000 must have been turned out. The supply generally exceeds the demand.

The lumber on the east coast is worth at the mills $9 per M.; that on the west coast $7. At the average of $8, the amount made last year would be worth $3,200,000. The value of shingles at $2 per M., was $515,000, and the lath at $1 per M., are worth $133-000.

We are enabled to present a nearly complete list of names of owners, with the amount of capital respectively, which will be of some interest, both at home and abroad. So far as the east coast is concerned, the figures are in the main entirely reliable, being upon the authority of one of the best men in the State who knows whereof he advises. Those for the west coast, thought not perhaps so strictly correct as the others, will as a general thing be found within bounds. We hope the statistics will prove an incentive to lumbermen to be more particular hereafter in furnishing information:

BLACK RIVER.

Name.	Capital.	Name.	Capital.
J. & J. Bayard......	$15,000	Davis' mill.........	$ 8,000
Sweetser & Bayard...	7,000	R. Wadham's mills..	10,000
Comstock mill.......	7,000	....	

MILL CREEK.

Name.	Capital.	Name.	Capital.
Bunce's mill..........	4,000	John H. Westbrook.	4,000
L. Brockway 2 mills................................			5,000

PORT HURON.

Name.	Capital.	Name.	Capital.
G. S. Lester.........	24,000	Avery..............	75,000
Haynes & Baird......	24,000	Bunce.............	24,000
Howard & Bachelor..	15,000	Hibbard...........	40,000
Fish, two mills..... .	35,000	Black River mill....	35,000
Welles..............	24,000		

LOCKPORT.

Farrand.. 10,000

BURCHVILLE.

Woods, two mills....	30,000	John S. Minor......	7,000

LEXINGTON.

Hubbard............	8,000	Stevens & Davis....	10,000
Jenks & Co..........	20,000	Hitchcock & Co.....	30,000

BARK SHANTY.

Oldfield.. 10,000

FORESTER.

Emely.. 50,000

GIBRALTAR.

Colin Campbell................................ 10,000

ALGONAC.

Daniels & Ripley.....	15,000	Smith..............	24,000

NEWPORT.

E. B. Ward.........	20,000	B. S. Horton......	10,000
Rust................	10,000		

ST. CLAIR.

Moore & Scott......	20,000	Oaks & Holland, two mills.............	40,000
W. Truesdale 2 mills.	60,000	St. Clair...........	30,000
E. Smith............	15,000		
Smith & Chamberlin..	5,000		

FORESTVILLE.

Name.	Capital.	Name.	Capital.
E. B. Ward..........	50,000	Breckinridge	2,000

VICKSBURG,

Williams & Mills, three mills........................55,000

CHEAOYGAN.

Three mills...100,000

CHERRY CREEK.

Peninsular Bank.................................. 15,000

HURON COUNTY.

Luddington..........	12,000	Smith & Co........	50,000
Hubbard & Co.......	50,000	W. R. Stafford....	15,000
Donahue............	30,000	Pt Austin Company	100,000
Armstrong & Co.....	10,000	Crawford & Co.....	10,000

BAY CITY.

Clark, Ballou & Co...	35,000	McEwing & Brother	30,000
Moore & Smith......	30,000	Bangor mills.......	35,000
Geo. Lord & Co......	24,000	Drake mills........	24,000
Saml. Pitts..........	30,000	Henry Raymond...	30,000
Beeson & Wheeler...	24,000	Catlin & Jennison..	10,000
Beebe & Atwood.....	10,000	Miller & Butterfield	14,000
Henry Doty.........	35,000	Frost & Bradley...	35,000

PORTSMOUTH.

J. J. McCormick....	10,000	Partridge mill.....	24,000
Portsmouth mill.....	15,000	H D Braddack & Co	14,000
Budd's mill..........	14,000	Watson & Southard	14,000

ZILWAUKEE.

J. J. Westervelt.................................. 35,000

CARROLLTON.

Name Unknown...................................35,000

EAST SAGINAW.

Name.	Capital.	Name.	Capital.
Garrison & Co........	24,000	Cushing & Co....	36,000
I. Hill..............	20,000	L. B. Curtis......	24,000
Holland.............	10,000	Wm. Gallagher...	14,000
Copeland & Co.......	10,000	Atwater mill......	30,000

SAGINAW CITY.

V. A. Payne........	30,000	G D Williams & Son	20,000
Curtis & King.......	30,000	D. Rust & Brother	50,000
New mill............	20,000		

TITTIBIWASSEE, PINE RIVER AND SWAN CREEK.

Eight mills.................................... 65,000

CASS, BAD, AND SHIAWASSEE RIVERS.

Seven mills.................................... 50,000

LAPEER.

D. Farrer...........	8,000	N. H. Hart......	21,000
W. Williams........	15,000	Rogers & Jenness.	24,000
Crofoot & Baldwin...	15,000	Smith & Jenness..	15,000
Manwaring & Co.....	21,000	Smith............	14,000
Wm. Peters.........	14,000	J. B. Wilson......	14,000
Thorp's mill.........	14,000	James Farrell....	10,000
H. D. Torner........	8,000	White & Peter...	10,000
Lawrence & M'Arthur	7,000	W. H. Crapo.....	60,000
Wm. Peter..........	30,000	H.L. Hemingway..	6,000
Sixteen small mills...	85,000		

PINE RUN.

McFarren....................................... 20,000

MONTROSE.

Name unknown.................................. 30,000

ALPENA AND VICINITY.

G. N. Fletcher & Co.	35,000	Smith & Chamberlain	15,000
Lockwood & Miner...	25,000	D. D. Oliver.......	5,000
Harris & Co.........	35,000	Whitmore & Co.....	25,000

SANILAC COUNTY.

Name.	Capital.	Name.	Capital.
J. L. Woods & Co.....	5,000	Stevenson & Davis...	20,000
Mason & Luce........	17,500		

AU SAUBLE HIGHLANDS.

Harris's mill..24,000

RIFLE RIVER, SAGANIN, COQUALIN, AND SAND BEACH.

Six mills..85,000

TUSCOLA COUNTY.

A. Watson..........	10,000	Edmunds & North...	14,000
W. A. Hart.........	10,000	Richardson & Bro....	14,000
Perry	5,000	Holmes..............	5,000
Others..............	30,000		

FLINT AND VICINITY.

Eleven mills 715,000

There are also others on the east slope of the lower peninsula, representing a capital of say—$120,000.

Beyond the lower peninsula, there are some very heavy manufactories, particularly around Green Bay, (Michigan) generally estimated at $1,000,000, but which it would be safe to put at—$750,000.

Total capital, including Detroit, - - $5,360,000

WESTERN SLOPE—OTTAWA COUNTY.

Name.	Capital.	Name.	Capital.
Ferry & Co..........	50,000	Plugger & Nyn......	24,000
W. M. Ferry, Jr......	50,000	Howard & Co........	14,000
Joseph Weld & Co....	30,000	Ryerson & Morris, 2 mills..............	65,000
T. W. White & Co...	50,000	Chapin, Marsh & Foss	50,000
Becker & Spoons....	40,000	Smith, Forbes & Co...	35,000
Richard Roberts.....	24,000	Trowbridge, Way & Son...............	65,000
Jno. Haire..........	24,000		
E. Jewitt...........	15,000		

Name.	Capital.	Name.	Capital.
J. B. Bailey	14,000	L. G. Mason & Co.	35,000
Porter & Slyfield	14,000	Beidler & Co.	40,000
C. Davies & Co.	50,000	Mears & Co.	24,000
Durkee, Truesdell & Co.	40,000	Hill & Co.	24,000
George Ruddmain	40,000	Colgrove & Co.	18,000
Lewis & Davis	24,000	Wm. Thompson	14,000
Eldridge & Co.	24,000	Harris & Co.	8,000
Carleton & Co.	24,000	Jno. Ford	8,000
Ferry & Son	40,000	Denton & Co.	14,000
Lind & Slater	50,000	Carleton & Co.	10,000
Young, Savedge & Co.	30,000	Jos. Dalton & Bro.	10,000
Amos Norton	40,000	S. Lawrence	12,000
Benj. Smith	30,000	Edward Dalton	8,000
Rhodes, Cloyn & Co.	24,000	E. W. Merrill & Co.	14,000
Hatch & Merritt	15,000	Reed & Co.	10,000
C. Hart	10,000	Brown & Grist	8,000

KENT COUNTY.

Name.	Capital.	Name.	Capital.
Jennison & Bro.	14,000	Reed & Plum	5,000
W. T. Powers	2,000	N. H. Withey	5,000
Seymour	24,000	Knickerbuck	4,000
Gooch & Webber	5,000	Robert Konkle	10,000
A. McFarland	4,000	A. Roberts & Son	25,000
Thos. Myers	21,000	White, Worden & Co.	25,000
George Funck	8,000	C. C. Comstock	9,500
S. Lapham	5,000	D. Porter	5,000
A. House	5,000	Chase, Harris & Co.	8,000
Farrell & Sons	10,000	C. W. Taylor	6,000
J. C. Clements	15,000	D. Caswell	12,000
T. Spencer	8,000	Hubbard, Hitchcock & Co.	16,000
Dewey & Co.	14,000		

NEWAYGO COUNTY.

Name.	Capital.	Name.	Capital.
Newaygo Company	80,000	J. M. Wood, 2 mills	25,000
Name unknown	24,000	James Botchford	10,000

Name.	Capital.	Name.	Capital.
R. P. Mitchell	5,000	Amos Bigelow,	4,000
Weaver	3,000		

STONY CREEK, OCEANA COUNTY.

Campbell, Wheeler & Co. 25,000

PERE MARQUETTE, BLACK CREEK AND BIG SAUBLE.

C. Mears & Co., 3 mills 95,000

SPRING CREEK.

Hopkins & Co. 24,000

MANISTEE.

Coles	80,000	John C. Haines	55,000
McVicker &Ingleman	24,000	John Stranch	40,000
One near Manistee	24,000		

GRAND TRAVERSE.

Hanna, Lay & Co.	32,000	A. S. Wadsworth	15,000

WHITE RIVER.

Amos Rathbone 24,000

MECOSTA.

Leonard, Ives, & Co. 20,000

MONTCALM COUNTY.

Bruce	10,000	E. Gregory & Co.	20,000
Slaght	14,000		

LELANAW COUNTY.

Averill & Son 2,000

BEC SCEE'S RIVER.

R. Gardner	15,000	Name unknown	2,000
Chamberlin & Co.	20,000	Harris & Co.	10,000

IONIA COUNTY.

Estimated Aggregate 100,000
All others, on West Slope, estimated 350,000
Capital Western Slope 2,669,500
Total Capital of State $8,029,5000

An intelligent gentleman who, at our instance, visited all the establishments around Saginaw, and procured statistics, reports the amount of lumber manufactured as follows:

Place.	No. of Mills.	Feet.
Bay City	11	20,000,000
Portsmouth	4	5,000,000
Zilwaukee	1	3,000,000
Carrollton	1	2,800,000
East Saginaw	8	19,750,000
Saginaw City	4	14,000,000
Bad River	2	4,500,000
Rafted Lumber		4,000,000
Total		73,050,000

Valuation, at $8.50 per M. $620,925

Of the above lumber, 63,000,000 has been shipped; the rest is now on the docks.

Shingles manufactured	25,000,000 at	$2.50	$62,500
Lath "	5,000,000 at	1.00	5,000
Oak Staves " and shipped	2,000,000 at	30.00	60,000
Add Lumber			620,925
Total			$748,425

The supply of pine in some few localities is becoming exhausted, and some few mills have ceased operating. This is the case at Lexington, but the machinery and capital have been taken elsewhere. At the present ratio of consumption, the supply of pine must rapidly become diminished, but profitable employment will then be found in the manufacture of hemlock and hard-wood. Some little has already been done in the way of turning out hemlock. The manufacture of hard-wood lumber is increasing very rapidly.

The copper interest of Michigan was first brought into public notice by the enormous speculations and the mad fever of 1845. The large spur of country which projects far out into the lake, having its base resting on a line drawn across from L'Anse Bay to Ontonagon, and the Porcupine Mountains for its spine, became the El Dorado of all copperdom of that day. In this year the first active operations were commenced at the Cliff Mine, just back of Eagle River harbor. Three years later, in 1848, work was undertaken at the Minnesota, some fifteen miles back from the lake at Ontonagon.

The history of the copper mines on Lake Superior shows that even the best mines disappointed the owners in the beginning. We give the facts relative to the three mines at present in the Lake Superior region to illustrate this. The Cliff Mine was discovered in 1845, and worked three years without much sign of success; it changed hands at the very moment when the vein was opened which proved afterward to be so exceedingly rich in copper and silver, producing now on an average 1,500 tons of stamp, barrel, and mass copper per annum.

The Minnesota Mine was discovered in 1848, and for the first three years gave no very encouraging results. The first large mass of native copper of about seven tons was found in a pit made by an ancient race. After that discovery much money was spent before any other further indications of copper were found. This mine yields now about 2,000 tons of copper per annum, and declared, for the year 1858, a net dividend of $300,000. The dividends paid since 1852 amount to upward of $1,500,000 on a paid-up capital of $66,000.

The same has been experienced at the Pewabic Mine. That mine commenced operations in the year 1855, with an expenditure of $26,357, which produced $1,080 worth of copper; the second year it expended $40,820, and produced $31,492 of copper; in 1857 $24,484 of expenses produced $44,058 worth of copper; 1858, the amount expended was $109,152, and the receipts for copper $76,538; the total expense amounts to $235,816, and the total receipts for copper to $153,168, leaving an excess of expenses amounting to $82,648, which is, however, amply covered by the extensive works established above and below ground at the mine.

The Pewabic will undoubtedly take its place among the dividend-paying mines of the present year.

It is scarcely ten years that mining has been properly commenced in that remote region. At that time it was difficult, on account of the rapids of St. Mary's River, to approach it by water with large craft. Being more than a thousand miles distant from the centre of the Union, destitute of all the requirements for the development of mines; every tool, every part of machinery, every mouthful of provisions had to be hauled over the rapids, boated along the shores for hundreds of miles to the copper region, and there often carried on the back of man and beast to the place where copper was believed to exist. Every stroke of the pick cost tenfold more than in populated districts; every disaster delayed the operations for weeks and months.

The opening of the Saut Canal has changed all this and added a wonderful impetus to the business, the mining interests, and the development of the Lake Superior country. Nearly one hundred different vessels, steam and sail, have been engaged the past season in its trade, and the number of these is destined largely to increase year by year, an indication of the growth of business and the opening up of the country. For the growth in the copper interest we have only to refer to the shipments from that region year by year. These, in gross, are as follows:

1853	2,535 tons.
1854	3,500 "
1855	4,544 "
1856	5,357 "
1857	6,094 "
1858	6,025 "
1859	6,245 "

The same facts of development would hold generally true, with regard to the other industrial interests of that vast country.

It remains yet almost wholly "a waste, howling wilderness." At Marquette, Portage Lake, Copper Harbor, Eagle River, Eagle Harbor, and Ontonagon, and the mines adjacent, are the only places where the primeval forests have given place to the enterprise of man, and these in comparison with the whole extent of territory embraced in this region, are but mere insignificant patches. What this country may become years hence, it would defy all speculations now to predict, but there seems no reason to doubt that it will exceed the most sanguine expectations.

The copper region is divided into three districts, viz., the Ontonagon, the most northern, the Keweenaw Point, the most eastern, and the Portage Lake, lying mostly below and partially between the range of the two. In the first are situated the Minnesota, the Rockland, the National, and a multitude of other mines of lesser note, profit, or promise. In the Cliff, the Copper Falls, and others. In the last are the Pewabic, Quincy, Isle Royale, Portage, Franklin, and numerous others. Each district has some peculiarities of product, the first developing the masses, while the latter are more prolific in vein-rock, the copper being scattered throughout the rock.

There have been since 1845 no less than 116 copper-mining companies organized under the general law of our State. The amount of capital invested and now in use, or which has been paid out in explorations and improvements, and lost, is estimated by good judges at $6,000,000. The nominal amount of capital stock invested in all the companies which have charters would reach an indefinite number of millions. As an offset to this, it may be stated that the Cliff and Minnesota mines have returned over

$2,000,000 in dividends from the beginning of their operations, and the value of these two mines will more than cover the whole amount spent in mining, and for all the extravagant undertakings which have been entered upon and abandoned. While success has been the exception and failure the rule in copper speculations, yet it must be admitted that these exceptions are remarkably tempting ones. Doubtless there is immense wealth still to be developed in these enterprises, and this element of wealth in the Lake Superior region is yet to assume a magnitude now unthought of.

The copper is smelted mainly in this city, Cleve land, and Boston, the works in this city being the largest. There is one establishment at Pittsburg which does most of the smelting for the Cliff Mine, we believe; one at Bergen, N. Y., and one at New Haven, Conn. There are two at Baltimore, but they are engaged on South American Mineral. The Bruce Mines on the Canada side of Lake Huron have recently put smelting works in operation on their location. Prior to this the mineral was barreled up and shipped to London, being taken over as ballast, in packet ships, at low rates.

The amount of copper smelted in this city we can only judge by the amount landed here, but this will afford a pretty accurate estimate. The number of tons landed here, in 1859, was 3,088. The copper yield of Lake Superior will produce between 60 and 70 per cent. of ingot copper, which is remarkably pure. The net product of the mines for 1859, is worth in the markets of the world nearly or quite $2,000,000. This large total shows the capabilities of this region and affords us some basis of calculation as to the value and probable extent of future development.

Beside the amount already noticed as landed here there were 1,268 tons brought to this city from the Bruce Mines, and sent on to London. The mineral of this location is of a different quality from that of Lake Superior and not near so productive of pure copper. The price of ingot copper in New York the past season has arranged from 20½ to 23½ cents per pound, averaging full 22½ cents.

There are indications that Michigan is slowly but surely taking the rank to which she is entitled in the manufacture as well as production of iron. The first shipment of pig iron of any consequence was made by the Pioneer Company in the fall of 1858. Dr. Russell, of this city, is turning out large quantities. His works went into operation about two years and a half ago, but were burned after running sixty days.

They were immediately rebuilt by the enterprising proprietor.

The Lake Superior iron has been proclaimed the best in the world, a proposition that none can successfully refute. Its qualities are becoming known in quarters where it would naturally be expected its superiority would be admitted reluctantly, if at all. It is now sent to New York and Ohio, and even to Pennsylvania—an agency for its sale having been established in Pittsburg. For gearing, shafting, cranks, flanges, and, we ought by all means, to add, car-wheels, no other should be used, provided it can be obtained.

A large amount of capital is invested in the iron interest in Michigan, as the following figures prove:

Pioneer	$150,000
Jackson	300,000
Collins	150,000
Cleveland	300,000
Lake Superior and Iron Mountain R. R. Co.	700,000
Northern Michigan Iron Company	110,000
Wyandotte Rolling Mills	236,000
Eureka Iron Company	117,000
Dr. G. B. Russell's	60,000
Ford & Philbrick's Steam Forge	25,000
	2,148,000

Marquette is the only point on Lake Superior

where the iron ore deposits have been worked. There are deposits of iron in the mountains back of L'Anse, but this wonderful region leaves nothing more to be desired for the present. At a distance of eighteen miles from the lake, are to be found iron mountains named the Sharon, Burt, Lake Superior, Cleveland, Collins, and Barlow, while eight miles further back lie the Ely and St. Clair mountains. Three of these mountains are at present worked, the Sharon, the Cleveland, and the Lake Superior, and contain enough ore to supply the world for generations to come. The mountains further back embrace tracts of hundreds of acres rising to a height of from four to six hundred feet, which, there is every reason to believe, from the explorations made, are solid iron ore. The extent of the contents of these mountains is perfectly fabulous, in fact, so enormous as almost to baffle computation. The ore, too is remarkably rich, yielding about seventy per cent. of pure metal. There are now in operation at Marquette three Iron Mining Companies, and two blast furnaces for making charcoal pig iron, the Pioneer and Meigs. The Pioneer has two stacks and a capacity of twenty tons of pig iron per day; the Meig sone stack, capable of turning out about eleven tons. The Northern Iron Company is building a large bituminous coal furnace at the mouth of the Chocolate River, three miles south of Marquette, which will be in operation early in the summer.

Each of the mining companies, the Jackson, Cleveland and Lake Superior, have docks at the harbor for shipment, extending out into the spacious and beautiful bay which lies in front of Marquette to a sufficient length to enable vessels of the largest dimension to lie by their side and to be loaded directly from the cars, which are run over the vessels and dumped into shutes, which are made to empty directly into the holds. The process of loading is therefore very expeditious and easy.

The amount of shipments of ore for 1859, from Marquette to the ports below, reaches 75,000 gross tons in round numbers, and the shipments of pig iron, 6,000 gross tons more. To this must be added the amount at Marquette when navigation closed, the amount at the mines ready to be brought down, and the amount used on the spot. This will give a total product of the iron mines of Michigan for the past year of between *ninety and one hundred thousand tons.* These mining companies simply mine and ship the ore and sell it. Their profit ranges between seventy-five cents and one dollar per ton.

The quality of the iron of Lake Superior is conceded by all to be the best in the world, as the analysis of Prof. Johnson, which we reproduce, shows. The table shows the relative strength per square inch in pounds.

Salisbury, Conn., iron	.58,009
Swedish (best)	.58,184
English cable	.59,105
Centre county, Pa	.59,400
Essex county, N. Y.,	.59,962
Lancaster county, Pa	.58,661
Russia (best)	.76,069
Common English and American	.30,000
Lake Superior	.89,582

The manufacture of pig iron at Marquette will probably be carried on even more extensively as the attention of capitalists is directed to it. The following may be considered a fair statement of the cost of producing one ton of pig iron at the Pioneer Iron Co.'s works:

1½ tons iron ore, at $1.50 per ton	$2 50
125 bushels charcoal at 7 cents per bushel	8 75
Fluxing	50
Labor	2 50
Incidental expenses	1 00
Cost at the works	15 00
Freight on R. R. and dockage	1 37
Cost on board vessel	$16 36

The quantity of wood required for charcoal for

both furnaces, is immense. The pioneer furnace requires 2,500 bushels of coal in twenty-four hours; and in blast as they are, day and night, for six months, and at a yield of forty bushels of coal to a cord of wood, it would require 15,000 cords of wood to keep them going. The company has had 120,000 cords chopped this season. This vast consumption of wood will soon cause the country to be completely stripped of its timber. Coal will then come into use. The business of manufacturing pig iron may be extended indefinitely, as the material is without limit, and the demand, thus far, leaving nothing on hand.

These facts exhibit the untold wealth of Michigan in iron alone, and point with certainty to an extent of business that will add millions to our invested capital, dot our State with iron manufactories of all kinds, and furnish regular employment to tens of thousands of our citizens, while our raw material and our wares shall be found in all the principal markets of the world.

The superior fish, found in such profusion in our noble lakes and rivers, while they afford a highly-prized luxury for immediate consumption, from one of our leading articles of export, and are very justly regarded as constituting one of our greatest interests.

It is estimated by men of intelligence that the

value of our yearly catch of fish is greater than that of all taken in fresh waters in the thirty-two remaining States of the Union. This may at first blush seem like a broad assertion, but it is no doubt strictly within bounds. If the claim be not too much of the nature of a truism, we may add that so far as quality is concerned the superiority of our finny tribes is even more strongly marked than in regard to quantity. In the sluggish streams that abound in "ten degrees of more effulgent clime," the fish partake of the slimy properties of their native element; it is only in the limpid waters of the North that they are found of flavor so unexceptionable as to please an epicurean taste, or exalt them to the dignity of a staple of commerce. Fish possess peculiar qualities to commend them as an article of food, independent of the arbitrary preference of the epicure. They are universally esteemed as a wholesome and nutritious diet. In that pleasant work, Irving's "Astoria," a tribe of Indians are described who subsisted entirely on fish, whose rotund appearance contrasted strongly with the physique of their brethren of the forest. The profusion with which the finny tribes propagate their species is a peculiarity said to be imparted to those who partake freely and regularly of them for food, a supposition which would seem to be strongly supported by facts. Fishermen are proverbial for the number of their descendants. One of the tribe who dries his nets in Sarnia, is the happy father of nineteen children, and we can cite numerous proofs almost equally striking in support of this theory.

The fisheries have always been a leading subject in the government policy of sea-board nations. They are a prime source of revenue, and have been the cause of numerous wars. The serious controversy between the United States and Great Britain concerning the Newfoundland fisheries, is still fresh in the memory of our readers. Recently the earnest attention of the French government has been directed to propositions for the artificial propagation of fish, as a means of affording good and cheap food to the people at a merely nominal cost. The gradual diminution of the species, as well as the ultimate extinction of the large birds and quadrupeds, is everywhere a condition of advanced civilization and the increase and spread of an industrial population. To provide a remedy for the evil, the science of pisciculture has latterly attracted no small degree of attention, and, at this time, gentlemen prominently identified with our fishing interest have it in contemplation to stock lakes in the interior of Michigan with a view to the prosecution of the science.

Most of the fish packed on Lake Huron, and rivers St. Clair and Detroit, find their way into the Ohio market. The trade with that State has rapidly increased, but in its early stages it had some difficulties to contend with, to one of which we will briefly allude. Some twelve or fourteen years ago, a large quantity of fish, not less than 8,000 to 10,000 barrels, which had been caught in Lake Superior, were in the possession of a single dealer, who had them stored in the large warehouse recently torn down at the Detroit and Milwaukee Railway depot. He had oportunities to dispose of them at $8 per barrel, but refused to sell them for less than $10, and the result was that they were kept so long that many of them spoiled. They were complained of as a nuisance, and 1,500 barrels were turned out into the river at one time. Part of the lot was, however, sent to Ohio, and the effect was, for a time, extremely prejudicial to our trade, requiring a great deal of explanation before the Cincinnati dealers could be again induced to stand in the position of customers. But when confidence once more became fairly restored, the circumstance seemed to have the effect to precipitate the trade between the two cities. At least it grew rapidly from that day, our neighbors purchasing freely of our staple articles and sending us sugar and molasses in return. Thus, as in Samson's time, honey was gathered from the carcass of the dead lion. Ohio has become a very large consumer of our fish, and her influence is being extended rapidly into Indiana.

The habits of fish are as interesting as anything in the animal economy, constituting a beautiful study for the lover of nature; but this branch does not come within the scope of our article, and we must content ourselves with a brief description of the principal varieties, particularly such as are held in highest repute for packing, with such statistics as we have been able to procure.

White-fish are more highly prized than any other kind found in our waters, being decidedly the most delicious in a fresh state, and when packed command a higher price than any other by $1 per bbl. They are found in the Straits and all the Lakes. They spawn in the fall, in the Straits, and in shoals and on reefs about the Lakes. They are caught in seines, gill nets, trap nets, and with spears; never with hooks. Those found in Detroit river come up from Lake Erie regularly in the fall to deposit their spawn. They were found in our lakes and rivers in vast quantities when the white men first visited their shores. They constituted, with other kinds, the principal food of the white and Indian voyagers as they coasted around the lakes, and were invaluable to the first settlers of the country, who, perhaps in some cases, but for the assistance they afforded, would have been compelled to relinquish their settlements. They could catch a supply at any time, and they then had an unfailing resort when their crops failed. White-fish were a great favorite with the Indians. They would give many times their weight in trout or any other species in exchange for them. It is said that a person can subsist longer upon them than upon any other kind.

Their ordinary weight is from 3 to 5 lbs, length 15 inches, though some have been caught weighing not less than 18 lbs. They are a beautiful fish, and when first taken out of the water and struggle and flounder in the sun, they exhibit all the colors of the rainbow, but they soon expire, and when dead they are of a delicate white color. The trout, pike, and muscalonge devour them without mercy. Some of these voracious kinds have been caught with the remains of six white-fish in them.

The Detroit River white-fish are more juicy and better flavored than those caught in the upper lakes, probably from the fact that they feed on more delicate food, but those found in Lake Superior surpass all others in size. They were once so numerous that eight thousand were taken at a single haul. At present a haul of one or two thousand is thought a very good one. In all the rivers they are growing scarce very gradually, but surely. The ratio of decrease cannot be arrived at with any degree of precision. A few years ago they were mostly taken with gill nets, and when they fell of in one place, a corresponding increase would be found in another. Now they are taken with trap nets along the shore. The trap nets are a decided advantage over gill nets. They allow the fish to be kept alive, and they are taken out at leisure; they are therefore of better quality.

Pickerel are also held in high esteem. They are good either fresh, or salted and dried, and for packing, rank next in value to white, although held nominally at the same price as trout when packed. They generally run up the rivers and lakes in the spring to spawn, where they are caught in considerable numbers. Average weight, 2 lbs; large, 20 lbs; common length, 15 inches.

Lake or Mackinaw trout are as voracious as pike. They are chiefly caught on Lake Huron with gill nets and hooks. Saginaw Bay appears to be a favorite resort with them. Some winters large quantities are caught in the Bay through the ice, with a decoy fish and spear. They spawn in the fall, generally in the bays and inlets. Average weight 5 lbs; large 75lbs.

Siscowits are mostly found in Lake Superior, and are preferred by some to any other kind. They are of the trout family, and for fat are unequaled; they are mostly taken in gill nets. They spawn in the fall, and are very superior for packing. They are also of some value for their oil. Common weight 4 pounds, length 16 inches.

Large herrings are very good fish, found only in the straits and large lakes. They spawn in the fall; but few are caught. Average weight 1¾ pounds; common length 10 inches.

In addition to the above the muskelonge—a large and delicious variety—black and white bass, rock bass, perch, sturgeon, and at least twenty other kinds, abound in our waters; a minute description of which we are compelled to forego. White-fish are taken both spring and fall, chiefly the latter; spring is the season for pickerel; trout are taken at all seasons.

Something over a year since some excitement was occasioned by a mode of fishing adopted by a party of fishermen on Detroit river, who stationed nets over a mile and a half in extent across the mouth of the stream, a proceeding that was not only calculated to destroy the value of the seine fisheries above, but which would ultimately have driven the fish out of the river altogether. A formidable opposition was of course arrayed against this unusual and unwarrantable proceeding, and the party found it expedient to desist, but the Legislature, which met shortly after, failed to pass an inhibitive measure. This action, or rather want of action, would have been considered extraordinary in a State less favored by nature.

We have fortunately been able to procure estimates of the amount of the catch at all the various fisheries, together with other leading statistics; and with the view of imparting to the subject a more general interest, we include two or three points beyond the limits of the State. The estimates are furnished by gentlemen of intelligence and experience, and may be relied on as substantially correct:

Sandusky fisheries, catch mostly sold fresh:

Whitefish, valuation	$50,000
Pickerel, bass, etc.	40,000
Value of seines and fixtures	16,000
Paid for wages	37,000

Maumee River, pickerel, white bass, etc., etc., mostly sold fresh.

Valuation	$50,000

Seines and fixtures $15,000
Paid for wages 12,000

Maumee Bay and Monroe County, Michigan, white fish and pickerel:

Valuation $20,000
Pounds, seines, and fixtures 9,000
Paid for wages 10,000

Detroit River, nearly all white:

Valuation $75,000
Seines, fishing grounds, and fixtures 40,000
Paid for wages 20,000

St. Clair River and Rapids, mostly pickerel:

Valuation $11,000
Cost of fixtures 2,000
Paid for wages 1,200

Port Huron to Point au Barque, 3,000 barrels, mostly white:

Valuation $25,000

Au Sauble 6,000, barrels, ¾ white, the rest trout:

Valuation $50,000
Boats, nets, etc. 13,000
Paid for wages 7,000

Thunder Bay and vicinity, above Sauble River, 6,000 barrels, mostly white:

Valuation $50,000

Saginaw Bay and River, 2,000 barrels pickerel and 1,500 white and trout.

Valuation $32,000

Tawas, 600 barrels, mostly white.

Valuation $5,000

Between Thunder Bay and Mackinac, 500 barrels, mostly white:

Valuation $4,500

Mackinac, including all brought there, 7,500 barrels, $\frac{3}{4}$ or $\frac{7}{8}$ white:

Valuation....................................$62,000

Beaver Islands and neighborhood, 7,000 barrels, nearly all white:

Valuation....................................$59,000

Green Bay in Michigan, 3,000 barrels, all white:

Valuation....................................$25,500

Island between De Tour and the Saut, 1,000 barrels, $\frac{3}{8}$ white, the rest trout:

Valuation.. $8,000

Green Bay in Wisconsin, 2,500 barrels white and 500 barrels pickerel, all packed:

Valuation....................................$25,000

Of the catch of Lake Huron, only an inconsiderable amount are sold fresh. On Detroit River about 4,000 barrels were packed last year.

Having procured specific information of the cost of outfit and amount paid for wages at the Sauble fisheries, we have taken such expenditures as the basis for those of all the upper lake fisheries in proportion to the catch, which in the main will doubtless prove substantially correct. At the Sauble last season there were sixteen boats employed for two months, and eight for the rest of the season. The value of the boats was $200 each, and the nets, etc., cost an additional sum of $600 for each, making the aggregate value of the boats and their outfit about $13,000. About forty men were employed on an average during the season, receiving a probable aggregate of $7,000 for wages. Taking these outlays, etc., as a fair average, and we have the following result:

From Port Huron to the Beavers, inclusive, together with Green Bay in Michigan, and the Saut Islands:

Cost of outfit........................$83,500
Amount paid for wages............... 45,000
Average number of men...........300

The amount shipped from Lake Superior, as appears from the report of the Superintendent of the Saut canal is 4,000 barrels. This is probably not a tithe of what might be done. The mouth of almost every stream in that region affords good fishing grounds, which is also true of most of the islands, particularly Isle Royale, where the siscowit is very abundant.

The fisheries on the east coast of Lake Michigan have for about six years past increased very rapidly in importance, some years gaining 100 per cent. on the year preceding. A few years since a party of Norwegians came on and embarked in the business, which they have prosecuted ever since with advantage and profit. Trained in the severe school of their rugged northern home, they exhibit the greatest daring, going out in their tiny craft during the heaviest gales. They frequently venture out twenty-five miles from shore, almost meeting their countrymen from the Wisconsin side of the lake, who are engaged in the same hazardous calling. We have the following returns:

Little Traverse, 600 barrels:

Valuation	$4,000
300 nets and 6 boats, worth	1,800
Paid for wages	575

Big Point Sauble, 1,500 barrels:

Valuation	$12,000
600 nets and 8 boats	3,600
Paid for wages	1,700

Little Point Sauble, 2,000 barrels:

Valuation	$16,500
750 nets and 10 boats	4,500
Paid for wages	2,000

White Lake, 1,500 barrels:

Valuation	$12,000
500 nets and 5 boats	3,000
Paid for wages	1,600

Grand Haven, 4,000 barrels:

Valuation	$32,800
800 nets and 8 boats	4,000
Paid for wages	5,000

Saugatuck, 2,000 barrels:

Valuation	$16,000
600 nets and 6 boats	3,600
Paid for wages	2,500

South Haven, 2,100 barrels:

Valuation	$16,800
600 nets and 6 boats	1,200
Paid for wages	2,500

St. Joseph's 3,500 barrels:

Valuation	$28,000
1,200 nets and 9 boats	7,500
Paid for wages	

New Buffalo, 300 barrels:

Valuation	$3,000
400 nets and 5 boats	2,600
Paid for wages	450

Michigan City, 3,000 barrels:

Valuation	$30,000
1,020 nets and 18 boats	8,000
Paid for wages	4,400

Showing an aggregate of 21,000 barrels, of which about 18,000 barrels are salted; valuation $169,800; value of fixtures $43,600; estimated amount paid for wages, $22,000.

The fishing grounds of Michigan City are almost

entirely within our State. The number of barrels include those sold fresh as well as salted, there being a considerable quantity of the former, in some of the fisheries last named, Michigan City and New Buffalo especially, from whence they are sent packed in ice to the different towns in Michigan; also to Lafayette and Indianapolis, Indiana, to Louisville, Kentucky, to Cincinnati, and also to Chicago, where they are repacked in ice, and some of them find their way to St. Louis, Cairo, etc. From St. Joseph and Grand Haven there are large quantities sent fresh to Chicago and Milwaukee, where they are repacked in ice.

At a fair estimate for the few small fisheries on this coast from which we have no return, together with those on the west coast of Lake Michigan, they are worth at least $60,000, but we have no data by which to form an estimate of the proportion packed.

The number of men employed, and the consequent expense, varies according to the method employed. With seines the occupation is very laborious, and requires a much stronger force than pound nets. One set of hands can manage a number of the latter. Some of the fisheries on Detroit and St. Clair rivers use seines altogether, to draw which, horse-power is brought into requisition in some cases. A double set of men are employed, working alternately day and night, and the exposure is a most disagreeable feature of the business, particularly in bad weather. The great bulk of the aggregate catch continues to be taken with seines or gill nets, but pound (or trap) nets are on the increase. They have been in use below Lake Huron more or less for the past four or five years, but it is only about two years since their introduction in the upper lakes. With these nets 100 barrels of white-fish have been taken at a single haul. Of course their general use must produce a material diminution in the supply.

As regards capital invested, there is in particular instances a wide difference. George Clark, Esq., nine miles below Detroit, has $12,000 invested in his grounds, owing mostly to the cost of removing obstructions. But this is an exception.

The barrels for packing constitute no inconsiderable item of this vast and important trade. Their manufacture is a regular branch in Port Huron, but most of them are made by the fishermen when not engaged in their regular vocation. They are made at all the villages and fishing stations on Lake Huron, pine being generally easy of access. The barrels are worth 62½ cents each; half-barrels, 50 cents. Over two-thirds of the packages used are halves, but our estimated totals of the catch represent wholes.

Formerly the nets used also to be made almost entirely by the fishermen, who usually procured the twine from Detroit. Latterly, many of them have been brought from Boston already made.

Salt is another large item. For packing and repacking, about one-fourth of a barrel is used to each barrel of fish. For the amount packed, therefore, in the fisheries we have described, about 20,000 barrels are used.

Total proceeds of Michigan fisheries	$620,000
Total proceeds of all enumerated	900,000
Total capital invested	252,000
Paid for wages	171,000
Aggregate of barrels salted, say 80,000 bbls.	
Cost of packages	70,000
Cost of salt	22,000

The catch at the Sauble and Thunder Bay showed a falling off last season, owing not to the want of fish, but to the unfavorable weather. At these points they congregate only from October to the close, and the weather being very rough last fall, the catch was comparatively light.

Mackinac has been famous as the greatest fishing point on the lakes. Gill nets are mostly in vogue. The work in that locality is mostly done by half-breeds, in the employ of the merchants, the latter furnishes the salt, and paying them in trade, of which the outfit generally constitutes a part. But with the late general depression, prices declined some thirty or forty per cent., and consequently the business, previously quite lucrative, lost its attraction for the time being. The merchants advanced the means in summer, and could not realize until the ensuing year. Small holders were obliged to sell, some of the time by forcing the market, and this added to the difficulty experienced by large holders in obtaining returns.

Much has been said in reference to the coal fields of Michigan, and within the past two or three years, explorations, with a view of developing these deposits, have been conducted in different portions of the State. There is no longer any doubt of the existence of a valuable field of coal in central Michigan. There have been openings at different points in the State; at Jackson and Sandstone, in Jackson county; at Owasso and Corunna in Shiawassee county; at Flint in Genesee county, and at Lansing, coal has been found deposited in veins of from twenty inches to four feet in thickness. Most of the openings have been upon veins outcropping at the surface of the ground, and there has been little difficulty in procuring samples of coal from these veins in many localities in the State. These deposits of coal found at, and near the surface, are producing coal in limited quantities in different localities, but no works have been prosecuted with a view to supplying any but a limited local demand. From the surface evidences of a coal field on the line of the Detroit and Milwaukee Road near Owasso, and from explorations and developments already made, some specimens of the coal having been produced and shipped to Detroit, it has been determined to prosecute the work at that point.

In Jackson county, however, the matter of mining has become an enterprise of some magnitude, and we are enabled to give some facts and figures which exhibit in some measure the importance to the State of this new branch of industry. There are several "workings" of coal in the vicinity of Jackson, and several companies have been formed for the purpose of mining coal. Considerable coal has been mined and sold from these different workings and mines. The principal mine, and one which in all its arrangements and provisions is equal to any mine in the country, is that of the Detroit and Jackson Coal and Mining Company. The works of this Company are at Woodville station on the line of the Michigan

Central Railroad, about three and a half miles west of Jackson city.

The mine is situated on the north side of the Railroad and about half a mile from the main track. The Coal Company have built a side track from the Central Road to the mouth of their shaft. The shaft from which the coal is taken is ninety feet deep, and at the bottom passes through a vein of coal about four feet in thickness. This vein has been opened in different directions for several hundred feet from the shaft, and with a tram-road through the different entries the coal is reached and brought from the rooms to the shaft, and then lifted by steam to the surface. This coal has been transported to different points in the State and is rapidly coming into use for all ordinary purposes, taking the place of many of the Ohio coals and at a reduced cost. The mine to which reference is made is within *four hours'* ride of Detroit, on the Central Road, and a visit of two hours (which can be accomplished any day, by taking the morning train, leaving the city at 9 45 and returning so as to reach here at half past six in the evening,) will repay any one for the trouble. The station is called Woodville, and is only three and a half miles west of Jackson.

Michigan, hitherto a heavy importer of salt, is in a fair way not only to have amply sufficient for her own wants, but something perhaps to spare. To aid in developing our saline resources, the Legislature wisely provided a bounty upon the production, which has already brought forth good fruits. At Grand Rapids, salt water has been discovered much stronger than that of the Syracuse springs, requiring only twenty-nine gallons to produce a bushel.—Arrangements have been almost perfected for commencing the manufacture upon a very extensive scale.

At Saginaw, within a few days, at the depth of 620 feet, copious volumes of brine were revealed. This is also stronger than any in New York. From some cause, it is sought to keep this information a secret, but it is fair to presume it would soon have leaked out. The salt both at Grand Rapids and Saginaw, is a beautiful article, of great purity.

When Nature formed the Grand River and Saginaw valleys, she seems to have been engaged in an animated contest with herself. The developments are such as to warrant the conviction that other and perhaps equally valuable salt springs lie hidden in the intervening space between those valleys. These and other discoveries plainly indicate that the employment of a large amount of capital in developing the latent resources of Michigan would amply "pay."

The inexhaustible plaster beds of Grand Rapids constitute one of the prime sources of prosperity of that enterprising metropolis of the Grand River Delta. Our whole State has also a great interest in the trade, the material being, it is admitted, a better fertilizer than the imported article.

CHAPTER XV.

Desirableness of a trip to the Lakes—Routes of travel—Interesting localities—Scenery—Southern coast—Portage Lake—Dr. Houghton—Ontonagon—Apostles' Islands—Return trip—Points of interest—St. Mary's River—Lake St. George—Point de Tour—Lake Michigan—Points of interest—Chicago.

A trip to the northern lakes, for variety and beauty of scenery to such as are seeking enjoyment and pleasure, possesses advantages over every other route of travel in the United States, and with the exception of the works of art and the classical associations of the old world, is unsurpassed by any on the globe. To such as are in quest of health, no comparison can be instituted, as it has been demonstrated that the Northwest, especially in the region of the lakes, possesses the most invigorating climate in the world. A reference to the mortuary tables removes all doubt on this point. In the town of Marquette, on Lake Superior, containing a population of over three thousand, there were during the last year but eight deaths, and only a portion of that number was from disease.

Our object in this chapter is to notice the various routes of travel to the interesting localities in the Northwest. During the summer months the most pleasant mode of conveyance is by water. The Hudson River boats, compared with which no inland steamers are superior, leave, every day, the foot of Courtland street for Albany. By taking passage on an evening boat, after a quiet night's rest the traveler will find himself at Albany the next morning, where he can take the cars for Buffalo, at which point he will be able to take a steamer for Detroit. From thence he can take a steamer for Superior City, passing through Lakes St. Clair and Huron, and up the Saut St. Mary to Lake Superior. On the route from the Saut he will pass the following points, Point Iroquois, White-Fish Point, Point Au Sable, Pictured Rocks, Grand Island, Marquette, Manitou Island, Copper Harbor, Eagle Harbor, Eagle River, Ontonagon, La Point, Bayfield and Point De Tour. The usual time occupied in passing over this route is about twenty-four hours. In leaving the Saut above the Rapids the steamer enters Lequamenon, passing Iroquois Point fifteen miles distant on the southern shore, while Gros Cap, on the Canada shore, can be seen about four miles distant. The porphyry hills, of which this point is composed, rise to a height of seven hundred feet above the lake, and present a grand appearance. North of Gros Cap is Goulais Bay, and in the distance a bold headland named Goulais Point can be seen. Indeed the whole north shore presents a scene of wild grandeur. Near the middle of Lequamenon Bay is Parisien Island which belongs to Canada; opposite to this island on the north is seen Croulee Point, an interesting locality in the vicinity of which are numerous islands. Still further on the steamer passes Mamainse Point, another bold headland once the seat of the works of the Quebec Copper Mining Company, but now abandoned in consequence of their unproductiveness; some fifteen or twenty miles further north, is located the Montreal Company's copper mine. The traveler has now fairly entered the vast mineral region of Lake Superior, and passes along a coast hundreds of miles in extent, "abounding in geological phenomena, varied mineral wealth, agates, cornelian, jasper, opal, and other precious stones, with its rivers, bays, estuaries, islands, presque isles, peninsulas, capes, pictured rocks, transparent waters, leaping cascades, and bold highlands, lined with pure veins of quartz, spar and amethystine crystals, full to repletion with mineral riches, reflecting in gorgeous majesty the sun's bright rays, and the moon's mellow blush; overtopped with ever verdant groves of fir, cedar, and mountain ash, while the back ground is filled up with moutain upon mountain, until, rising in majesty to the clouds, distance loses their inequality resting against the clear vault of Heaven."

On the southern shore, beyond White Fish Point, immense sand hills can be seen rising from four hundred to one thousand feet in height. After passing Pictured Rocks, which we have elsewhere described, the steamer approaches Grand Island, the shores of which present a magnificent appearance. This island is about one hundred twenty-five miles from the Saut and is about ten miles long and five wide. It is wild and romantic. The cliffs of sandstone broken into by the waves form picturesque caverns, pillars, and arches of great dimensions. Forty-five miles further is the town of Marquette one of the most flourishing places on the borders of the lake, and the entrepot of the vast mineral wealth in that region. Near this place are the Carp and Dead rivers, both which have rapids and falls of great beauty. Sailing in a northwestern direction the steamer passes Standards Rock, a solitary and dangerous projection, rising out of the lake at the entrance of Keweenaw Bay. At the head of this bay stands the harbor of L'Anse a short distance from which are located a Roman Catholic and Methodist mission house and church, both of which, on each sides of the bay where they are located, are surrounded by Indian tribes and settlements.

Passing along, the steamer enters Portage Lake an extensive and beautiful sheet of water extending nearly the entire breadth of the peninsula of Keweenaw Point, which is a large extent of land jutting out into Lake Superior, from ten to twenty miles wide and sixty in length. This whole section abounds in silver and copper ores. After passing Manitou Island, Copper Harbor, one of the best on the lake is reached. At this place there is a flourishing village. The next points are Agate Harbor, Eagle Harbor, and Eagle River Harbor. It was at this point that the lamented Dr. Houghton was drowned in October 1845. He was the State Geologist of Michigan, and while coming down from a portage to Copper Harbor, with his four Indian companions *du voyage*, the boat was swamped in a storm about a mile and a half from Eagle River. Two of the *voyageurs* were saved by being thrown by the waves upon the rocks ten feet above the usual level of the waters.

The next point, three hundred and thirty-six miles from the Saut, is Ontonagon situated at the mouth of a river of the same name. A flourishing town is located here having several churches. In its vicinity are the Minnesota, Norwich, National, Rockland, and several other copper mines of great productiveness; silver is also found intermixed with the copper ore, which abounds in great masses. La Point, four hundred and ten miles from the Saut and eighty-three from Superior City, which is next reached, is situated on Madeline Island, one of the group of the Twelve Apostles. It was settled at an early day by the Jesuit Missionaries and the American Fur Traders. The population is mixed, consisting of Indians, French, Canadians and Americans. It has long been the favorite resort of the "red man" as well as the "pale face," and possesses a historic interest to travelers. The adjacent islands of the Twelve Apostles grouped together a short distance from the main land, present during the summer months a most lovely and beautiful appearance. Cliffs from one to two hundred feet, may be seen rising above the waters, crowned with the richest foliage. Passing Rayfield, a village on the mainland, and Ashland, a settlement at the head of Chag-wamegon Bay, and the Maskeg and Montreal Rivers, the steamer, after round-ing Point de Tour, enters Fon du Lac, a noble bay at the head of Lake Superior, twenty miles in width and fifty miles in length, on the shore of which stands Superior City, near the mouth of St. Louis River. This is a flourishing place, possessing great commercial importance, and which, at no distant day, must be connected with the mouth of the Columbia River and Puget Sound. On the return trip coasting along the northwest, the steamer passes numerous points of interest. At the extreme west end of Lake Superior, seven miles northwest from Superior City, stands the village of Portland. Along the shore northward are bold sandy bluffs and highlands which are supposed to be rich in mineral wealth. Encampment, the name of a river, island, and village, is a romantic spot. Immense cliffs of greenstone are to be seen rising from two hundred to three hundred feet above the water's edge; northward along the shore porphyry abounds in great quantity. This point is noted for the singular agitation of the magnetic needle. Hiawatha, Grand Portage, Pigeon Bay, Pie Island, Thunder Cape, and Thunder Bay, surrounded by grand scenery; Isle Royale, Fort William, a strong post of the Hudson Bay Company. Black Bay, Nopigon Bay, on the extreme north of the lake. St. Ignace Island, State Islands, Pic

Island Michipicoten Island, formely the seat of Lake Superior Silver Mining Company of Canada. Montreal Island, Carabon Island and other points of interest.

Re-entering the Saut the steamer shapes her course for Mackinaw. The Garden River settlement, an Indian village ten miles below the Saut, is on the Canada shore. A mission church and several dwellings occupied by Chippewa Indians may be found here. The St. Mary's River presents the finest scenery. A traveler in describing it says, "There is a delicious freshness in the countless evergreen islands that dot the river in every direction from the Falls to Lake Huron." The next point is Church's Landing on Sugar Island, opposite to which is Squirrel Island belonging to the Canadians. Lake George twenty miles below the Saut is an expansion of the River which at this point is five miles wide. The steamer soon enters the Nebish Rapids, after passing Lake George, and the main land of Canada, stretching out to the north in a dreary wilderness, is lost sight of. Sugar Island which is a large body of fertile land belonging to the United States, near the head of St. Joseph's Island is next reached, and then in succession, Nebish Island, Mud Lake, another expansion of the river, Lime Island, Carltonville, St.

Joseph's Island, a large and fertile body of land belonging to Canada, once the site of a fort; Drummond Island, belonging to the United States, and Point De Tour, at the mouth of the river, the site of a lighthouse and settlement. The other points of interest are Round Island, Bois Blanc, at the head of Lakes Huron and Mackinac, all of which we have elsewhere described. At east the steamer enters the Straits of Mackinaw, and the site of the old fort and town heave in view. These straits are from four to twenty miles in width, and extend east and west about twenty miles.

Lake Michigan now spreads out its beautiful sheet of water, second in size to Superior, and invites the traveler to sail along its shores and among its islands. The points of interest are, La Gros Cap, a picturesque headland; Garden and Hog Islands, Great and Little Beaver Islands, Fox Island, on the west of which is the entrance to Green Bay, and on the east the entrance to Grand Traverse Bay, the Great or north Manitou, and the Little or south Manitou Islands, Kewawnee, Two Rivers, Manitoulin and Sheboygan, Port Washington, Milwaukee, Racine, Waukegan and other places of minor importance. After passing the localities on the western shore, at length Chicago is seen in the distance, stretching along for miles and presenting a fine appearance. From this point the traveler can return to New York, by way of Detroit, through Canada on the railroad, or he may if he chooses take a southern route. Such are the facilities for travel that the tourist will be at no loss during the entire season in finding excellent steamers and good accommodations. Steamers of the first class leave Cleveland on Mondays, Tuesdays, Thursdays and Fridays of each week, for Lake Superior, touching at the various ports on the route. Persons in the West or South, who may desire to visit the lakes can thus be at any time accommodated.

Should the tourist prefer taking another route from Buffalo, instead of passing over Lake Erie and up the Detroit River, he can go direct to Collingwood at the foot of Georgian Bay, and from thence can take steamer for Saut St. Mary, Chicago or any other point he may desire in the Northwest.

THE END.

www.ingramcontent.com/pod-product-compliance
Lightning Source LLC
LaVergne TN
LVHW020100110826
845151LV00001B/31

* 9 7 8 1 4 2 5 5 4 4 5 2 2 *